Behavioral Social Choice

Behavioral Social Choice looks at the probab[...]
decision making rules. The authors challenge n[...]
wisdom about social choice processes, and seek to restore faith in the possibility
of democratic decision making. In particular, they argue that worries about the
supposed prevalence of majority rule cycles that would preclude groups from
reaching a final decision about what alternative they prefer have been greatly
overstated. In practice, majority rule can be expected to work well in most real-
world settings. Furthermore, if there is a problem, they show that the problem
is more likely to be one of sample estimates missing the majority winner in
a close contest (e.g., Bush–Gore) than a problem about cycling. The authors
also provide new mathematical tools to estimate the prevalence of cycles as a
function of sample size. They provide new insights into how alternative model
specifications can change our estimates of social orderings.

Michel Regenwetter is Associate Professor of Psychology and Political Science
at the University of Illinois at Urbana-Champaign (UIUC). Dr. Regenwetter has
published over 20 scholarly articles in leading academic journals in his field,
including *Journal of Experimental Psychology: Learning, Memory and Cognition*, *Journal of Mathematical Psychology*, *Management Science*, *Mathematical
Social Sciences*, *Psychological Review*, *Psychometrika*, *Social Choice and Welfare*, and *Theory and Decision*. Dr. Regenwetter has served as guest associate
editor for *Management Science*, and since 2003, he has been a permanent member of the editorial board of *Journal of Mathematical Psychology*.

Bernard Grofman is Professor of Political Science at the University of California,
Irvine. He is coauthor of *A Unified Theory of Party Competition* (with James
F. Adams and Samuel Merrill III, Cambridge University Press, 2005), *A Unified
Theory of Voting* (with Samuel Merrill, III, Cambridge University Press, 1999),
and *Minority Representation and the Quest for Voting Equality* (with Lisa
Handley and Richard G. Niemi, Cambridge University Press, 1994).

Professor A. A. J. Marley, a Fellow of the American Psychological Society, was
Chair of the Department of Psychology at McGill University from 1992 to
2001 and is now Adjunct Professor at the University of Victoria and Professor
Emeritus of McGill University. He was Editor of the *Journal of Mathematical
Psychology* and Section Editor for *Mathematics and Computer Sciences* of the
International Encyclopedia of the Social and Behavioral Sciences (2001). He
is the editor of *Choice, Decision and Measurement: Essays in Honor of R.
Duncan Luce* (1997).

Ilia M. Tsetlin is an Assistant Professor of Decision Sciences at INSEAD. His
research has appeared in academic journals such as *Management Science, Operations Research, Journal of Risk and Uncertainty*, and *Social Choice and
Welfare*.

To our families

Behavioral Social Choice

Probabilistic Models, Statistical Inference, and Applications

MICHEL REGENWETTER
University of Illinois at Urbana-Champaign

BERNARD GROFMAN
University of California, Irvine

A. A. J. MARLEY
University of Victoria

ILIA TSETLIN
INSEAD

CAMBRIDGE
UNIVERSITY PRESS

CAMBRIDGE UNIVERSITY PRESS
Cambridge, New York, Melbourne, Madrid, Cape Town, Singapore, São Paulo

Cambridge University Press
40 West 20th Street, New York, NY 10011-4211, USA

www.cambridge.org
Information on this title: www.cambridge.org/9780521829687

First published 2006

Printed in the United States of America

A catalog record for this publication is available from the British Library.

Library of Congress Cataloging in Publication Data

Behavioral social choice : probabilistic models, statistical inference, and applications /
Michel Regenwetter ... [et al.].
    p. cm.
Includes bibliographical references and indexes.
ISBN-13: 978-0-521-82968-7 (hardback)
ISBN-10: 0-521-82968-2 (hardback)
ISBN-13: 978-0-521-53666-0 (pbk.)
ISBN-10: 0-521-53666-9 (pbk.)
1. Social choice – Mathematical models.   2. Decision making – Mathematical
models.   3. Voting – Mathematical models.   4. Probabilities – Mathematical
models.   I. Regenwetter, Michel.   II. Title.
HB846.8.B44   2006
302′.13′01 – dc22   2005023291

ISBN-13   978-0-521-82968-7 hardback
ISBN-10   0-521-82968-2 hardback

ISBN-13   978-0-521-53666-0 paperback
ISBN-10   0-521-53666-9 paperback

Contents

Figures and Tables

FIGURES

TABLES

Acknowledgments

Regenwetter performed the research and writing that went into this book while he was a graduate student in the program in Mathematical Behavioral Sciences in the School of Social Sciences at the University of California, Irvine, as a post-doctoral fellow in the Department of Psychology at McGill University, as an Assistant Professor of Business Administration at the Fuqua School of Business, Duke University, briefly as a scholar in residence at the Center for the Study of Democracy at the University of California, Irvine, and as an Assistant Professor in the Departments of Psychology and Political Science, University of Illinois at Urbana-Champaign. He completed his work on the book while an Associate Professor in the Departments of Psychology and Political Science, University of Illinois at Urbana-Champaign.

Grofman carried out the research for this book while a Professor in the Department of Political Science and a member of the Institute for Mathematical Behavioral Sciences at the University of California, Irvine; and while he was a scholar in residence in the Department of Political Science, and a Fellow of the Institute for Advanced Study, at the University of Bologna (Italy). He completed his work on the book while a Professor in the Department of Political Science and a member of the Institute for Mathematical Behavioral Sciences at the University of California, Irvine.

Marley carried out the research and writing for this book while he was a Professor of Psychology at McGill University (Canada), a Fellow of the Hanse-Wissenschaftskolleg (Delmenhorst, Germany), and a visiting researcher in the Department of Economics at the University of Groningen

(The Netherlands); he completed his work on the book while a Professor Emeritus at McGill University (Canada) and an Adjunct Professor in the Department of Psychology, University of Victoria (Canada).

Tsetlin performed the research and writing for this book while he was a Ph.D. student in Decision Sciences at the Fuqua School of Business, Duke University. He completed his work on the book while an Assistant Professor of Decision Sciences at INSEAD (France and Singapore).

We are pleased to acknowledge the financial support of the following: The National Science Foundation, Grant # SBR-97-30076 (to Michel Regenwetter), Grant # SBR-97-30578 (to Bernard Grofman and A. A. J. Marley), and Grant # SBR-98-18756 (to Michel Regenwetter and Aleksandar Pekeč); NSERC Canada Collaborative Grant # CGP-0164211 (to A. A. J. Marley with J. Aczel, H. Joe, C. Genest, I. J. Myung, H. Colonius); NSERC Canada Discovery Grant # RGPIN 8124-98 (to A. A. J. Marley); the Center for Decision Making and Risk Analysis at INSEAD (to Tsetlin); the INSEAD Alumni Fund (to Tsetlin); The Fuqua School of Business, Duke University (to Regenwetter and Tsetlin); the Institute for Mathematical Behavioral Sciences and the Center for the Study of Democracy, the University of California, Irvine (Grofman, Marley and Regenwetter); the Department of Psychology and the Faculty of Science, McGill University, Montreal, Canada (to Marley and Regenwetter); the Hanse-Wissenschaftskolleg, Delmenhorst, Germany (to Marley); and the Netherlands' Organization for Scientific Research (to Marley).

Various aspects of this work have benefited from helpful comments and suggestions at various times by the following individuals (listed alphabetically): James Adams, William Batchelder, François Bavaud, Steven Brams, Martin Chabot, Robert Clemen, Eric Cosyn, Xinyuan Dai, Jean-Paul Doignon, Jean-Claude Falmagne, Scott Feld, Peter Fishburn, Wulf Gärtner, William Gehrlein, Yung-Fong Hsu, Harry Joe, Craig Leth-Steensen, Duncan Luce, Michael Munger, Louis Narens, Robert Nau, Reinhard Niederée, Prasanta Pattanaik, Aleksandar Pekeč, Donald Saari, James Smith, Reinhard Suck, Robert Winkler, Hsiu-Ting Yu, and various anonymous referees and journal editors. We would like to thank Mark Berger for help in data extraction, Peter Karcher for help in computer programming and computer simulations, Clover Behrend for secretarial and bibliographic assistance, and Chantale Bousquet for her long-distance secretarial support. Hsiu-Ting Yu provided us with extensive assistance with LaTeX, and performed most of the work in generating the subject and author indices.

For access to data which we have used in this book, or drawn on for closely related projects, we wish to thank the Interuniversity Consortium for Political and Social Research (University of Michigan), as well as Steven Brams, Peter Fishburn, John Little, Jack Nagel, Helmut Norpoth, and Nicholas Tideman. Some of these data sets were available on CD-ROM (ICPSR), some were provided to us directly, and some were available through being reprinted in the author(s)' publications.

The material in this book represents a synthesis of previous work by the authors (some of it joint with other scholars). The following nine papers are the most important of the papers that we draw upon (in some cases quite heavily):

1. J.-P. Doignon and M. Regenwetter. "An approval-voting polytope for linear orders." *Journal of Mathematical Psychology*, **41**:171–188, 1997.

2. M. Regenwetter, J. Adams, and B. Grofman. "On the (sample) Condorcet efficiency of majority rule: An alternative view of majority cycles and social homogeneity." *Theory and Decision*, **53**:153–186, 2002.

3. M. Regenwetter and B. Grofman. "Approval voting, Borda winners and Condorcet winners: Evidence from seven elections." *Management Science*, **44**:520–533, 1998a.

4. M. Regenwetter and B. Grofman. "Choosing subsets: A size-independent probabilistic model and the quest for a social welfare ordering." *Social Choice and Welfare*, **15**:423–443, 1998b.

5. M. Regenwetter, B. Grofman, and A. A. J. Marley. "On the model dependence of majority preferences reconstructed from ballot or survey data." *Mathematical Social Sciences (special issue on random utility theory and probabilistic measurement theory)*, **43**:453–468, 2002.

6. M. Regenwetter, A. A. J. Marley, and B. Grofman. "A general concept of majority rule." *Mathematical Social Sciences (special issue on random utility theory and probabilistic measurement theory)*, **43**:407–430, 2002.

7. I. Tsetlin and M. Regenwetter. "On the probabilities of correct or incorrect majority preference relations." *Social Choice and Welfare*, **20**:283–306, 2003.

8. I. Tsetlin, M. Regenwetter and B. Grofman. "The impartial culture maximizes the probability of majority cycles." *Social Choice and Welfare*, **21**:387–398, 2003.

9. M. Regenwetter, A. A. J. Marley, and B. Grofman. "General concepts of value restriction and preference majority." *Social Choice and Welfare*, **21**:149–173, 2003.

We are indebted to all of these journals for granting us reprint permission as follows:

Materials from Doignon and Regenwetter (1997) are reprinted from *Journal of Mathematical Psychology*, volume 41, pages 171–188, Copyright (1997), with kind permission from Elsevier.

Materials from Regenwetter, Adams, and Grofman (2002a) are reprinted from *Theory and Decision*, volume 53, pages 153–186, Copyright (2002), with kind permission of Kluwer Academic Publishers.

Materials from Regenwetter and Grofman (1998a) are reprinted by permission, Regenwetter and Grofman, Approval voting, Borda winners and Condorcet winners: Evidence from seven elections, *Management Science*, volume 44, issue 4, pages 520–533, Copyright (1998), the Institute for Operations Research and the Management Sciences, 901 Elkridge Landing Road, Suite 400, Linthicum, MD 21090 USA.

Materials from Regenwetter and Grofman (1998b), Tsetlin and Regenwetter (2003), Tsetlin, Regenwetter and Grofman (2003), and Regenwetter, Marley and Grofman (2003) are reprinted from Social Choice and Welfare, Choosing subsets: A size-independent probabilistic model and the quest for a social welfare ordering, volume 15, pages 423–443, Copyright (1998); On the probabilities of correct or incorrect majority preference relations, volume 20, pages 283–306, Copyright (2003); The impartial culture maximizes the probability of majority cycles, volume 21, pages 387–398, Copyright (2003); General concepts of value restriction and preference majority, volume 21, pages 149–173, Copyright (2003); with kind permission by Springer-Verlag.

Materials from Regenwetter, Grofman, and Marley (2002b) and from Regenwetter, Marley, and Grofman (2002c) are reprinted from Mathematical Social Sciences, volume 43, pages 453–468 and pages 407–430, Copyright (2002), with kind permission from Elsevier.

Chapter 1 draws heavily on Tsetlin et al. (2003) and on Regenwetter and Grofman (1998b). Chapter 2 draws heavily on Regenwetter et al. (2002c) and Regenwetter et al. (2003) and also makes use of a small portion of Regenwetter et al. (2002a). Chapter 3 integrates large parts of Regenwetter et al. (2002b) and Regenwetter et al. (2003). Chapter 4 draws on portions of Doignon and Regenwetter (1997), and more substantially on Regenwetter and Grofman (1998a) and on Regenwetter et al.

(2002b). Chapter 5 draws on Regenwetter et al. (2002a), and heavily on Tsetlin and Regenwetter (2003). Chapter 6 draws in part on Regenwetter and Grofman (1998a) and Regenwetter and Grofman (1998b). We are particularly grateful to James Adams for permission to use some material in Regenwetter et al. (2002a); and to Jean-Paul Doignon for permission to report some of the theorems in Doignon and Regenwetter (1997).

Introduction and Summary

Behavioral Social Choice Research

This book develops conceptual, mathematical, methodological, and empirical foundations of *behavioral social choice research*. Behavioral social choice research (or, more briefly, *behavioral social choice*) encompasses two major interconnected paradigms: the development of *behavioral social choice theory* and the evaluation of that theory with empirical data on social choice behavior.

The fundamental purpose of a behavioral theory of social choice processes is the development of descriptive models for real actors' social choice behavior and the statistical evaluation of such models against empirical data. Our notion of behavioral social choice research builds on and, at the same time, complements much of classical social choice theory in the tradition of leading figures such as the Marquis de Condorcet, Duncan Black, Kenneth Arrow, and Amartya Sen. Most classic approaches follow an axiomatic, normative line of reasoning. They formulate desirable properties of "rational" social choice and provide numerous "possibility" or "impossibility" theorems that classify groups of such axioms into whether or not they lead to 'feasible' aggregation procedures, given various theoretical assumptions about the nature, domain, and distribution of individual preferences (McLean and Urken, 1995). A principal task of behavioral social choice research is to evaluate such normative benchmarks of rational social choice against empirical evidence on real world social choice behavior. Consistently throughout this book we attempt to evaluate

1

our models against a wide range of empirical evidence drawn from large-scale real-world data sets from three different countries. To the extent that classical/normative theories fail to be descriptive of observed social choice behavior, they motivate and inspire the development of (alternative) behavioral theories that complement classical approaches by descriptively capturing the social choice behavior of real actors.

We see our work as building on the pioneering literature that integrates formal models with the analysis of real world social choice data (e.g., Chamberlin et al., 1984; Felsenthal et al., 1986, 1993; Felsenthal and Machover, 1995; Laver and Schofield, 1990; Niemi, 1970; Riker, 1958). We provide a general probabilistic modeling and statistical sampling and inference framework for the descriptive theoretical and empirical investigation of social choice behavior of real-world decision makers, but we place a major emphasis on majority rule decision making (Condorcet, 1785). Our general framework is formulated in terms of an extremely broad domain of permissible preference representations and it is applicable to an extremely broad range of empirical rating, ranking, and choice paradigms.

Six Major Contributions

While we conceptualize behavioral social choice theory as encompassing a very broad spectrum of research paradigms,[1] we focus here exclusively on the foundations for such a theory. Our main contributions are sixfold:

1. We argue for the limited theoretical relevance and demonstrate the lack of empirical evidence for cycles in mass electorates by replacing "value restriction"[2] and similar classic domain restriction conditions, as well as the "impartial culture" assumption, with more realistic assumptions about preference distributions.
2. We expand the classical domains of permissible preference states by allowing for more general binary preference relations than linear or weak orders and by considering probabilistic representations of preference and utility.
3. We develop methodologies to (re)construct preference distributions from incomplete data, that is, data which do not provide either complete rankings or complete sets of pairwise comparisons.

---

[1] For example, in addition to the study of committee voting and mass election processes, we see behavioral social choice theory as encompassing the empirical study of coalitions, of information pooling (such as occurs in juries), and of a wide variety of other collective choice processes.

[2] A definition of this (and related) terms is provided later in the text.

4. We highlight the dependence of social choice results on assumed models of preference or utility.
5. We develop a statistical sampling and Bayesian inference framework that usually places tight upper and lower bounds on the probability of any majority preference relation (cycle or not).
6. We demonstrate that in situations where sampling may be involved, misestimation (i.e., erroneous evaluation) of the majority preferences is a far greater (and much more probable) threat to democratic decision making than majority cycles.

Conceptually, our work is heavily influenced by the foundations of behavioral economics and behavioral decision theory (see, e.g., Akerlof, 1984; Allais, 1953; Camerer et al., 2004; Harless and Camerer, 1994; Kahneman and Tversky, 1979; Kahneman et al., 1982; Luce, 1992, 2000; Luce and Suppes, 1965; Luce and von Winterfeldt, 1994; Plott and Levine, 1978; Shleifer, 2000; Simon, 1955; Smith, 1976, 1994; Suppes, 1961; Thaler, 1993a,b; Tversky, 1969; Tversky and Kahneman, 1974, 1981). Similar to much theoretical work in those fields, our approach to behavioral social choice theory is descriptive, yet mathematically formal. Also, like those fields, our approach draws theoretically, conceptually, and methodologically on mathematical psychology and statistics. In particular, we seek to build upon the early integrative perspective to the decision sciences of two outstanding theorists, Duncan Luce and Patrick Suppes (see esp. Luce and Suppes, 1965).

We recognize that, by concentrating on foundational work here, we omit other important and, in our opinion, 'higher order' aspects of a full-fledged behavioral theory, such as issues of strategic behavior that are so central to much ongoing work on social choice.[3] While we do not investigate the behavioral ramifications of game theoretic models here, we do believe that future descriptive work on strategic social choice behavior can build on the general foundations that we lay here.

We now briefly elaborate on our six major contributions.

1 Majority Cycles in a New Light. Majority rule has played an important role in the history of social choice theory. We believe it is fair to say that majority rule continues to be broadly viewed as the most important (or at least most influential) benchmark of rational social choice, while at the same time being put into question by important theoretical classical

---

[3] Since most of our data analyses use survey data on mass electorates, we do not believe that our substantive empirical conclusions are likely to be affected by our implicit assumption that the data are sincere reflections of the voter preferences.

work. In particular, our work complements three major theoretical developments in classical social choice theory that bear heavily on the study of majority rule decision making: Arrow's impossibility theorem and two subsequent strands of research that were motivated by Arrow's result, namely the literature on domain restrictions and the literature that draws on the impartial culture assumption.

ARROW'S THEOREM AND CYCLES. Arrow's famous "impossibility theorem" (1951) eliminates majority rule because one can easily construct hypothetical preference distributions under which majority rule violates one of Arrow's axioms, namely transitivity.[4] (However, see Saari's recent work, 1999, 2001b, 2001c for a novel theoretical perspective on Arrow's theorem and on majority cycles in particular.) In fact, the possibility of majority cycles continues to be a major reason why so many social choice scholars (and those influenced by them) argue that majority rule decision making is flawed. Yet, Arrow's approach requires an ideal social choice procedure to satisfy a certain set of axioms under all *possible* distributions of preferences (i.e., all possible preference profiles) over a given domain of possible preferences states, and proves that such a procedure fails to exist.[5] Behavioral social choice research can bring a new perspective to Arrow's theorem if it demonstrates that *actual* (voting) data are such that majority rule is overwhelmingly transitive. One interpretation of such an empirical result is that, for real data, one does not need to assume Arrow's condition that the social welfare function (choice procedure) is defined over all possible voter profiles. To phrase it differently, in this approach the feasibility of Arrow's ideal is no longer a theoretical question alone, but rather it becomes primarily an empirical and pragmatic one. If we take the pragmatic view that democratic decision making needs to be feasible only for actual preference distributions observed in the real world (i.e., the domain of the social choice function consists only of those distributions that have actually been observed), rather than for all conceivable

---

[4] The simplest example of the paradox of cyclical majorities, also called the "Condorcet paradox," occurs with three voters choosing among three alternatives. Label the alternatives as A, B, and C, assume that voter 1 has preference order ABC, voter 2 has preference order BCA and voter 3 has preference order CAB. Then majorities prefer A to B and B to C, which might lead us to expect that a majority prefers A to C. But this is not the case. Instead, a majority prefers C to A, and therefore these majority preferences form a cycle, i.e., group preferences are not transitive even though the individual preferences are transitive.

[5] One can avoid the impossibility result either by generalizing the approach to *nondeterministic* methods, leading to a *probabilistic dictator* (Pattanaik and Peleg, 1986; Tangiane, 1991), or by considering an infinite set of voters (Fishburn, 1970a).

distributions, then majority rule remains a strong contender to Arrow's challenge. In this book, we consider a number of real world preference distributions and find no conclusive empirical evidence that would substantiate the existence of majority cycles. One of our theoretical aims is thus to develop descriptively adequate constraints on preference distributions that explain the absence of majority cycles, that is, to answer Gordon Tullock's (1981) question "Why so much stability?"

DOMAIN RESTRICTIONS AND CYCLES. The literature on domain restrictions such as Sen's "value restriction" and Black's "single peakedness" (Black, 1958; Sen, 1966, 1970; see Gärtner, 2001, for a nice overview of that and related work) studies ways in which the domain of feasible individual preferences can be constrained in such a way that, for example, majority cycles are eliminated, regardless of the distribution of preferences over that restricted domain. Behavioral social choice research places a premium on the analysis of real world data. We present and analyze survey data from national election studies in three countries.[6] Although we discuss noteworthy exceptions that have to do with extremely homogenous national subpopulations, we find these empirical distributions to violate every imaginable domain restriction condition because of the fact that every permissible preference state (say, strict weak order) is reported by a very large number of respondents. Therefore, in our approach, rather than restricting the *domain* of permissible preferences, we restrict the *distribution* of preferences (and, in fact, vastly enlarge the domain of permissible preferences). We expect that in general, at least for mass electorates, every preference state that a voter is allowed to report will be reported by some (and possibly many) voters, no matter how 'strange' or 'irrational' we might consider that preference state to be. Nonetheless, we also expect that the *distribution* of such preference states will be such that majority rule is transitive.

THE IMPARTIAL CULTURE AND CYCLES. The literature on the impartial culture and related distributions (DeMeyer and Plott, 1970; Gehrlein and Fishburn, 1976b; Gehrlein and Lepelley, 1999, 2001; Jones et al., 1995; Klahr, 1966) investigates the probability that majority rule leads to a cycle, when preferences are randomly sampled from a given probability distribution over a given domain of permissible preferences, as one varies

---

[6] We refer to the distributions of choices (votes) in these surveys as "realistic" because, while they are likely to closely resemble the actual population distributions that the surveys were drawn from, our arguments hold without having to claim that the surveys accurately reflect the exact distribution of preferences in all details.

the number of candidates and/or the number of voters. An *impartial culture* is a uniform distribution over linear or weak orders and consists, itself, of a complete majority tie among all candidates. We call such distributions *cultures of indifference*. While random samples drawn from cultures of ndifference generate majority cycles with high probability, we show that samples drawn from any other culture will have majority cycles with probability approaching zero as the sample size increases, unless the culture itself has a cycle built in. One of the policy reversals suggested by this change of perspective is that <u>high</u> turnout (not, as is commonly claimed, <u>low</u> turnout) is desirable when using majority rule. In our empirical work, we show that none of our empirical preference distributions even remotely resembles a random sample from an impartial culture.[7]

Classical approaches fail to describe empirical data on preference distributions for mass electorates, and are often construed as suggesting overly pessimistic policy implications regarding the feasibility of democratic decision making. To summarize our discussion of cycles in somewhat simplistic terms, all three sets of results, Arrow's theorem, Sen's value restriction, and the impartial culture assumption, place constraints that are too strong, each in its own way. Arrow requires a procedure that not only 'works' in practice, but that 'works' under all conceivable circumstances. Sen's value restriction and similar domain restrictions rule out preference states that will invariably be held by some large number of people.[8] The impartial culture requires extreme symmetry on the distribution of preferences and the slightest violation of that symmetry completely upsets the policy implications one would draw. We believe that a behaviorally adequate theory of majority rule requires an extremely broad domain of permissible preference states and a descriptively adequate theory of real-world preference distributions, as well as adequate probabilistic modeling and statistical analysis tools to investigate empirical data. Much of this book is dedicated to that task. In particular, we replace classical assumptions by conditions stated in terms of "net preferences" over a very broad domain of permissible preferences to obtain results (in particular, about cycles) that we consider much more behaviorally realistic and that fare well in their evaluation against empirical data.

2 Generalizing Majority Rule. Our behavioral approach dictates that we reach beyond the deterministic linear or weak order individual

---

[7] None of them looks like a random sample from an intransitive culture either.

[8] In particular, we conjecture that such observations cannot simply be attributed to measurement error or other noise.

preferences, commonly assumed in classical theories, to include a broad range of mathematical representations of preference or utility that have been proposed and used in the decision sciences.

The various representations of "preference" that have been studied in the decision sciences include linear, weak, partial orders and semiorders, as well as probability distributions over such orders. All of these are special cases of binary relations and probability distributions over binary relations. Most mathematical representations of "utility" (as opposed to preference) rely on real-valued functions that map objects into their (possibly vector-valued) utility values. A very general conceptual framework to represent and quantify the variability of utilities is provided by random utility theory. Here, the utility of an object is (the value of) a random variable (or a random vector). Preference relations are in close correspondence with utility functions, and probability distributions over preference relations are in close correspondence with utility random variables, that is, random utility models. Just as probability distributions over preference relations generalize and include deterministic preference relations, so do random utilities generalize and include real-valued deterministic utility functions. In this book we formulate and investigate majority rule (for finitely many candidates/choice alternatives) in terms of arbitrary binary preference relations, probabilistic binary preference relations, arbitrary real (possibly vector) valued utility functions, and arbitrary real (possibly vector) valued random utility representations. In so doing, we integrate deterministic with probabilistic representations of preference, and we allow for multiple possible representations of utility, including random utility models.

We make no assumptions about where the randomness comes from. Probabilities may capture random error, random sampling, probabilistic mechanisms inside the decision maker's head, or they may simply quantify the 'proportion' of the population that satisfies some property. In particular, we require no independence assumptions. Since people interact and communicate, we allow individual preferences to be interdependent and/or systematically biased in the following sense: In a probability distribution over preference relations, interdependencies can be quantified through setting the probabilities of certain preference orders very high or very low; in the random utility framework, the interdependent nature of utilities is captured and quantified through the joint distribution of the utility random variables. We also make no assumptions about that joint distribution.

Our very general and unifying mathematical framework also establishes a close link between social choice theory and the other areas of the decision sciences, especially individual choice theory. Furthermore, this approach allows us to derive results at a level of mathematical generality that includes and combines many known social choice theoretic results as special cases of a much broader framework.

3 (Re)constructing Preference Distributions. We argue that majority rule decision making has received limited empirical investigation because hardly any empirical data provide the input that is technically required to compute majority rule outcomes. Therefore, 'empirical' majority outcomes are usually hypothetical in nature to the extent that their computation from most available data requires various simplifying assumptions. We use a probabilistic approach to the measurement and inference of preference distributions from incomplete and/or randomly sampled empirical data in such a fashion as to encompass a multitude of empirical choice, rating, and ranking paradigms. In particular, our approach allows us to use the kinds of ballot data that are available from many real elections (e.g., plurality bloc voting, the single transferable vote, the alternative vote, and approval voting) and the kinds of data that are frequently collected in surveys (e.g., thermometer ratings and proximity data in national election studies) to make inferences about the distribution of underlying preferences. We illustrate our general approach with a particular emphasis on "feeling thermometer" survey data and on "approval voting" (i.e., "subset choice") election ballot data.

4 Model Dependence. We discuss the fundamental problem of model dependence of social choice results. As mentioned above, theoretical results about majority rule outcomes may dramatically change as one moves from one model of preferences and their distributions to another. For instance, our theoretical view of behaviorally appropriate domains of preference relations and preference distributions minimizes the likelihood of cycles and reverses a common policy recommendation about voter turnout. In the empirical domain we show how the analysis of empirical data may crucially depend on the implicit or explicit modeling assumptions that enter the analysis. When we analyze the same set of data with multiple competing models, we find that the inferred preferences and preference distributions can be dramatically different across models. Nonetheless, by and large, the nature of the majority preference relation is not dramatically affected. Moreover, virtually all our analyses of all data sets in this book share the common conclusion that majority preferences are transitive. (The exceptional analyses, i.e., those that do not rule out a cycle, do not provide strong evidence for the presence of a cycle either.)

5 A General Sampling and Inference Framework. Classical social choice theory relies on statistics largely in work on sampling from the impartial culture or other cultures of indifference. We develop a statistical sampling and Bayesian inference framework for the theoretical and empirical investigation of majority rule decision making in samples drawn from practically any distribution over any family of binary relations (over finitely many candidates). This allows us to place upper and lower bounds on the probability of any majority outcome (cycle or not) in a sample given almost any population, or in the population given almost any sample. Our method provides, by and large, very tight bounds on these probabilities. In particular, it allows us to place tight bounds on the probability of a cycle in a fashion that reaches far beyond the traditional cultures of indifference used in classical sampling work. More importantly, using this method, as long as we know the pairwise preference margins among each pair of candidates in a random sample, we can place upper and lower bounds on the probability of any conceivable majority preference relation in the population from which this sample was drawn. We believe that this constitutes a major milestone in our ability to study majority rule outcomes, both theoretically and empirically. To our knowledge, this is also the first full-fledged statistical framework for the investigation of classical social choice concepts such as, in this book, majority rule decision making. At a practical level, this book provides tools that can be applied to a variety of real world data sets in order to address a range of important issues.

6 Majority Preference Misestimation. There is, however, one aspect of our approach and findings that raises an important caveat about the processes of democracy. We argue that one must think of ballot casting and counting as noisy processes, which correctly record a given voter's current preference with probability less than one.[9] "Preference misestimations" (by which we mean erroneous estimates of the population majority preference) can also arise in estimating preferences from incomplete voting or survey sample data.[10] While we are not the first to note these issues,

---

[9] Also, we can think of the choices of individual voters (e.g., whether or not to vote, and, if to vote, whom to vote for) as nondeterministic (i.e., probabilistic) processes. Furthermore, we believe that many voters experience uncertainty about candidates' utilities and/or their own preferences, and thus the 'correct' preference of a voter may have to be conceptualized either as a statistic of a probability distribution over possible preference states, or as being a random draw from such a distribution.

[10] Note that the term "preference misestimation," as we use it, should not be confused with either strategic misrepresentation of preferences, as used in game theory, or with

we are the first to suggest, and empirically illustrate, that preference mis-estimations may pose a far greater threat to democratic decision making than majority cycles. Our analytic results show how to precisely assess both the likelihood of cycles and of majority preference misestimations using real-world data for which voter preferences between any pair of alternatives are known or can be estimated.

In illustration of these latter points, consider the uncertainties of the 2000 United States presidential election that transfixed America and the world from election day in November until early December 2000. In this context, we observe that, clearly, nobody was ever concerned about the possibility of a majority cycle among Bush, Gore, and Nader in that election. "Who won Florida?", "Who won the majority of the electoral college votes?" were the questions. The issue was whether or not the outcome of the election might 'accidentally' misestimate the electorate's 'true' preferences by reversing the top two choices. Hence, the central questions regarding that election concern accuracy of the assessment of majority preferences. With only two strong candidates, the possible occurrence of majority cycles was simply not an issue.[11]

SUMMARY

Throughout the book, we assume that the set of candidates/options/alternatives, that voters/survey respondents rate/rank/choose from, is finite.[12] We begin each chapter with a chapter summary, which we keep as informal and as nonmathematical as possible. In principle, each chapter can be read independently of the others. Whenever material from another chapter plays a critical role, we refer back to the chapter (definition,

---

Althaus' (1998, 2003) misrepresentation of public opinion due to "information effects." According to Althaus, the uneven social distribution of political knowledge in mass publics may distort the assessment of collective opinion in surveys.

[11] This is the concern which underlies the statutes mandating election recounts in various American states whenever the winning candidate's margin of victory falls below some specified threshold.

[12] Scholars interested in cycles have also studied what happens when the alternatives can be thought of as points in an *n*-dimensional space, giving us an infinite set of possible alternatives. The key result is that, in two or more dimensions, we can expect that the entire space of alternatives will be in a majority rule cycle (McKelvey, 1976, 1979). However, if we impose some constraints, e.g., voting one issue dimension at a time (Shepsle and Weingast, 1981) or ruling out pairwise votes involving alternatives that are highly similar to one another, or setting limits on how many alternatives may be considered (Feld and Grofman, 1996; Feld et al., 1989; Miller et al., 1989), we can avoid cycling (always, in the first case; almost always in the second and third cases).

theorem, and/or equation) in question. Keeping the chapters somewhat independent of each other, however, entails a small amount of repetition across chapters.

The book has three parts.

Part I consists of two mainly theoretical chapters, each of which also contains a short section illustrating applications of the theoretical points and analytic tools, developed in the chapter, to real-world data. Chapter 1 deals with theoretical arguments bearing on the prevalence of cycles. Chapter 2 presents a very general probabilistic approach to defining majority rule that is consistent with a broad range of deterministic and probabilistic representations of preference and utility.

Part II also consists of two chapters, each of which develops models bearing on how one may construct underlying voter/actor preferences from data that do not necessarily provide full rankings or full information about pairwise preferences. The first of these chapters is primarily data oriented, while the second is both data and theory oriented. Chapter 3 shows that the majority outcomes constructed from survey data may be affected by the implicit or explicit model used in the analysis. Chapter 4 expands the same logic to "subset choice" data.

Part III consists of two chapters. Chapter 5 studies majority rule both theoretically and as applied to data, in a statistical sampling and a Bayesian inference framework. Chapter 6 reviews the key theoretical and empirical results in the earlier chapters and discusses a variety of topics for future research.

We now give a more detailed summary of each of the six chapters.

Part I

Chapter 1 deals with theoretical arguments bearing on the prevalence of majority cycles.

One of social choice theory's classic preoccupations has been with *majority rule cycles*. There is a considerable body of theoretical work estimating the probability of such cycles, the best known estimates being derived from random samples drawn from a uniform distribution over all linear (or weak) orders, i.e., from the impartial culture (Black, 1958; Riker, 1982; Shepsle and Bonchek, 1997).[13] The theoretical literature

---

[13] This distribution has been extensively studied. For linear orders, see, e.g., Black (1958); DeMeyer and Plott (1970); Garman and Kamien (1968); Gehrlein and Fishburn (1976a,b); Klahr (1966); Niemi and Weisberg (1968). For weak orders, see, e.g., Fishburn and Gehrlein (1980); Jones et al. (1995); Tangian (2000); Van Deemen (1999).

based on the impartial culture suggests that the probability of cycles increases as the number of alternatives increases, approaching a certainty of finding a cycle as the number of alternatives gets very large (Shepsle and Bonchek, 1997). In contrast, for only three alternatives, the probability of cycles has been estimated to approach about .088. However, the empirical literature yields virtually no evidence of majority cycles in voter preferences over major candidates or parties. The few cycles that have been observed tend to be among alternatives that are low-ranked and amongst which voters are not readily able to discriminate.[14] The failure to find almost any cycles in survey data (and equally few cycles in legislative roll call data, even when we include contrived cycles due to strategic voting of the sort described by Riker, 1958) led the economist Gordon Tullock (1981, see also Grofman and Uhlaner, 1985; Niemi, 1983) to ask the question: "Why so much stability?" This kind of contrast between most contemporary theoretical results and available empirical data is an important force driving the theoretical and empirical aspects of this book.

The first part of Chapter 1 considers the flaws in using theoretical and simulation results based on the impartial culture and closely related distributions as the basis for the claim that cycles are of practical importance. While it is widely acknowledged that the impartial culture is unrealistic, conclusions drawn from the use of that culture are nevertheless still widely reproduced in textbooks. We demonstrate analytically that the impartial culture is the "worst case scenario" among a very broad range of possible voter preference distributions, where by "worst case scenario" we mean the one most likely to produce majority cycles. More specifically, we show that any deviation from the impartial culture over linear orders reduces the probability of majority cycles in infinite samples unless the culture from which we sample is itself intransitive. Indeed, if the underlying culture contains no majority ties and no majority intransitivities, then infinite samples will have majority cycles with probability zero. By extension, sufficiently large electorates will encounter the Condorcet paradox with probability arbitrarily close to zero.

Moreover, since the impartial culture implies that, in the population, social preference is a complete tie, we argue that results drawn from it are of little practical importance.[15] Consequentially, we argue for the need for

---

[14] The potential for cycles among (such minor) candidates that voters can hardly discriminate is, of course, consistent with the results obtained from the impartial culture.

[15] The common use of sampling in applied statistics is to calculate a statistic in a random sample, with the hope that this statistic will be a good 'guess' of some population

analyses based on distributions of the highly nonuniform sort encountered in real-world data.

The second part of Chapter 1 considers another key theoretical argument that seemingly leads to the inevitability of cycles, namely Sen's (1970) famous value restriction condition. This classic condition is sometimes interpreted as providing a necessary condition for transitive majority preferences, and therefore, since this condition is essentially never met with real world data, as predicting that cycles are inevitable. After briefly showing that the claim that value restriction is necessary to avoid cycles rests on a misinterpretation of Sen, we show that, in fact, value restriction merely provides a sufficient condition for transitive majority preferences. We then develop extensions of Sen's never-best (*NB*, single-troughedness), never-middle (*NM*, polarization), and never-worst (*NW*, single-peakedness) conditions. These extensions are defined in terms of a cancellation of opposite preference orderings so as to generate "net preference probabilities." A straightforward generalization of Sen's value restriction, which we call "net value restriction," plus a "net preference majority" condition, are then shown to be both necessary and sufficient for transitive majorities when preferences are linear orders. We illustrate the results of the chapter with data from three German National Election Studies. Sen's value restriction is violated in each of these data sets, but nevertheless the majority preferences are transitive in each set. We show how our net value restriction condition accounts for such absence of majority cycles. We also show that, with extremely high (statistical) confidence, none of these data sets was a random sample from an impartial culture.

Chapter 2 presents a general probabilistic approach to defining majority rule. The mathematical formulation in that chapter provides the

---

parameter. Hence, if we think of the majority preference relation in a random sample from some distribution as a sample statistic aimed at estimating the majority preferences in the population that this sample was drawn from, then the study of majority cycles in random samples from a uniform distribution becomes highly suspect: A population with a uniform distribution has in fact a complete majority tie among all candidates and, therefore, anything other than a majority tie in a random sample will be a sample outcome that does not match the population parameter (majority tie) we are trying to recover. In particular, note that a uniform distribution over linear orders includes an even number of orders as each order and its inverse are included. Then, if we draw random samples of odd size from that distribution over linear orders (this is the standard procedure in this strand of literature), then it is impossible for the sample majority preference to match the population majority preference (a complete tie) for any sample size (in particular for arbitrarily large odd sample size).

basic theoretical tool kit for the remainder of the book. We develop a general concept of majority rule for finitely many choice alternatives that is consistent with arbitrary binary preference relations, real-valued utility functions, probability distributions over binary preference relations, and random utility representations. The underlying framework is applicable to virtually any type of choice, rating, or ranking data, not just the linear orders or paired comparisons assumed by classic majority rule social welfare functions. We begin with a general definition of majority rule for arbitrary binary relations that contains the standard definition for linear orders as a special case. Then we develop a natural way to project, three elements at a time, from arbitrary binary relations onto the set of linear orders in such a way that the majority preferences are preserved. By defining majority rule in terms of the theoretical primitives that are common to virtually all models of choice, rating, or ranking, we provide a common ground for the theoretical and empirical analysis of majority rule within a panoply of basic and applied research paradigms. Furthermore, in direct contrast to work on domain restrictions in social choice theory, we dramatically expand the domain of permissible preferences (or utility functions).

The second part of Chapter 2 generalizes Sen's (1966, 1970) seminal concept of value restriction and our related results of Chapter 1 to general binary relations. Again, while Sen's condition restricts the domain of permissible preference states by ruling out certain states, we continue to use the extremely broad domain introduced earlier, and instead restrict the distributions of preferences in appropriate ways. When individual preferences are allowed to be more general than the linear orders considered in Chapter 1, then neither net value restriction nor net preference majority is necessary for transitive majority preferences. Net value restriction is sufficient for transitive strict majority preferences, but not sufficient for a transitive weak preference majority. Net majority is sufficient for a transitive preference majority only if the preference relation with a net majority is a weak order. An application of our results to four U.S. National Election Study data sets reveals a transitive preference majority in each case, despite a violation of Sen's original value restriction condition (in fact, despite a violation of any possible domain restriction condition). However, a similar analysis of Communist voters in the 1988 French National Election Study reveals that this extremely homogeneous group satisfies Sen's value restriction because certain preference states fail to be reported by any of the Communist respondents. This finding may suggest that domain restriction conditions could be behaviorally adequate descriptions of certain highly homogeneous subgroups of national electorates.

Part II

Chapter 3 begins by discussing the fact that virtually no social choice procedure or survey research study reports complete pairwise comparisons or a complete linear order of the choice alternatives for each voter, as required in order to evaluate standard majority rule. Thus, majority rule can almost never be computed directly from ballots or survey data; in particular, the *Condorcet criterion*, which requires that a majority winner be elected whenever it exists, cannot usually be applied directly to the available 'raw' data. Building on these facts, and using our general definition of majority rule developed in Chapter 2, we show that any (re)construction of majority preferences from ballot or survey data is sensitive to the underlying implicit or explicit model of decision making. This methodology is illustrated by developing semiorder representations of 100-point "thermometer" evaluations of candidates in several multicandidate U.S. presidential elections. The distribution of preferences depends on the utility discrimination threshold we use in the translation of thermometer scores into semiorders. However, the fact that majority preferences are transitive turns out not to be affected by the choice of threshold in these data. We also discover in this context that our general concept of net value restriction is often technically violated, yet still 'very nearly satisfied' by the semiorder distributions, and, in fact, we find transitive majorities in all cases.

Chapter 4 continues the discussion of how to compute majority preference relations from 'incomplete data,' i.e., data that do not provide the full rankings or complete paired comparisons which are technically required as input for majority rule computations. We focus on "subset choice," i.e., choice situations where one fixed set of choice alternatives (candidates, products) is offered to a group of decision makers, each of whom is requested to pick a preferred subset containing any number of alternatives. In this context, we merge three choice paradigms, namely "approval voting" from political science, the "weak utility model" from mathematical psychology, and "majority rule social welfare orderings" from classical social choice theory. We primarily use a probabilistic choice model, called the *size-independent model*, proposed by Falmagne and Regenwetter (1996), that is built upon the notion that each voter has a (possibly latent) personal strict linear order (or complete ranking) of the alternatives and chooses a subset (possibly nondeterministically) at the top of the linear order. Using our extension of Sen's (1966) theorem about value restriction, discussed in Section 1.2, we provide necessary and sufficient conditions for this empirically testable choice model to yield a transitive majority preference order. Furthermore, we develop a method for computing Condorcet winners from such subset choice probabilities. We also introduce an alternative model, Regenwetter's (1997) *topset voting model*, for inferring preference distributions (and majority orders) from subset choice data. This model is built on the idea that each voter is indifferent between her/his approved candidates and indifferent between all other candidates, while preferring all approved candidates to those not approved. We illustrate the application of both models to seven real and mock elections conducted under approval voting.

Our empirical illustrations, again, fail to find convincing evidence for majority cycles. Two data sets allow for the possibility of cyclical majority preferences consistent with the size-independent model. However, in both cases, the model yields several different possible majority relations, and the cycles occur only in a relatively small part of the solution space of the model.

Part III

Chapter 5 studies majority rule both theoretically and as applied to data, in a statistical sampling and a Bayesian inference framework. Conceptually, the work in this chapter is closely related to the notion of *Condorcet efficiency*: The Condorcet efficiency of a social choice procedure is defined usually as the probability that the outcome of this procedure coincides with the majority winner (or majority ordering) in random samples, given that a majority winner exists (or given that the majority ordering is transitive in the sample). Consequently, it is in effect a conditional probability that two sample statistics coincide, given certain side conditions. We raise a different issue of Condorcet efficiency: What is the probability that the outcome of a social choice procedure applied to a sample matches the majority preferences of the population from which the sample was drawn? Whenever a sample majority preference relation matches the population's majority preference relation, we call this sample majority relation the "correct majority relation"; otherwise, we call it an "incorrect majority relation." We apply the same logic to the majority winner. While majority cycles may pose a threat to democratic decision making, actual decisions based (intentionally or inadvertently) upon a misestimated majority preference relation may be far more expensive to society.

Chapter 5 presents a rather elegant method of bounds that leads to theoretical results about the likelihood of both cycles and of preference misestimations for samples drawn from virtually any distribution. Based on any given paired comparison probabilities or ranking probabilities in a population (i.e., "culture") of reference, we derive upper and lower bounds on the probability of a correct or incorrect majority social welfare relation in a random sample (with replacement). We also show how to go in the opposite direction, from sample to population, by presenting upper and lower bounds on the (posterior) probabilities of the permissible majority preference relations in the population given what is observed in a sample. Our approach uses a Bayesian updating and inference framework.

We argue that sampling needs to be seen in a broad sense: Data generated or gathered under conditions of uncertainty need to be thought of as a sample (possibly biased) from some underlying distribution. More precisely, any process with an uncertain outcome is, technically, a random variable. Every collection of repeated and independent observations of such outcomes is a random sample. Therefore, as a first approximation, it is very natural to think of ballot counts as being random samples.

We are able to show that, for real-world social choice data, preference misestimation – a situation where a sampling process generates observed choices, which are different from the (majority) preferences of the population – is a far more important phenomenon than (majority) cycles. We demonstrate this fact by looking at the likelihood of both cycles and incorrect social preference outcomes in samples drawn from a number of real world data sets, including U.S. and French presidential elections and German legislative elections, involving three or more candidates or parties. We find no evidence of cycles in any of the populations we examine. Moreover, in general, we show that the potential for incorrect assessments and inferences about majority preferences or candidate/party rankings, derived from sampling, dramatically overwhelms the potential for obtaining sample majority cycles; the latter has previously been the sole concern of social choice theorists interested in sampling models. This means that we ought to worry about misestimation, especially when dealing with heterogeneous groups and small sets of data. We show that variations in preference homogeneity among "stratified" population sub-samples have important consequences for the relative importance of preference misestimation and cycles (e.g., on our examples of Middle Class, Communist-leaning, Socialist-leaning, and other subgroups of voters in France).

Chapter 6 argues that this book makes two important broad contributions to the decision sciences. First, we provide the formal underpinnings

for various social choice processes viewed probabilistically in terms of inferences from many types of voting or survey data, and provide a bridge
between social choice theory as developed primarily by economists and
random utility models as developed by both economists and psychologists.
Many social choice concepts have been defined only for linear or weak
order preferences, while decision theorists and psychologists study much
more general representations such as partial orders, real valued utility
functions, probabilistic preference relations, and random utility representations. In particular, we show how majority rule may be studied in many
empirical settings where the data do not provide the required full ranking
or full paired comparison information that is needed to apply the traditional definition of majority rule. Thus, the theoretical work reported in
this book provides the basis for a better integration of social choice theory
with the rest of the decision sciences in terms of a nonparametric random
utility and probabilistic preference framework. We do not know of any
other work in social choice theory that has explicitly attempted to reach
such a general integrative point of view as ours, although there is some
work on integrating multiple deterministic representations of preferences
and comparing multiple aggregation methods, most notably the seminal
work of Donald Saari (1994, 1995).

Second, we believe that our work makes an important contribution to
the reconciliation of normative and descriptive viewpoints, and counters
the pessimism of scholars such as Riker (1982) regarding the possibility of
democratic decision making. In particular, we argue that the implications
of results such as Arrow's impossibility theorem, Sen's value restriction
theorem, and analytic and simulation results about the likelihood of cycles under the assumption of the impartial culture and other cultures of
indifference, need to be understood in the light of evidence about actual
distributions of voter preferences. For example, impossibility results tell
us what may happen; they do not tell us how likely such events are to
occur. We show both analytically and empirically that preference misestimations (e.g., inference errors in estimating population rankings) are
considerably more likely to be a problem than cycles.[16] With regard to

---

[16] Note that when we talk about majority cycles we mean cycles in preferences, not
contrived cycles based on strategic manipulation of ballots. There is an important literature on the latter, beginning with Riker (1961; 1965). The idea is that, although there is
no cycle among the voter preferences, strategic voting by a subset of the voters can create
the appearance that there is a cycle. Empirical evidence about such claims is discussed in
Mackie (2003).

majority cycles and mass electorates, we therefore conclude that democratic decision making is possible![17]

Chapter 6 also considers directions for further research in behavioral social choice. These include extensions beyond majority rule to its leading normative contender the Borda rule (and related scoring rules), and to (nonmajoritarian) procedures for selecting more than one alternative, such as electoral rules aimed at proportional representation (e.g., the single nontransferable vote); extensions to types of data other than thermometer scores and subset choice ballots; and work in experimental behavioral social choice, building on the research tradition of Vernon Smith, Charles Plott, and others, but also integrating recent work on deliberative democracy.

---

[17] Note that some arguments have been made that majority cycling *over time* can be desirable. The most prominent example is the Madisonian argument (e.g., by Miller, 1983) that every time you cycle you change the nature of the winning coalition, thus preventing the permanent tyranny of a given majority.

I

PROBABILISTIC MODELS OF SOCIAL CHOICE BEHAVIOR

1

The Lack of Theoretical and Practical Support
for Majority Cycles

Chapter Summary

This chapter demonstrates the limited theoretical and empirical relevance of two common topics in theoretical work on majority cycles, namely the "impartial culture" (and related distributions), and Sen's "value restriction" condition (and similar domain restrictions on feasible preferences). One can view the impartial culture and value restriction conditions as two opposite extremes: given a family of binary preference relations (traditionally either linear or weak orders), the impartial culture assumption states that each preference is possible and occurs with equal probability, whereas domain restrictions such as value restriction, single-peakedness, or others, rule out certain preference states entirely and assume that the remaining preference states can occur with any well defined probability. We show that both extremes are behaviorally inadequate descriptions of social choice data and we shift our focus to conditions that neither rule out certain preference states, nor require preference states to follow a uniform distribution. Instead, we study other constraints on so-called "net preference probabilities," their theoretical implications for majority rule decision making, as well as their descriptive empirical validity.

Many papers have studied the "Condorcet paradox" (of majority cycles) using the so-called "impartial culture" assumption or related distributional assumptions. (For formal definitions of the various relevant cultures, see Appendix A.) Under the *impartial culture* assumption, a voter preference profile (i.e., frequency distribution of preferences) is a random sample, with replacement, from a uniform distribution over linear orders or weak orders. While it is widely acknowledged that the impartial culture assumption is unrealistic, conclusions drawn from that culture are nevertheless still widely reported and reproduced in textbooks (e.g., Shepsle and Bonchek, 1997).[1] In this chapter, we argue that the impartial culture is the <u>worst case scenario</u> (with respect to majority rule outcomes in random samples) among a very broad range of possible voter preference distributions. More specifically, we show that <u>any</u> deviation from the impartial culture over linear orders <u>reduces</u> the probability of majority cycles in infinite samples, unless we sample from an inherently intransitive culture, i.e., a culture with an intransitive majority preference. We prove this statement for the case of three candidates and we discuss the conjecture that the statement extends to any finite number of candidates.

Another important body of research on majority cycles investigates restrictions on feasible preferences. One of the most important of such restrictions is Sen's "value restriction" condition (see the definition later in the text). Unfortunately, there appears to be a misperception among some researchers that Sen's (1969, 1970) value restriction condition is both necessary and sufficient for the avoidance of majority cycles.[2] This misperception suggests an unduly pessimistic view about the prevalence of majority cycles, in that Sen's condition is rarely satisfied in large-scale

---

[1] However, most recent research papers either avoid or downplay the policy implications of results based on this assumption.

[2] It is well known (Van Deemen, 1999) that it is misleading for anyone to characterize Sen's original value restriction conditions as 'necessary and sufficient conditions on a (single) preference profile for majority rule to be transitive.' Sen's (1970) statements are much more subtle. First, Sen (1970) uses the term 'necessary condition' in a rather peculiar way, by limiting himself to conditions that can be expressed without reference to any actual assignment of voter frequencies to the preferences that are allowed to occur in the profile. See his Definition 10*9 (Sen, 1970, p. 183) of 'necessary condition,' and his subsequent comments. In other words, Sen's necessary and sufficient condition on preference profiles is a condition that guarantees majority preferences to be transitive, no matter what frequency (or probability) distribution we assign to the preference relations that are allowed to occur in the profile. Sen acknowledges that other natural definitions of 'necessary condition' are possible (p. 183). We believe that many people in the field use the term 'necessary condition' in a different way, namely in the way that we use it here.

Sen's notion of necessity is too strong if it is to be checked on a single assignment of frequencies (probabilities) to the preference relations in the profile. Even for linear orders, it is easy to show that there are specific (probability) distributions (over preference relations) that simultaneously violate NB, NM, and NW, yet are transitive according to majority rule. Consider for example, two voters with preference ordering abc, plus one voter with each of the preference orderings acb, bac, bca, cab, and cba, respectively. The transitive majority is abc, yet all of Sen's value restriction conditions are violated in the sense that each alternative is ranked at each position at least once.

real-world data.[3] However, we may still have transitivity of majority preferences when Sen's value restriction does not hold.

In order to account for possible transitivities in settings where value restriction is violated, we provide new results that generalize Sen's theorem to "net preference probabilities" (for closely related concepts, see Feld and Grofman, 1986b; Gärtner and Heinecke, 1978). This generalization involves two observable properties each of which is sufficient, and at least one of which is necessary, for the existence of a transitive majority preference relation for a given probability distribution on linear orders. The conditions are called "net value restriction" and "net preference majority" and are much weaker than Sen's value restriction condition. To constrast our conditions with Sen's conditions in a nutshell: While Sen's conditions place constraints on the domain of possible preference relations without constraining the possible preference distributions on that domain, our conditions place no constraints on the domain of possible preferences but instead place constraints on the possible distributions of preferences on that domain.[4]

Paralleling our theoretical discussion, we provide empirical illustrations of the two main points, namely that the impartial culture is an unrealistic assumption, and that Sen's value restriction is not needed to avoid cycles. We look at some of the few data sets that provide linear orders from a large number of individuals. Using these data sets we also demonstrate that our conditions of net preference majority and net value restriction are able to explain the absence of majority cycles despite the violation of Sen's conditions. Our illustrative data also show that it is generally behaviorally unrealistic to place constraints on the domain of possible preferences, since every permissible preference state (here, every linear order) is reported by a substantial number of voters in these data. Instead, our approach of constraining the possible distributions of preferences over the full domain (via our net value restriction and net preference majority conditions) proves to be successful in providing descriptively valid constraints.

The chapter is organized as follows: Section 1.1 shows how the impartial culture and related assumptions form a worst case scenario for the

---

[3] Of course, if we consider sufficiently politically homogenous subpopulations then the condition may hold. We see this in the Communist subgroup in Chapter 2.

[4] To be more precise: Sen considers strict weak order preferences and domain constraints within that family. In this chapter, we consider strict linear order preferences, without any constraint on the permissible preferences within that family. In Chapter 2 we expand the domain to the familly of all (finite) binary relations.

assessment of the probability of majority cycles. Section 1.2 discusses our generalizations of Sen's value restriction conditions in terms of net preference probabilities. Section 1.3 provides several empirical illustrations which underscore our theoretical points. The impartial culture assumption is consistently violated and majority preferences are consistently transitive, despite the fact that Sen's conditions are violated in each data set. Section 1.4 concludes with a synthesis and discussion.

This chapter assumes that individual preferences are (strict) linear orders or sometimes (strict) weak orders. (Here and throughout, we assume that the number of choice alternatives, or candidates, is finite.) Starting with Chapter 2 we allow individual preference states to be arbitrary (asymmetric) binary relations. We give formal definitions of all relevant binary relations in Appendix B. Here we briefly introduce the concepts of linear orders and weak orders, that are central to the present chapter. A *strict linear order* is a transitive, asymmetric, and complete binary relation. There is a well-known one-to-one correspondence between strict linear orders on alternatives and *(complete) rankings, without ties,* of alternatives.[5] In this chapter we use the terms strict linear order, linear order, and ranking interchangeably. A *weak order* is a transitive and strongly complete binary relation. A *strict weak* order is the asymmetric part of a weak order (i.e., ties are not counted as a 'preference both ways' but as a 'lack of strict preference either way'). There exists a wellknown one-to-one correspondence between weak or strict weak orders and *rankings, with possible ties,* of alternatives. Unless it is important to emphasize the difference, we use the terms weak order and strict weak order interchangeably in this section. We also treat both as synonymous with 'ranking with possible ties.' Every strict linear order is a strict weak order, but not conversely.

1.1 THE IMPARTIAL CULTURE AND MAJORITY CYCLES: A WORST CASE SCENARIO

One of social choice theory's classic preoccupations has been with "majority rule cycles." The simplest example of the "paradox of cyclical majorities," also called the *Condorcet paradox,* occurs with three voters choosing among three alternatives, here labeled *a, b,* and *c.* Let voter 1 have preference order *abc,* voter 2 have preference order *bca,* and voter

---

[5] A *ranking, without ties,* of *n* many choice alternatives is a one-to-one mapping from the choice alternatives onto $\{1, 2, \ldots, n\}$.

3 have preference order *cab*. Then, majorities prefer *a* to *b* and *b* to *c*, which might lead us to expect that a majority prefers *a* to *c*. But this is not the case. Instead, a majority prefers *c* to *a*, and therefore these majority preferences form a cycle, i.e., they are not transitive.[6]

Much analytical/theoretical work on majority rule has been devoted to the probability of cycles occurring in samples (groups of people) of different sizes. The most widely used probability distribution of preferences to generate the random profiles has been the impartial culture. The *impartial culture* is a uniform distribution over linear orders (Black, 1958; DeMeyer and Plott, 1970; Garman and Kamien, 1968; Gehrlein and Fishburn, 1976a,b; Guilbaud, 1952; Klahr, 1966; Niemi and Weisberg, 1968) or weak orders (Fishburn and Gehrlein, 1980; Jones et al., 1995; Tangian, 2000; Van Deemen, 1999). The impartial culture is an example of a *culture of indifference*, by which we mean that every pairwise majority (in the population) is a majority tie (see also Appendix A). While the bulk of research on the Condorcet paradox was done two or more decades ago, there continue to be occasional refinements in the literature.

The theoretical literature on the impartial culture suggests that the probability of cycles increases as the number of alternatives increases, approaching a certainty of finding a cycle as the number of alternatives gets very large (Riker, 1982; Shepsle and Bonchek, 1997). Even for only three alternatives, the probability of cycles has been estimated to approach about 8.8% as the number of voters approaches infinity. An overview of cycling probabilities under the impartial culture, compiled by Riker (1982), is provided in Table 1.1. The table shows the probability of a majority cycle as a function of the number of voters (horizontal dimension) and the number of candidates (vertical dimension). These are probabilities of cyclical majority outcomes in random samples drawn with replacement from a uniform distribution over linear orders, i.e., the traditional impartial culture.

Some researchers have also investigated the probabilities of majority cycles in samples drawn from a uniform distribution over weak orders. For three alternatives that probability has been estimated to approach 5.6% as the number of voters approaches infinity (e.g., Jones et al., 1995; Van Deemen, 1999). From here on, we sometimes use the abbreviation *infinite sample* to refer to the limiting case of samples of size *n* as $n \to \infty$.

---

[6] Note that the individual preferences satisfy transitivity, even though transitivity is violated at the level of aggregated majority rule.

TABLE 1.1: *Probabilities of Majority Cycles in Samples Drawn from the Impartial Culture (uniform distribution over linear orders)*

Number of Candidates	Number of Voters					
	3	5	7	9	11	∞
3	.056	.069	.075	.078	.080	.088
4	.111	.139	.150	.156	.160	.176
5	.160	.200	.215			.251
6	.202					.315
∞	≈ 1.00	≈ 1.00	≈ 1.00	≈ 1.00	≈ 1.00	≈ 1.00

Source: Riker (1982) (p. 122).

Without loss of generality the reader can assume that all samples are drawn with replacement.

Although the theoretical literature suggests that majority cycles should be ubiquitous (at least if there are many alternatives), the empirical literature yields virtually no evidence of cycles among voter preferences over major candidates or parties (see esp. Brady, 1990; Chamberlin et al., 1984; Dobra, 1983; Dobra and Tullock, 1981; Feld and Grofman, 1988, 1990, 1992; Kurrild-Klitgard, 2001; Niemi, 1970; Niemi and Wright, 1987; Radcliff, 1997; Regenwetter and Grofman, 1998a; Van Deemen and Vergunst, 1998). Moreover, the few cycles that have been observed tend to be among alternatives that are low-ranked and among which voters are not readily able to discriminate. The failure to find almost any cycles in survey data (and equally few cycles in legislative roll call data, even when we include contrived cycles due to strategic voting of the sort described by Riker, 1958) led the economist Gordon Tullock (1981; see also Grofman and Uhlaner, 1985; Niemi, 1983) to ask the question: "Why so much stability?"

As we mentioned above, Jones et al. (1995) ran Monte Carlo simulations in which they drew random samples from a uniform distribution over weak orders. They concluded that making preferences more 'realistic' by allowing for weak order preferences (instead of linear order preferences) reduces the probability of cycles significantly. They argued that this more 'realistic' representation of preferences leads to cycle probabilities that are more consistent with the fact that cycles are rarely encountered empirically. In our view, by focusing on the switch from linear orders to weak orders, these authors missed the core problem with the impartial culture assumption. We argue here that changing the distribution in any fashion (whether we call it 'realistic' or not) away from an impartial culture over linear orders will automatically have the effect of reducing the probability of majority cycles in infinite samples as long as the underlying culture itself does not have an intransitive majority preference relation. In other words, we conjecture (and prove for three candidates) that in all cases but the degenerate case that presumes the Condorcet paradox from the start, the impartial culture over linear orders is the worst case scenario. Here, and even more so in Chapter 5, we demonstrate that, in sampling processes based on some real-world data, cycles will occur with probability near zero for sufficiently large samples.

Section 1.1 is organized as follows. Subsection 1.1.1 provides some useful background information and a primer on our argument. Subsection 1.1.2 contains three theorems. Theorem 1.1.1 states that if the weak majority preference of the culture is transitive then, for three candidates, the probability of cycles in infinite samples is nonzero only for a culture of indifference. Theorem 1.1.2 shows that, for three candidates, the impartial culture over linear orders maximizes the probability of cycles in the class of all cultures of indifference over weak orders. Combining Theorems 1.1.1 and 1.1.2 yields Theorem 1.1.3, which can be summarized as follows: in the case of three candidates the impartial culture over linear orders maximizes the probability of cycles in infinite samples drawn from any culture over weak orders which does not have a weak majority intransitivity built in from the start. Subsection 1.1.3 states the conjecture that the same result holds regardless of the number of candidates, and provides several arguments for its support. All proofs are in Appendix C.

1.1.1 Background

Fifteen years before Jones et al.'s (1995) paper on the Condorcet paradox in samples from a weak order distribution, Fishburn and Gehrlein (1980) analytically derived the probability of cycles for three, four, and five candidates in infinite samples drawn from any mixture of the impartial culture over linear orders and impartial cultures over weak orders with a fixed number of ties.[7] From their formula it follows that (for three, four, or five candidates) the impartial culture over linear orders maximizes the probability of cycles among all mixtures of the impartial culture over linear orders and impartial cultures over weak orders with a fixed number

---

[7] Fishburn and Gehrlein (1980) have unfortunately been largely ignored in the literature. In particular, they are not cited in Jones et al. (1995). For an earlier study based on computer simulations, see Bjurulf (1972).

of ties (see also Appendix A for more details).[8] Jones et al. (1995) report Monte Carlo simulation results that are consistent with these analytical formulae, but which expand these results to finite samples and to more than five candidates (see also Timpone and Taber, 1998, for more details). Jones et al. conclude that for large samples ($n > 501$), "highly indifferent electorates are most likely to find Condorcet winners" (Jones et al., 1995, p. 141). The parallel finding for infinite samples was already stated in Fishburn and Gehrlein (1980): "... it is seen that the likelihood of the [Condorcet] paradox decreases as individual indifference increases" (Fishburn and Gehrlein, 1980, abstract).

Gehrlein (1999, p. 38) shows that the impartial culture over linear orders for three candidates maximizes the probability of cycles in samples drawn from any *dual culture* (where only linear orders are possible, and each linear order has the same probability as its reverse linear order).[9] Thus, for three candidates and linear order individual preferences, any deviation from a 'symmetric' distribution (e.g., a distribution that is invariant with respect to relabelings of the candidates) also reduces the probability of cycles.

All these results suggest that the traditional impartial culture over linear orders is a worst case scenario in the sense that it maximizes the probability of cycles, at least in infinite samples.[10]

However, all sampling results that we are aware of compare the impartial culture only to particular other cultures of indifference and therefore are only special case results. Thus, the first question we pose is whether the impartial culture maximizes the probability of cycles among all cultures of indifference. Our ultimate question in this section is whether the

---

[8] Although all the necessary mathematics is present in Fishburn and Gehrlein (1980), the final formula for the case of three candidates appears explicitly only in Lemma 1 of Gehrlein and Valognes (2001).

[9] For three candidates, the dual culture is a culture of indifference over linear orders. Therefore, Gehrlein (1999) proves that the impartial culture maximizes the probability of cycles compared to any culture of indifference over *linear orders* for three candidates. See also Appendix A.

[10] The existing research on the *impartial anonymous culture* (where only linear orders are possible, and each profile is equally probable) also supports this thesis: for three candidates and infinite sample size, the probability of cycles for the impartial anonymous culture is $\frac{1}{16}$ (Gehrlein and Fishburn, 1976b), which is less than the probability of cycles for the impartial culture over linear orders (0.088).

   In the *maximal culture* (where a positive integer L is selected, and, for each linear order, the number of voters having that linear order is drawn from a uniform distribution on the integers $\{1, 2, \ldots, L\}$), the probability of cycles is no less than $\frac{11}{120}$ (Gehrlein and Lepelley, 1997). (Notice that the maximal culture does not have a fixed number of voters.) See also Appendix A for more details on these cultures.

impartial culture maximizes the probability of cyclic samples among all cultures that are not already cyclic to start with. To the best of our knowledge, the answer to that question has not been provided in the literature.[11]

Our main theorem (Theorem 1.1.3) proves that, in the case of three candidates, the impartial culture is indeed the worst case scenario in the sense that it maximizes the probability of majority cycles in infinite samples drawn from any culture with transitive weak majority preferences. (A culture has a *weak majority preference* of candidate *a* over candidate *b* if there are at least as many people who prefer *a* to *b* as people who prefer *b* to *a*.) Results of this type are known (for three alternatives) for the dual culture (Gehrlein, 1999) (this requires maximization over two variables) and for the mixture of the impartial culture over linear orders and the impartial culture over weak orders with exactly one tie (Fishburn and Gehrlein, 1980; Gehrlein and Valognes, 2001) (this requires maximization over a single variable). However, it is not obvious that the same result holds for all cultures of indifference over weak orders. In general, there are 13 possible weak orders with 4 restrictions, and therefore to find a distribution with a maximal probability of cycles in infinite samples we need to maximize over 9 variables. One restriction is that the sum of the probabilities of all 13 weak orders equals 1, and three more restrictions are imposed by the requirement that we are dealing with a culture of indifference, i.e., that all three pairwise majority preferences in the culture are ties.

We concentrate on the case of three candidates not only because of its analytic tractability, but also because transitivity is a property over triples. If the probability of a cycle is zero for each triple among *m* candidates, then the majority relation over all *m* candidates is transitive with probability one. After proving the theorem for the case of three candidates, we present strong intuitive arguments for the conjecture that the impartial culture over linear orders must be the worst case regardless of the number of candidates.[12]

---

[11] While we generalize dramatically beyond the usual distributional assumptions, we continue to assume that the underlying culture has a transitive majority preference relation. Otherwise, large samples will simply reproduce the cycle that has been assumed in the first place. More specifically, if one were to draw random samples from a distribution which already contains majority cycles, then random samples would display the same cycles with probability one as sample size approaches infinity.

[12] Recall that all results in this section assume that individual preferences are linear orders or weak orders. Chapter 5 shows, for a very broad range of preference representations, how to compute the probability of majority cycles in samples of any size from any culture in which majority preferences are not tied. The results in that chapter show that if the culture has neither ties nor intransitive majority preferences, then the probability of majority cycles goes to zero as sample size approaches infinity.

1.1.2 For Three Candidates the Impartial Culture Generates the Most Cycles

We first present our notation. Here and throughout, we refer to a fixed finite set C of choice alternatives that can be interpreted as candidates, parties, or consumption bundles. Let $\mathcal{SWO}$ be a collection of strict weak orders over C. For any two candidates a, b, and any voter with preference relation $B \in \mathcal{SWO}$, the standard notation aBb means that a person in the state of preference B finds that a is *better than* b. Denote the probability of each strict weak order $B \in \mathcal{SWO}$ in the culture by p_B. We use the word "population" in the statistical sense and in a fashion interchangeable with the word "culture." Any given population probability distribution over $\mathcal{SWO}$ is conceptualized as a set of parameters $p = (p_B)_{B \in \mathcal{SWO}}$ in the closed interval $[0, 1]$ with the restriction that $\sum_{B \in \mathcal{SWO}} p_B = 1$. For example, suppose $B = abc$, a complete linear order which formally captures a state of preference of a person who likes a best, b second best, and c least. Then p_{abc} denotes the probability that a person drawn at random from the culture is in the preference state abc. To make the notation more readable, we write p_{aBb} for $\sum_{B \in \mathcal{R}} p_B$ where $\mathcal{R} = \{B \in \mathcal{SWO}$ such that $aBb\}$. So, in the special case when only complete linear orders of three candidates have positive probability, we have $p_{aBb} = p_{abc} + p_{acb} + p_{cab}$. In the general case allowing for indifference, we write aEb if and only if neither aBb nor bBa holds. In other words, aEb denotes the situation where a and b are *equivalent* (hence the notation). A person in this state of preference has no strict preference either way, i.e., s/he is indifferent between the two options. If a person is indifferent between a and b, but prefers each of them to c, we write $aEbBc$. Given any population, captured by the probability distribution p over strict weak orders, we say that a is preferred to b by a *weak majority* in the population if $p_{aBb} \geq p_{bBa}$. We use boldface to denote random variables and regular font to denote numbers. Suppose that we draw a random sample of size n with replacement from the distribution p. Analogous to the notation for p, we write $\mathbf{N}_{aBb}$ for the number of people who prefer a to b in such a random sample. We also write $P(\mathbf{N}_{aBb} > \mathbf{N}_{bBa})$ for the probability that a majority in the sample prefers a to b.

We denote the probability of cycles in infinite samples drawn from a distribution p by $P_c^\infty(p)$.[13] For three alternatives a, b, c, this probability

---

[13] Since the probability of a majority tie between the two alternatives in an infinite sample is zero (unless everybody is indifferent between these two alternatives), looking for majority intransitivities is equivalent to looking for majority cycles.

is given by the following function:

$$P_c^\infty(p) = \lim_{n \to \infty} \left(\begin{array}{l} P\Big((N_{aBb} > N_{bBa}) \cap (N_{bBc} > N_{cBb}) \cap (N_{cBa} > N_{aBc}) \Big) \\ + P\Big((N_{aBb} < N_{bBa}) \cap (N_{bBc} < N_{cBb}) \cap (N_{cBa} < N_{aBc}) \Big) \end{array} \right).$$

(1.1)

The result of the first theorem can be summarized as follows: Suppose individual preferences are strict weak orders over three alternatives and that the population weak majority preference is transitive. Then, in the limit (as $n \to \infty$), the probability of a cyclical majority preference in a sample is different from zero only if all three alternatives are majority tied in the underlying population.[14]

Theorem 1.1.1 *Let $C = \{a, b, c\}$ and let $p : B \mapsto p_B$ be a probability distribution on strict weak orders over C. Suppose that the weak majority preference relation is transitive, i.e., for every relabeling $\{x, y, z\} = \{a, b, c\}$*

$$\left. \begin{array}{l} p_{xBy} - p_{yBx} \geq 0 \\ p_{yBz} - p_{zBy} \geq 0 \end{array} \right\} \Rightarrow p_{xBz} - p_{zBx} \geq 0.$$

Then $P_c^\infty(p)$ is different from zero only if all pairs of candidates are majority tied:

$$P_c^\infty(p) > 0 \Rightarrow \left\{ \begin{array}{l} p_{aBb} = p_{bBa}, \\ p_{bBc} = p_{cBb}, \\ p_{aBc} = p_{cBa}. \end{array} \right.$$

The proof of this theorem is in Appendix C.

It is important to realize that the assumption of a transitive weak majority preference in the population holds for the impartial culture (and any culture of indifference) since the majority preference relation in such cultures is a complete tie, hence transitive. Recalling Equation (1.1), the theorem implies that, as sample size goes to infinity, cycles are possible only if samples are drawn from a culture of indifference.

Our second theorem establishes that, for three candidates, the impartial culture over linear orders maximizes the probability of cycles within the class of all cultures of indifference.

---

[14] A similar result, based on more specialized assumptions, is given in Williamson and Sargent (1967).

Theorem 1.1.2 *Let $C = \{a, b, c\}$ and let $p : B \mapsto p_B$ be a probability distribution on strict weak orders over C, satisfying a culture of indifference, i.e., $p_{aBb} = p_{bBa}$, $p_{bBc} = p_{cBb}$, and $p_{aBc} = p_{cBa}$. Then $P_c^\infty(p)$ reaches its maximum at the following values:*

$$p_{abc} = p_{acb} = p_{cab} = p_{bac} = p_{bca} = p_{cba} = \frac{1 - p_{aEbEc}}{6};$$

$$0 \le p_{aEbEc} < 1,$$

i.e., for the impartial culture over linear orders, possibly plus 'total indifference' (p_{aEbEc}).

The proof of this theorem is in Appendix C.

It is straightforward to show that, for $n \to \infty$, the probability p_{aEbEc} does not influence the probabilities of possible majority preference relations (as long as $p_{aEbEc} < 1$). In other words, only the relative probabilities of those weak orders that are not the total indifference relation $aEbEc$ are relevant for determining the probability of any possible majority preference relation (unless everyone is completely indifferent).

Combining Theorems 1.1.1 and 1.1.2 we now prove that, for three candidates, the impartial culture over linear orders (possibly plus 'total indifference') maximizes the probability of cycles compared to *any* culture over strict weak orders with a transitive weak majority preference relation.

Theorem 1.1.3 *Let $C = \{a, b, c\}$ and let $p : B \mapsto p_B$ be a probability distribution on strict weak orders over C. Suppose that the weak majority preference relation is transitive, i.e., for every relabeling $\{x, y, z\} = \{a, b, c\}$,*

$$\left. \begin{array}{l} p_{xBy} - p_{yBx} \ge 0 \\ p_{yBz} - p_{zBy} \ge 0 \end{array} \right\} \Rightarrow p_{xBz} - p_{zBx} \ge 0.$$

Then $P_c^\infty(p)$ reaches its maximum at the following values of p:

$$p_{abc} = p_{acb} = p_{cab} = p_{bac} = p_{bca} = p_{cba} = \frac{1 - p_{aEbEc}}{6};$$

$$0 \le p_{aEbEc} < 1,$$

i.e., for the impartial culture over linear orders, possibly plus 'total indifference' (p_{aEbEc}).

Theorem 1.1.3 follows directly from Theorems 1.1.1 and 1.1.2.

It is quite important to notice that Theorem 1.1.3 is valid only for an infinite sample size. For any specified (fixed), but large enough finite sample size it is easy to find a population in which the probability of cycles in samples of that specified size is arbitrarily close to $\frac{1}{2}$ and therefore much higher than the probability of cycles for the impartial culture. For example, consider the following distribution: $p_{abc} = \frac{1}{2} + 2\epsilon$, $p_{cab} = \frac{1}{4} - \epsilon$, $p_{bca} = \frac{1}{4} - \epsilon$. Choosing $\epsilon > 0$ small enough, we can force the probability of cycles to be as close to $\frac{1}{2}$ as we wish: For this distribution, the probability that a randomly drawn voter prefers a to b is $\frac{3}{4} + \epsilon$, and the probability that the voter prefers b to c is also $\frac{3}{4} + \epsilon$. Thus, in a large sample, almost for sure, a beats b by a majority and b beats c by a majority. However, the probability that a randomly drawn voter prefers a to c is $\frac{1}{2} + \epsilon$. Therefore, for small ϵ the probability that a beats c by a majority (in a sample) is close to $\frac{1}{2}$, and the probability that c beats a by a majority is also close to $\frac{1}{2}$. In the latter case, where a beats b, b beats c, and c beats a, we obtain a cycle.[15] Notice, however, that if ϵ is specified first then we can, in turn, always find n large enough to make the probability of cycles as close to zero as we wish (Theorem 1.1.1) because the probability of abc as the majority ordering in the sample will approach 1.0.

1.1.3 Does the Impartial Culture Generate the Most Cycles Regardless of the Number of Candidates?

We do not know of a rigorous proof of a theorem analogous to Theorem 1.1.3 for more than three candidates. We offer the following arguments for the conjecture that the impartial culture over linear orders (possibly plus 'total indifference') is the worst case for any number of candidates.

- If we have m candidates, then the number of possible majority relations in infinite samples is $2^{m(m-1)/2}$ (because majority ties have probability zero). Only $m!$ of these majority relations are linear orders, i.e., transitive. Thus, there are $2^{m(m-1)/2} - m!$ possible intransitive majority relations in infinite samples. An intransitive majority relation can occur in an infinite sample only if there is a triple that has a majority cycle in that sample. On the other hand, the argument given in the proof of Theorem 1.1.1 implies that if only one triple of alternatives is majority

---

[15] We formally develop results like this in Proposition 5.1.1 of Chapter 5. The results for the present example follow from Equation (5.3).

tied in the underlying culture, then a majority cycle in an infinite sample must include that triple. It is plausible that, in order for the total probability of cycles to be maximized, we ought to give every one of the $2^{m(m-1)/2} - m!$ potential intransitivities a positive probability. For that we need a culture of indifference for each triple. The only way to have a probability distribution on weak orders, whose marginal distribution on any triple of objects is a culture of indifference, is to have a culture of indifference on the full set of weak orders.[16]

- It is plausible that, in order for the total probability of cycles to be maximized, the probability of cycles in any given triple should also be maximized. Together with Theorem 1.1.2, this suggests that we need to have the impartial culture over linear orders on each triple. This rules out all strict weak orders with one or more ties for each triple and consequently all strict weak orders with one or more ties. Consequently, we conjecture that the probability of cycles is maximized for a population where only linear orders have positive probability.

- Because relabeling (permuting) the alternatives has no impact on the overall probability of cycles, a basic symmetry argument suggests that the extremum should also be reached at a culture that is itself symmetric with respect to every relabeling of the candidates. Therefore, we expect that the probability of cycles is maximized by a culture which is symmetric with respect to every relabeling of the candidates. In particular, consistent with this argument, in the case of three candidates the impartial culture is the unique symmetric distribution among dual cultures (Gehrlein, 1999) and, as we have shown, it maximizes the probability of cycles.

- The second and third arguments above together suggest that the probability of cycles is maximized for a symmetric (with respect to every relabeling of candidates) distribution over linear orders, that is, for the impartial culture over linear orders.

In conclusion, this section shows for three candidates, and conjectures for any number of candidates, how moving away from the impartial culture (within cultures of indifference) in virtually any fashion will automatically reduce the probability of cycles. We also show that, for transitive cultures which are not cultures of indifference, when restricted to any given triple, the probability of cycles can be made arbitrarily close to

---

[16] This follows immediately by substituting the relevant quantities in the pertinent definitions.

zero by choosing a sufficiently large sample. In the next section we move from restrictive hypothetical distributions that predict a prevalence of majority cycles to the other extreme, namely restrictive theoretical domain constraints that rule out the occurrence of majority cycles. We then replace domain restrictions by restrictions on the distribution of preferences which we expect to be behaviorally descriptive of actual data.

1.2 NET VALUE RESTRICTION AND NET PREFERENCE MAJORITY

Now we introduce basic concepts such as weak stochastic transitivity and the weak utility model, as well as redefine concepts from the social choice literature such as "Condorcet winner" and "majority preference relations" in terms of probabilistic representations of linear order preferences. Then we state Sen's (1969, 1970) value restriction condition (Definition 1.2.7) and provide a probabilistic reformulation (Definition 1.2.8). We also generalize Sen's value restriction condition to what we call "net preference probabilities" (Definitions 1.2.10 and 1.2.13), so as to provide necessary and sufficient conditions for transitive majority preferences based on individual linear order preferences (Theorem 1.2.15).

1.2.1 Majority Rule and Probabilistic Preferences

A majority vote is *transitive* if the following property holds: Whenever candidate c has a majority over d and d has a majority over e, then c has a majority over e. Unless we explicitly ask voters to perform paired comparisons, it is not quite clear what this statement should mean in general. Yet, hardly any empirical ballots or survey responses provide full information on all paired comparisons. Thus, we need to take a more general perspective, as we do now.

Transitivity of votes is closely related to what the psychological and statistical choice literature calls "weak stochastic transitivity," and to the well-known "weak utility model" (Luce and Suppes, 1965). This latter model assumes that in a binary choice paradigm each paired comparison has a well-defined probability of a choice for each alternative (i.e., the choice of a given alternative is the outcome of a Bernoulli trial). The following definitions are from Luce and Suppes (1965).

Suppose that an individual (possibly drawn at random from a population) is asked to choose one candidate from a pair of candidates. Let p_{cd} denote the probability of a choice of c when c and d are being offered.

Definition 1.2.1 A *weak utility model* is a set of binary choice probabilities for which there exists a real-valued function w over $\mathcal{C}$ such that

$$p_{cd} \geq \frac{1}{2} \Leftrightarrow w(c) \geq w(d).$$

When $\mathcal{C}$ is finite, then the weak utility model is equivalent to weak stochastic transitivity of the binary choice probabilities, which we define next.

Definition 1.2.2 *Weak stochastic transitivity of binary choice probabilities* holds when

$$p_{cd} \geq \frac{1}{2} \ \ \& \ \ p_{de} \geq \frac{1}{2} \ \implies \ p_{ce} \geq \frac{1}{2}.$$

Throughout this section we assume that individual preferences take the form of linear orders. This assumption will be dropped in Chapter 2. We write Π for the collection of all (strict) linear orders over $\mathcal{C}$. For a given probability distribution $\pi \mapsto \mathbb{P}(\pi)$ over Π, we write $\mathbb{P}_{cd} = \sum_{(c,d) \in \pi} \mathbb{P}(\pi)$ for the marginal pairwise ranking probability of c being ranked ahead of d.

There exists a substantial literature trying to explain probabilities of (observable) binary choices by probabilities of (latent and unobserved) rankings through

$$p_{cd} = \mathbb{P}_{cd}. \tag{1.2}$$

Given a set of binary choice probabilities, it is not trivial to answer the question whether probabilities on rankings exist that satisfy (1.2). This question is commonly studied under the label "binary choice problem" and plays an important role in mathematical psychology as well as in operations research (Block and Marschak, 1960; Bolotashvili et al., 1999; Campello de Souza, 1983; Cohen and Falmagne, 1990; Dridi, 1980; Fishburn, 1990, 1992; Fishburn and Falmagne, 1989; Gilboa, 1990; Grötschel et al., 1985; Heyer and Niederée, 1989, 1992; Koppen, 1995; Marley, 1990; Marschak, 1960; McFadden and Richter, 1970; Suck, 1992).

In the probabilistic framework it is appealing and straightforward to define an aggregate preference relation through "c is aggregately preferred to d if and only if the choice probability $p_{cd} \geq \frac{1}{2}$ (in the Bernoulli trial)." Such a preference relation is transitive if and only if weak stochastic transitivity holds. Thus, for probabilistic binary choice (with $|\mathcal{C}|$ finite), the existence of a transitive social welfare order, weak stochastic transitivity, and the weak utility model are equivalent. The function w in Definition 1.2.1 thus defines what we call a (majority) *social welfare function*.

Another important normative concept in the social choice literature, besides that of a majority weak order guaranteed by weak stochastic transitivity, is that of the "majority winner." A *Condorcet winner* (also known as *Condorcet candidate*, or a *majority winner*) is usually defined as the candidate(s) (if they exist) who would receive majority support against every other candidate if they were to compete pairwise (Black, 1958; Condorcet, 1785; Felsenthal et al., 1990; Young, 1986, 1988). The Condorcet winner is the most commonly accepted normative criterion for a social choice procedure that is required to select a single alternative.[17]

Since we usually lack data on binary comparisons, we formally define weak stochastic transitivity and the concept of a Condorcet winner in terms of (latent and unobserved) probabilistic rankings.[18]

Definition 1.2.3 A probability distribution $\mathbb{P}$ on Π satisfies *weak stochastic transitivity (for rankings)* if and only if the induced marginal (pairwise) ranking probabilities satisfy

$$\mathbb{P}_{cd} \geq \frac{1}{2} \quad \& \quad \mathbb{P}_{de} \geq \frac{1}{2} \quad \Longrightarrow \quad \mathbb{P}_{ce} \geq \frac{1}{2}.$$

Definition 1.2.4 Given a probability $\mathbb{P}$ on Π, candidate $c \in C$ is a *Condorcet winner* if and only if

$$\mathbb{P}_{cd} \geq \frac{1}{2} \quad \forall d \in C - \{c\}.$$

These concepts of weak stochastic transitivity and of a Condorcet candidate are compatible with the idea that, if the voters were indeed asked to do a paired comparison, they would actually base their decision on a latent preference ranking and would choose the alternative (in the Bernoulli process) that is ranked ahead of the other in the sampled preference ranking.[19]

---

[17] The arguably second most commonly accepted normative benchmark, and main competitor of the Condorcet winner, is the Borda winner. The latter is strongly advocated by some researchers, e.g., Saari (1994; 1995).

[18] In fact, we usually also lack information on full rankings. The subsequent chapters discuss this situation in detail.

[19] It should be noted that the reverse approach has also been modeled where only paired comparison probabilities are given, and ranking probabilities are constructed from those paired comparison probabilities (e.g., Marley, 1968).

Definition 1.2.5 Consider a probability $\mathbb{P}$ on Π. We define a *weak majority preference relation* $\succsim$ and a *strict majority preference relation* $\succ$ through

$$c \succsim d \quad \Leftrightarrow \quad \mathbb{P}_{cd} \geq \mathbb{P}_{dc} \Leftrightarrow \mathbb{P}_{cd} \geq \frac{1}{2}, \tag{1.3}$$

$$c \succ d \quad \Leftrightarrow \quad \mathbb{P}_{cd} > \mathbb{P}_{dc} \Leftrightarrow \mathbb{P}_{cd} > \frac{1}{2}. \tag{1.4}$$

Observation 1.2.6 *The weak majority preference relation $\succsim$, as defined in Definition 1.2.5, is reflexive and strongly complete (and thus complete). Therefore, $\succsim$ is a weak order if and only if it is transitive. The strict majority preference relation $\succ$, as defined in Definition 1.2.5, is asymmetric (and thus antisymmetric). Therefore, $\succ$ is a strict weak order if and only if it is negatively transitive. More generally, $\succ$ is a strict partial order if and only if it is transitive. Furthermore, $\succ$ is a strict weak order if and only if $\succsim$ is a weak order.*

The proof is in Appendix C.

When $\succsim$ is transitive, then $\succ$ is also transitive. However, $\succ$ may be transitive when $\succsim$ is not: Suppose that preferences are linear orders and that $\mathbb{P}(\{(a, b), (b, c), (a, c)\}) = \mathbb{P}(\{(a, b), (c, b), (c, a)\}) = \frac{1}{2}$. Then, $\succ = \{(a, b)\}$, which is transitive. On the other hand, $\succsim = \{(a, a), (a, b), (a, c), (b, b), (b, c), (c, c), (c, a), (c, b)\}$, which is intransitive.

Chapter 2 develops more general definitions of Condorcet winner and majority preference relations for a broad range of deterministic and/or probabilistic representations of preference or utility.

Sen's "value restriction" is a sufficient condition for the existence of a transitive social welfare ordering. We first state its formal definition, and then translate the condition into probabilistic terms.

Definition 1.2.7 Suppose that each voter has a strict linear preference order. Given a collection of voters, a triple of alternatives satisfies *NW* (*never worst*) if and only if there is one alternative among the three that is not ranked worst (i.e., third) among the three by any of the voters; *NM* (*never middle*) if and only if there is one alternative among the three that is not ranked in the middle (i.e., second) among the three by any of the voters; *NB* (*never best*) if and only if there is one alternative among the three that is not ranked best (i.e., first) among the three by any of the voters. Sen's *value restriction* holds if and only if every triple of alternatives satisfies either *NW*, *NM*, or *NB*.

The underlying intuition of value restriction is that in each triple of candidates there should be at least one about which all voters agree that s/he is not the worst, or not the middle, or not the best.

We now translate the *NB*, *NM*, and *NW* conditions into probabilistic terms for linear order preferences. (In Chapter 2, we further generalize these concepts to a much broader framework.)

1.2.2 Probabilistic Reformulation and Generalizations of Sen's Value Restriction

Definition 1.2.8 Consider a probability $\mathbb{P}$ on Π. For any given triple of alternatives, we say that the marginal ranking probabilities induced by $\mathbb{P}$ on that triple satisfy $NW(c)$ if and only if the (marginal) probability for c to be ranked worst (in the triple) is zero. When $NW(c)$ holds, c is said to be (*almost surely*, abbreviated a.s.) *never worst*. $NM(c)$ and $NB(c)$ are defined analogously. $\mathbb{P}$ is (*a.s.*) *value restricted* if and only if in each triple $\{x, y, z\} \subseteq \mathcal{C}$ there exists c with either $NW(c)$, $NM(c)$, or $NB(c)$. In that case, we also say that (*a.s.*) *value restriction* holds.

The following theorem is a variation of Sen's theorem on value restriction (Sen, 1966, 1969, 1970), generalized to probabilistic terms.

Theorem 1.2.9 *Given a probability $\mathbb{P}$ on Π, consider the relations $\succsim$ and $\succ$ of Definition 1.2.5. If $\mathbb{P}$ is (a.s.) value restricted, then 1) the weak majority preference relation $\succsim$ is a weak order, 2) the strict majority preference relation $\succ$ is a strict weak order, and 3) if $\mathbb{P}_{cd} \neq \mathbb{P}_{dc}, \forall c \neq d$, then the strict majority preference relation $\succ$ is a strict linear order. Thus, (a.s.) value restriction implies transitivity.*

We now move from domain restrictions to restrictions on the distribution of preferences, or, more specifically, on the "net preference probabilities" over the full domain. The following definitions are critical throughout the rest of this section. (Again, Chapter 2 generalizes these concepts much further.)

Definition 1.2.10 Given a probability $\mathbb{P}$ on Π, and denoting by π^{-1} the reverse order of π, the *net ranking probability* (*net preference probability*) NP (induced by $\mathbb{P}$) is defined as

$$NP(\pi) = \mathbb{P}(\pi) - \mathbb{P}(\pi^{-1}).$$

The *net margins* (*net pairwise preference probabilities*) are defined as $NP_{cd} = \mathbb{P}_{cd} - \mathbb{P}_{dc}$. (See Feld and Grofman, 1988, for a similar concept.)

Net marginal ranking probabilities of triples are defined analogously. We also write NP_π for $NP(\pi)$, and NP_{cde} for the net marginal ranking probability that c is ranked before both d and e, and that d is ranked before e. The following observation follows immediately from these notational conventions.

Observation 1.2.11 *Given NP on Π and $\succsim$ and $\succ$ on $\mathcal{C}$ as above, we have*

$$c \succsim d \Leftrightarrow NP_{cd} \geq 0, \quad c \succ d \Leftrightarrow NP_{cd} > 0.$$

We now define *NW*, *NM*, and *NB* for net probabilities on linear orders.

Definition 1.2.12 Given NP on Π as before, for any triple $\{c, d, e\} \subseteq \mathcal{C}$,

$$NP \text{ satisfies } NW(c) \quad \Leftrightarrow \quad NP_{edc} \leq 0 \ \& \ NP_{dec} \leq 0,$$
$$NP \text{ satisfies } NM(c) \quad \Leftrightarrow \quad NP_{ecd} \leq 0 \ \& \ NP_{dce} \leq 0 \Leftrightarrow NP_{ecd} = 0,$$
$$NP \text{ satisfies } NB(c) \quad \Leftrightarrow \quad NP_{cde} \leq 0 \ \& \ NP_{ced} \leq 0.$$

When NP satisfies $NB(a)$, we often also say for short that *Net NB(a)* is satisfied. The same applies to the other conditions and choice alternatives.

Definition 1.2.13 NP is *marginally value restricted* for the triple $\{x, y, z\} \subseteq \mathcal{C}$ if and only if there exists an element $c \in \{x, y, z\}$ such that NP satisfies $NW(c)$ or $NB(c)$ or $NM(c)$. If this property is satisfied, then *marginal net value restriction* holds on the triple $\{x, y, z\}$. *Net value restriction* holds on $\mathcal{C}$ if marginal net value restriction holds on each triple. When net value restriction holds, we also say that the *net value restriction condition* is satisfied.

REMARK. If NP on Π satisfies $NW(c)$ for a triple $\{c, d, e\} \subseteq \mathcal{C}$, then

$$NP_{ecd} \leq 0 \quad \Rightarrow \quad NP \text{ satisfies } NB(e),$$
$$NP_{ecd} \geq 0 \quad \Rightarrow \quad NP \text{ satisfies } NB(d).$$

Similarly, $NB(c)$ implies either $NW(d)$ or $NW(e)$. Also, $NM(c)$ means that $NP_{ecd} = 0$ and thus it means that at most two rankings have strictly positive NP values, and that $NW(d)$ or $NW(e)$ holds. At most three elements in

$\{cde, ced, dce, dec, ecd, edc\}$ have strictly positive net preference probabilities. Furthermore, net value restriction is weaker than value restriction:

- $\mathbb{P}$ satisfies $NW(c) \Rightarrow N\!P$ satisfies $NW(c)$, but not conversely,
- $\mathbb{P}$ satisfies $NB(c) \Rightarrow N\!P$ satisfies $NB(c)$, but not conversely,
- $\mathbb{P}$ satisfies $NM(c) \Rightarrow N\!P$ satisfies $NM(c)$, but not conversely.

Clearly, domain restrictions imply distributional restrictions, but the converse does not generally hold.

We need a further definition before we can state our key theorem on necessary and sufficient conditions for weak stochastic transitivity on probability distributions over linear orders.

Definition 1.2.14 Given $N\!P$ on Π as before, $\pi \in \Pi$ has a *net preference majority* if and only if

$$N\!P(\pi) > \sum_{\substack{\pi' \in \Pi - \{\pi\}, \\ N\!P(\pi') > 0}} N\!P(\pi'). \tag{1.5}$$

Similarly, for any triple $\{c, d, e\} \subseteq C$, cde has a *marginal net preference majority* if and only if

$$N\!P_{cde} > \sum_{\substack{\pi' \in \{ced, dce, dec, ecd, edc\}, \\ N\!P_{\pi'} > 0}} N\!P_{\pi'}.$$

We say that the *net majority condition* holds if there is a linear order that has a net preference majority.

The following theorem is similar in spirit to Lemma 2 of Feld and Grofman (1986b).[20]

Theorem 1.2.15 *The weak majority preference relation $\succsim$ defined in Definition 1.2.5 is transitive if and only if for each triple $\{c, d, e\} \subseteq C$ at least one of the following two conditions holds:*

1. *$N\!P$ is marginally value restricted on $\{c, d, e\}$ and, in addition, if at least one net preference is nonzero then the following implication is true (with possible relabelings):*

$$N\!P_{cde} = 0 \Rightarrow N\!P_{dce} \neq N\!P_{ced}.$$

---

[20] Note that their treatment omits certain knife-edge situations caused by possible ties.

2. $\exists \pi_0 \in \{cde, ced, dce, dec, ecd, edc\}$ *such that* π_0 *has a marginal net preference majority.*

Similarly, the strict majority preference relation $\succ$ *is transitive if and only if for each triple* $\{c, d, e\} \subseteq C$ *at least one of the following two conditions holds:*

1. *NP is marginally value restricted on* $\{c, d, e\}$.
2. $\exists \pi_0 \in \{cde, ced, dce, dec, ecd, edc\}$ *such that* π_0 *has a marginal net preference majority.*

The proof is in Appendix C.

1.3 EMPIRICAL ILLUSTRATIONS

This section provides brief empirical illustrations based on survey preference data. First, these data can be shown clearly not to originate from an impartial culture. Also, for these data, Sen's value restriction is violated, but nevertheless, majority preferences are transitive. We show how our net value restriction condition (and, incidentally, <u>not</u> the net majority condition) accounts for the absence of majority cycles in these data.

It is difficult to find empirical data that provide either complete paired comparisons or complete linear orders of all choice alternatives as technically required by any standard definition of majority rule, including the one we use in this section. We consider three national survey data sets from Germany in which complete linear orders of three major parties were reported for all respondents (Norpoth, 1979). These three major parties are the Social Democratic party (S), the Christian Democratic parties (C), and the Free Democratic party (F). The data under consideration are 1969, 1972, and 1976 German National Election Study (GNES) data sets.

Figure 1.1 displays the results for the 1969 GNES (this survey distribution was reported by Norpoth, 1979). The graph shows all possible linear order preference states, as well as the relative frequencies of their occurrences in the 1969 GNES. We identify relative frequencies with probabilities and provide the net probabilities in parentheses. The inset table provides the pairwise net probabilities. For instance, $NP_{CF} = .6$. Linear orders and paired comparisons with positive net probabilities are shaded in grey.

First of all, we can test the hypothesis that the survey data set originated from a uniform distribution over linear orders. We use the following likelihood ratio test. Writing N_π for the frequency with which the linear order π was observed in the survey, and writing $N = \sum_{\pi \in \Pi} N_\pi$ for the

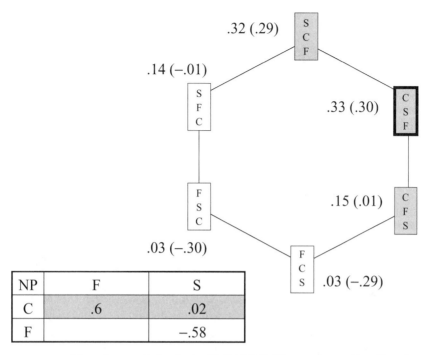

FIGURE 1.1: Net value restriction in the 1969 GNES. The graph provides all ranking probabilities and net probabilities (in parentheses). The inset table provides the pairwise net probabilities NP_{CF}, NP_{CS}, and NP_{FS}. Linear orders and paired comparisons with positive net probabilities are shaded in grey. The linear order with boldface frame is $\succ$, the majority preference relation.

total sample size (in the 1969 survey, $N = 818$), the likelihood L_{IC} of the observed data under the impartial culture assumption is given by

$$L_{IC} = \left(\frac{1}{6}\right)^N,$$

whereas the likelihood L_{MN} of the data under an unconstrained multinomial distribution $\pi \mapsto p_\pi$ is given by

$$L_{MN} = \prod_{\pi \in \Pi} p_\pi^{N_\pi}. \tag{1.6}$$

The maximum likelihood estimates $\hat{p}_\pi$ of the values p_π are simply the relative frequencies in the observed data, i.e., $\hat{p}_\pi = \frac{N_\pi}{N}$. Therefore, to test the hypothesis that the observed data are a random sample from a uniform distribution, as opposed to a random sample from an unconstrained multinomial distribution, we simply substitute the maximum likelihood estimates $\hat{p}_\pi$ for the probabilities p_π in Equation (1.6) and compute the

G^2 statistic given by

$$G^2 = -2ln\left(\frac{L_{IC}}{L_{MN}}\right). \tag{1.7}$$

Since there are 6 linear orders, whose probabilities add up to one, there are 5 degrees of freedom in the numerator. There are no free parameters in the denominator. Thus, we compare the resulting value of the G^2 statistic in Equation (1.7) against a chi-square distribution with 5 degrees of freedom, χ_5^2. For the 1969 GNES, we obtain $G^2 = 478$. The p-value of this statistic, $P(\chi_5^2 \geq 478) < 10^{-100}$, is minuscule, which shows that the survey is very significantly different from a random sample of an impartial culture. Similarly, in the 1972 GNES ($N = 1595$) and the 1976 GNES ($N = 1872$), the corresponding p-values are minuscule. In other words, from a classical statistical hypothesis testing point of view, we reject with virtual certainty the hypotheses that the 1969, 1972, or 1976 German national electorates were impartial cultures.

In the 1969 GNES survey, there is no majority cycle even though Sen's value restriction condition is violated. Sen's condition would require the existence of a candidate and a position such that the probability of this candidate being ranked at that position is zero. The smallest such proportion in the survey is .06, namely the proportion (probability) that F is ranked first. Given the large number of respondents, a proportion of .06 is clearly not a statistical accident, and so we omit a formal statistical test. Our net preference majority condition is also violated.[21] However, the net probabilities satisfy $NB(F)$ and $NW(C)$, and thus our net value restriction condition holds. The resulting majority social welfare order is $C \succ S \succ F$. This linear order has a boldface frame in Figure 1.1.

Figures 1.2 and 1.3 display the results for the 1972 and 1976 GNES, respectively (these survey distributions were also reported by Norpoth, 1979). The inset table in each of these figures provides the pairwise net probabilities. Linear orders and paired comparisons with positive net probabilities are shaded in grey. In each case, Sen's value restriction condition and our net preference majority condition are violated. Sen's condition would require the existence of a candidate and a position, such that the probability of this candidate being ranked at that position is zero. In these data sets, the smallest such probabilities are .06, .07 and .08, respectively, each for the probability that F is ranked first. In both cases,

---

[21] Actually, the order CSF 'almost' satisfies our net majority condition (at the accuracy given in the figure) because it satisfies (1.5) in Definition 1.2.14 with equality instead of strict inequality.

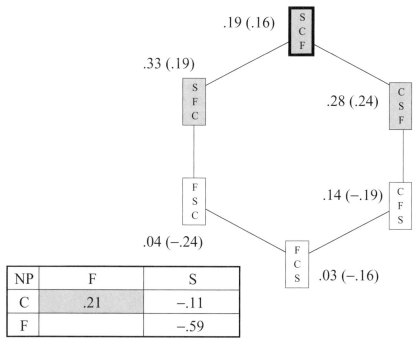

NP	F	S
C	.21	−.11
F		−.59

FIGURE 1.2: Net value restriction in the 1972 GNES. The graph provides all ranking probabilities and net probabilities (in parentheses). The inset table provides the pairwise net probabilities NP_{CF}, NP_{CS}, and NP_{FS}. Linear orders and paired comparisons with positive net probabilities are shaded in grey. The linear order with boldface frame is ≻, the majority preference relation.

given the large number of respondents, these proportions are clear violations of the net majority condition.[22]

However, the net probabilities in each data set satisfy $NB(F)$ and $NW(S)$. Thus, our net value restriction condition holds in both cases. The resulting majority social welfare order is $S ≻ C ≻ F$ for both data sets. The latter linear order is marked with a boldface frame.

In summary, we have the following results:

1. These survey data do not at all look like random samples from a uniform distribution, i.e., from an impartial culture. This reinforces the already commonly held view that the impartial culture is unrealistic and nondescriptive of empirical data on social choice behavior.

[22] Feld and Grofman (1988, 1990, 1992) discuss evidence of the degree to which candidate preference rankings in actual elections satisfy value restriction, and find value restriction never to be satisfied in any of the elections they examine.

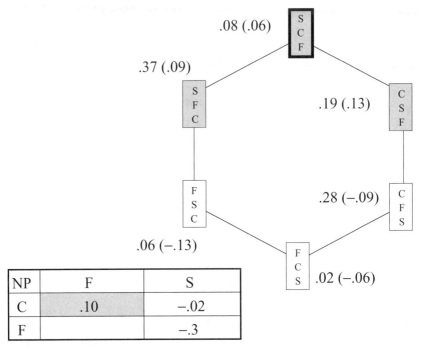

NP	F	S
C	.10	−.02
F		−.3

FIGURE 1.3: Net value restriction in the 1976 GNES. The graph provides all rank-ing probabilities and net probabilities (in parentheses). The inset table provides the pairwise net probabilities NP_{CF}, NP_{CS}, and NP_{FS}. Linear orders and paired comparisons with positive net probabilities are shaded in grey. The linear order with boldface frame is $\succ$, the majority preference relation.

2. There are no majority cycles in any of these three surveys. This finding cross-validates the overall pattern of findings in the limited empirical literature on majority cycles, mentioned at the beginning of this chapter, that has failed to find compelling evidence for the occurrence of cycles in real elections.

3. Sen's value restriction condition is violated in all three surveys and thus cannot be relied upon as an explanation for the absence of cycles in these data. More generally, because every strict linear order is reported as a preference state of a substantial number of respondents, any other domain restriction condition would also be ruled out by these data.

4. The net majority condition does not hold in any of these surveys.

5. In each survey, net value restriction holds. In the 1969 data set, NP satisfies $NB(F)$ and $NW(C)$, which guarantees the existence of a transitive majority social welfare order. The majority ordering is

$C \succ S \succ F$. In the 1972 and 1976 data sets, N^p satisfies $NB(F)$ and $NW(S)$, which guarantees the existence of a transitive majority social welfare order. The majority ordering is $S \succ C \succ F$ in both cases. Net value restriction is thus a theoretically attractive constraint on the (net probability) distribution of preferences that predicts transitivity of majority preferences and it is behaviorally descriptive of all three GNES data sets. Therefore, it provides a convincing descriptive theoretical account for the absence of cycles in these data.

1.4 DISCUSSION

Section 1.1 examines the probability of majority cycles when sampling from an impartial culture or other culture of indifference. Several papers (Fishburn and Gehrlein, 1980; Jones et al., 1995; Van Deemen, 1999) suggest that majority cycles (i.e., the Condorcet paradox) become less probable when the impartial culture over linear orders is replaced by a culture that allows for individual indifference. We agree that it is more realistic to move from strict linear order preferences to strict weak order preferences by allowing for individual voter indifference between some or all candidates. However, any culture of indifference, i.e., any culture that requires a complete majority tie at the level of the population, is empirically unrealistic. Both the impartial culture over linear orders, as well as the impartial culture over strict weak orders, and even any probability mixture of the two, are cultures of indifference. Therefore the impartial culture over weak orders remains a 'near worst case' scenario.

We prove the following very general result for the case of three candidates, and conjecture that a parallel result holds for any number of candidates: The impartial culture over linear orders maximizes the probability of majority cycles in infinite samples, among all cultures over weak order preferences that do not already presume some inherent weak majority intransitivity to begin with. While cultures of indifference are 'near worst case' scenarios, even among such cultures over linear orders, we can make the probability of majority cycles as close to zero as we wish by deviating appropriately from the impartial culture (Gehrlein, 1999). Therefore, reducing the probability of the paradox does not crucially rely on moving from linear order preferences to weak order preferences.

Much more importantly, rather than showing, as Jones et al. (1995) do, that under certain circumstances the probability of the paradox can be somewhat reduced, we actually show that under most reasonable circumstances there is no paradox: As Theorem 1.1.1 indicates, if the underlying culture contains no majority ties and no inherent majority intransitivities, then infinite samples will have majority cycles with probability zero. By extension, sufficiently large electorates will encounter the Condorcet paradox with probability arbitrarily close to zero. In other words, while enlarging the domain from linear or strict weak orders reduces the likelihood of cycles slightly, once we move away from cultures of indifference to arbitrary distributions without ties or cycles at the level of the culture, we completely eliminate the Concorcet paradox for infinite samples. In all such cases, the issue of majority cycles becomes theoretically irrelevant.

Looking ahead, in Chapter 5 we derive very general results that apply to virtually any culture over virtually any type of preference relations and that further support the same points at a general level. For example, we show that if there are m many candidates, and if the pairwise margin is at least 10 percent for any pair of candidates (i.e., for any pair a, b, the difference between the number of people who prefer a to b and those who prefer b to a is at least 10 percent of all voters), then an electorate of 951 voters is sufficient to avoid a Condorcet cycle with probability at least $1 - (.001)^{\frac{m(m-1)}{2}}$. We discuss this pairwise constraint in much more detail in Chapter 5, e.g., in Table 5.1. As a consequence, a sampling framework will allow for the Condorcet paradox in large voter profiles only in two circumstances: Either the paradox already exists at the level of the culture, or the profiles are generated from a culture where sufficiently many pairs of alternatives are majority tied (at the level of the culture).[23]

Section 1.2 provides theoretical constraints on the distribution of preferences that are necessary and sufficient for majority preferences to be free of cycles. Sen's value restriction condition is the inspiration for these constraints, but we significantly modify that condition. While Sen's condition is a domain restriction condition that rules out certain preference states, we do not rule out any preference states, but instead formulate constraints at the level of preference distributions. More specifically, we use net probabilities to let opposite orders cancel each other, and then we check whether, in net probability terms, any candidate out of a triple tends to be net never best, net never middle, or net never worst. Our results show that even when we have tremendous diversity in voter preferences, violating Sen's value restriction, and therefore potentially giving rise to

---

[23] This holds regardless of the exact mathematical representation of preferences, i.e., regardless of the domain, as long as this domain is sufficiently large, say <u>all</u> linear, weak, or partial orders.

cycles, this diversity can in large part 'cancel out' at the aggregate, with the 'noncanceled' preferences yielding transitive majority preferences. To the extent that these conditions are theoretically adequate, they again imply that majority cycles are theoretically irrelevant.

Finally, using three national election surveys, Section 1.3 shows that empirical preference distributions do not look at all as if they originated from an impartial culture. Rather, some preference relations occur much more frequently than others and a preference relation and its opposite never occur with equal probability. Moreover, these data violate Sen's original value restriction condition because every permissible linear order is reported by a large number of respondents. Nonetheless, each of the three survey data sets yields transitive majority preferences. In each data set, our net preference majority condition is also violated, but our net value restriction condition provides a descriptive theoretical account for the absence of majority cycles.

Looking at these results in terms of behavioral theories of social choice, we find that both the impartial culture assumption, and Sen's approach of constraining the domain of possible preference states, are behaviorally unrealistic and empirically invalidated by our data. In contrast, our alternative approach of constraining the possible preference distributions on the full domain is behaviorally realistic and descriptive of the empirical data. An important insight gained from these findings is that confronting theoretical ideas (such as the impartial culture assumption or Sen's value restriction condition) with empirical data can critically inform us on aspects of such assumptions that are behaviorally inappropriate and that may stand in the way of developing more 'elegant' theoretical models. Not only is our net value restriction descriptive of empirical data, it also shares much of the mathematical elegance of Sen's original domain restriction condition. In addition, in contrast to the pessimistic predictions stemming from the impartial culture assumption, our conditions make optimistic predictions regarding transitivity (i.e., 'well-behavedness') of majority preferences: We conjecture, and support with various empirical analyses throughout the book, that, at least for mass electorates, majority cycles are only of very limited (if any) empirical relevance.

In the next chapter we turn to a dramatic expansion of the domain of permissible preferences by generalizing our results beyond the case where individual preferences are linear or weak orders. That chapter reviews a broad range of deterministic and probabilistic representations of preferences and utilities. We define majority rule in a framework that is sufficiently general to incorporate those diverse probabilistic preference relations and random utility representations.

2

A General Concept of Majority Rule

Chapter Summary

In focusing on linear and weak orders, the literature on social choice has by and large ignored the vast literature in other areas of the decision sciences covering a multitude of mathematical representations of preference and/or utility. This broad range of mathematical representations is particularly important for the development of descriptive, behavioral models, because deterministic linear or weak orders are often too restrictive to serve as descriptive representations of individual preference. Here, we develop a general concept of majority rule for finitely many choice alternatives that is consistent with arbitrary binary preference relations, real-valued utility functions, probability distributions over binary preference relations, and random utility representations. The underlying framework is, at least in principle, applicable to virtually any type of choice, rating, or ranking data, not just the linear orders or paired comparisons traditionally studied. Our general definition of majority rule for arbitrary binary relations contains the standard definition for linear orders as a special case.

Section 1.2 of Chapter 1 discusses a probabilistic generalization of Sen's (1966, 1970) classic value restriction condition over linear orders. Here, we develop generalizations of net value restriction and net preference majority for general binary relations. It turns out that, in general, neither net value restriction nor net preference majority is necessary for majority preferences to be transitive. Net value restriction is sufficient for transitive strict majority preferences, but not sufficient for transitive weak majority preferences. Net majority is sufficient for transitive majorities only if the preference relation with a net majority is a weak order.

We provide a brief illustration of our general concepts using four data sets involving probability measures on weak orders over three major political candidates that we obtained from U.S. national election surveys (ANES) (Sapiro et al., 1998), just as we use German national election survey (GNES) data over political parties to illuminate our results on strict linear orders in Chapter 1. In each of these four surveys we find transitive majorities even though, in each case, Sen's original value restriction condition is violated. In each case, our net value restriction and/or net majority conditions provide a simple explanation for the transitivity of majority preferences. In addition, we consider a fifth data set on a politically homogeneous subpopulation from a French national election study (FNES) (Pierce, 1996). For that subpopulation we find Sen's original value restriction condition (and thus also our generalizations of that condition) to be satisfied. It thus appears that, while domain restrictions of any kind are consistently violated by all our data sets on national electorates, they may provide adequate descriptive theories for certain extremely homogeneous subpopulations such as the French Communists.

The chapter is organized as follows: Section 2.1 introduces a general concept of majority rule that is applicable to a broad variety of representations of preference or utility. Section 2.2 briefly discusses generalizations of the impartial culture and other cultures of indifference to the much broader domain of preference and utility representations offered by this chapter. Section 2.3 uses the general definition of majority preference relations of Section 2.1 to generalize Sen's value restriction conditions to a similarly broad class of preference representations in a fashion that replaces domain restrictions by net probability distribution restrictions on a very broad domain. Section 2.4 provides several empirical illustrations of our theoretical results, and Section 2.5 concludes the chapter with a discussion and synthesis of our findings.

2.1 A GENERAL DEFINITION OF MAJORITY RULE

Much of the work in social choice theory on the topic of preference aggregation involves one or more of the following restrictions on the domain of study:

- Beginning with Arrow's *Social Choice and Individual Values* (Arrow, 1951, 1963), social choice theories have tended to posit that actors have linear order or weak order preferences. More general binary preference relations have largely been ignored. Noteworthy exceptions include Blair and Pollak (1979), Blau (1979), and Brady and Ansolabehere (1989). These authors discuss a palette of representations ranging from linear orders to the family of all transitive binary relations.

- Until recently, much of the work in social choice posited deterministic preferences rather than allowing for probabilistic preferences. Here, there are a number of notable exceptions, including the literature on probabilistic voting schemes (Coughlin, 1992; Enelow and Hinich, 1984, 1989; Fishburn and Gehrlein, 1977; Fishburn, 1975, 1984; Intriligator, 1973; Schofield and Tovey, 1992). Note that we may treat relative frequencies of deterministic preferences as a special case of a probability measure over preference relations.

- To our knowledge, the social choice literature has not treated the various deterministic and probabilistic representations of preferences and their relationship to various deterministic and probabilistic representations of utility in a unifying way. For instance, very few social choice results have been explicitly stated in terms of random utility representations. Noteworthy exceptions include Falmagne and Regenwetter (1996), Regenwetter (1997), and Tangian (2000).

We continue to focus on majority rule since it is historically the most important preference aggregation mechanism. Our generalization of the concept of majority rule (for a finite number of choice alternatives) is applicable to all binary preference relations, real-valued utility functions, probability distributions over binary preference relations, and random utility representations.

The definition of majority rule for "binary preferences" can be informally stated as follows. For a profile of binary preference relations (possibly with repetitions), alternative c is majority preferred to alternative d if and only if the total number of preference relations in which c is preferred to d exceeds the total number of preference relations in which d is preferred to c. Much of the social choice literature has dealt with deterministic preferences. Because probability distributions over binary relations contain relative frequencies/tallies as a special case, we make use of a probabilistic framework.

Here, given a probability distribution over binary preference relations, alternative c beats d by a majority if and only if the total probability of those relations in which c is 'strictly better than' d exceeds the total probability of those relations in which d is 'strictly better than' c. We essentially make use of this definition already in Chapter 1, when we assume that individual preferences are (randomly drawn from distributions over) linear orders (or, in some cases, weak orders).[1]

There are several reasons for developing a definition of majority rule that is fully general in the way specified above.

1. The literature on preference and utility provides considerable evidence that actual preferences are much more general than linear or weak orders, and this literature discusses a panoply of utility representations (Fishburn, 1970b; Kahneman and Tversky, 1979; Loomes and Sugden, 1982; Luce, 1959; Luce and von Winterfeldt, 1994; Luce and Suppes, 1965; Tversky, 1969; Tversky and Kahneman, 1986). Indeed, sometimes this literature even suggests that individual preference need not be transitive (Gehrlein, 1989; Tversky, 1969; Vila, 1998). Consequently, a descriptively adequate theory of social choice behavior must be reformulated in a fashion that is consistent with descriptive models of individual preference and choice.

2. Mathematical generality is desirable in and of itself: all binary relations, not just linear and weak orders, as well as probability distributions over binary relations, should be accounted for.

3. Similarly, it is desirable to have a concept of majority rule that is general enough to be well defined in terms of any type of real-valued (possibly multicriteria, i.e., vector-valued) utility functions and their generalizations to random (or possibly random vector-valued) utilities.

4. Most election ballot data and most preferences recorded in public opinion surveys fail to explicitly require or record all, or even any, pairwise comparisons. Thus, if we wish to 'reconstruct' majority preferences from empirical data, we need a general framework that permits such inferences. This chapter (and, more generally, this book) provides exactly such a framework.

This section has two subsections.

Subsection 2.1.1 offers a general concept of "majority rule" in terms of arbitrary binary preference relations. We begin that subsection with a

---

[1] Indeed, our approach allows for cycles at the individual preference level. Considering just the pair c, d the cycle 'c (strictly) preferred to d, d (strictly) preferred to e, e (strictly) preferred to c' would be tallied for 'c strictly better than d,' and the reverse cycle 'c (strictly) preferred to e, e (strictly) preferred to d, d (strictly) preferred to c' would be tallied for 'd strictly better than c.'

general definition of "net preference probability," which is key to most of the subsequent theorems. This definition (Definition 2.1.1) generalizes Definition 1.2.10 of Chapter 1 from probability distributions over complete linear orders to probability distributions over arbitrary binary relations. We use the idea of net preference probabilities to define majority preference relations for finitely many choice alternatives in a way that is consistent with all binary preference relations, and with probability distributions over such binary preference relations. This is done in Definition 2.1.3, which expands the domain of individual preference relations on which the majority preference relations $\succ$ and $\succsim$ (Definition 1.2.5, Chapter 1) are defined from linear orders to arbitrary binary relations. Most of the existing literature focuses on linear order preferences. We link our results on general binary relations to that work by proving that there is a unique way to translate a net probability distribution on general binary relations over triples into a net probability distribution over linear orders on the same triples that preserves pairwise net preference probabilities (Theorem 2.1.5). This result essentially allows us to translate tallies on (probability distributions over) binary relations into tallies on (probability distributions over) linear orders in a fashion that preserves majority rule.

Subsection 2.1.2 discusses utility and random utility representations. We begin by summarizing known results on deterministic real-valued representations of various types of binary preference relations (Theorem 2.1.8). We also review previous work on the corresponding relationship between probability distributions over preference relations, on the one hand, and random utilities, on the other (Theorem 2.1.10). As a consequence of these representations, our general definition of majority rule in terms of preference relations naturally extends to utility functions and random utility representations (Observations 2.1.12 and 2.1.14).

2.1.1 Majority Rule Based on General Binary, Deterministic or Probabilistic, Preferences

Most commonly used mathematical representations of preference (as opposed to utility) take the form of binary (order) relations. Here we present results for linear orders, strict weak orders, semiorders, interval orders, strict partial orders of dimension $\leq k$ (for some k), and even arbitrary binary relations on finitely many choice alternatives. We state most of our results in terms of arbitrary binary relations (which we project down to the family of asymmetric binary relations, with a mathematical 'trick' and without loss of generality for our results on majority rule). Of course, because the various types of orders are special cases of binary relations, the results consequently apply to them as well.

Here, as everywhere else in the book, we focus on a basic finite set C of choice alternatives (commodities, political candidates). A binary relation B on C is a set $B \subseteq C^2$. For $(x, y) \in B$, we also write xBy (as in 'x *is better than* y').[2] Given a binary relation B, we write $B^{-1} = \{(y, x)|\ xBy\}$ and $\bar{B} = C^2 - B$. Appendix B provides axiomatic definitions of all standard binary relations, such as partial orders,[3] interval orders, semiorders, weak orders, and linear orders. Besides the classical cases in which preferences belong to one of these families of binary relations, we also allow individual preference to be any binary relation. By covering all binary relations, we are able to derive the existence or nonexistence of transitive majority preference relations even when many members of a population have cyclic (individual) preferences. In other words, we allow for the possibility that society may be 'rational' even when many individuals are not.

As already pointed out, majority rule is usually defined in terms of hypothetical pairwise competitions of each candidate against each of the others. In contrast to that conventional definition of majority rule, virtually no social choice procedure explicitly requires or records pairwise comparisons or complete rankings. Therefore, expanding on the logic of Section 1.2, we redefine majority rule in terms of different primitives: the distribution of (possibly unobservable) utilities or preferences in the population at large. As we also discuss in that section, what really matters in majority rule is whether c is (strictly) preferred to d more often than d is (strictly) preferred to c, or vice versa. Therefore, we now generalize net preference probabilities from linear orders to arbitrary binary preference relations.

Definition 2.1.1 A probability distribution on a collection $\mathcal{B}$ of binary relations is a mapping $P : \mathcal{B} \to [0, 1]$ where $B \mapsto P(B)$ and $\sum_{B \in \mathcal{B}} P(B) = 1$. Writing, as before, $B^{-1} = \{(b, a)|aBb\}$ for the reverse of B, and given

[2] As in Chapter 1, we ignore the detailed semantic distinctions between strict and weak individual preference, i.e., between indifference and incomparability, because these distinctions do not affect majority rule outcomes.

[3] In addition to their use in combinatorics and operations research, strict partial orders are also studied in much detail in the mathematical social sciences. For instance, Falmagne (1997) and others develop stochastic processes on (strict) partial orders to study the evolution of preferences over time (see also Böckenholt, 2002). Regenwetter et al. (1999) successfully analyze a national election panel with two time points using strict weak orders. There is also continued interest in (strict) partial orders in economic theory (see Duggan, 1999, for a recent example).

a probability distribution P on a collection $\mathcal{B}$ of binary relations, the *net preference probability* (on $\mathcal{B}$) of $B \in \mathcal{B}$, $NP^{\mathcal{B}}(B)$, is given by

$$NP^{\mathcal{B}}(B) = \begin{cases} P(B) - P(B^{-1}) & \text{if } B^{-1} \in \mathcal{B}, \\ P(B) & \text{otherwise.} \end{cases}$$

The second line in the above equation in effect treats $P(B^{-1})$ as being zero when B^{-1} does not technically belong to $\mathcal{B}$. However, most 'natural' choices of $\mathcal{B}$, such as the families of all (strict) linear, (strict) weak, semi-, interval, or (strict) partial orders, are closed under inversion, i.e., for $B \in \mathcal{B}$, we have $B^{-1} \in \mathcal{B}$, and thus they do not invoke the second line.

We also call the mapping $NP^{\mathcal{B}} : \mathcal{B} \to [-1, 1]$ *a net (preference) probability distribution*. The binary net preference probability of (the preference of) a over b is

$$NP^{\mathcal{B}}_{ab} = \sum_{\substack{B \in \mathcal{B} \\ a B b}} NP^{\mathcal{B}}(B). \tag{2.1}$$

(The empty sum is assumed to be equal to zero.)

In order to be able to state our results succinctly for many different classes of relations at once, we use the following convention (mathematical 'trick'):

Definition 2.1.2 Consider any probability distribution P on a nonempty collection $\mathcal{B}$ of binary relations on $\mathcal{C}$ and the corresponding net probability distribution $NP^{\mathcal{B}}$ defined in Definition 2.1.1. Writing $AS(D) = D - (D \cap D^{-1})$ for the asymmetric part of a binary relation D, define the *net probability distribution* NP (without the superscript) on the set of all asymmetric binary relations on $\mathcal{C}$ as follows: for any asymmetric binary relation $B \subseteq \mathcal{C}^2$ (not necessarily in $\mathcal{B}$),

$$NP(B) = \sum_{\substack{D \in \mathcal{B} \\ B = AS(D)}} NP^{\mathcal{B}}(D), \tag{2.2}$$

where an empty sum is set to be zero. The corresponding *binary net preference probability* NP_{ab} of (the preference of) a over b is given by

$$NP_{ab} = \sum_{\substack{B \in \mathcal{B} \\ a B b}} NP(B). \tag{2.3}$$

Notice that with this definition $NP_{ab} = NP^{\mathcal{B}}_{ab}$. In other words, (1) we embed the collections Π of strict linear orders, $\mathcal{SWO}$ of strict weak orders, $\mathcal{SO}$ of semiorders, $\mathcal{IO}$ of interval orders, and $\mathcal{SPO}$ of strict partial orders naturally in the collection of all asymmetric binary relations; (2) we collapse all binary relations into their asymmetric part because relationships of the form $a\,Ba$ are not relevant for binary net preference probabilities, and relationships of the form $a\,Bb\,Ba$ cancel out with themselves in the binary net preference probabilities.

This mathematical trick allows us to treat $\mathcal{SWO}$ and $\mathcal{WO}$ (the collection of weak orders) as interchangable and to treat $\mathcal{SPO}$ and $\mathcal{PO}$ (the collection of partial orders) as interchangeable. In particular, whenever we refer to a probability distribution on binary relations, we can, without loss of generality for majority rule outcomes, assume that the probabilities of symmetric relations (i.e., relations B such that $B^{-1} = B$) or reflexive relations (i.e., relations B such that $I \subseteq B$) are zero, since we project those relations down to their asymmetric parts.[4] This convention is used whenever we leave out the superscript $\mathcal{B}$ from $\mathsf{N}^{\mathcal{B}}$.[5]

We now proceed to provide a general definition of majority rule based on a set $\mathcal{B}$ of arbitrary binary preference relations. (In order to be able to keep track of particular cases, we state the definition with the superscript.) Grandmont (1978) develops somewhat related concepts. This definition generalizes the definitions of weak and strict majority preference relations of Definition 1.2.5 from linear orders to arbitrary binary relations.

Definition 2.1.3 Given a probability distribution P on a set $\mathcal{B}$ of binary relations over a finite set $\mathcal{C}$ and given the corresponding net preference

---

[4] For instance, the asymmetric part of a symmetric relation is the empty set, i.e., the strict weak order representing complete indifference between the choice alternatives. More interestingly, the asymmetric part of the (reflexive) weak order $\{(a,a),(a,b),(b,b),(b,c),(c,c),(a,c)\}$ on the set $\{a,b,c\}$ is the strict weak order $\{(a,b),(b,c),(a,c)\}$.

[5] Some authors distinguish '$a\,Bb$ and $b\,Ba$' (often referred to as 'indifference' between a and b) from 'neither $a\,Bb$ nor $b\,Ba$' (often referred to as 'incomparability' of a and b). As we mention in Footnote 2, and paralleling Chapter 1, we do not make use of this distinction here, because it is inconsequential for the analysis of majority preferences. For instance, suppose that 2/3 of the population has the weak order $\{(a,a),(b,b),(c,c),(a,b),(a,c),(b,c),(c,b)\}$ and the remaining 1/3 of the population has the weak preference order $\{(a,a),(b,b),(c,c),(b,c),(c,a),(b,a)\}$. Using Definition 2.1.2, we treat that situation as if 2/3 of the population had the strict weak order preference $\{(a,b),(a,c)\}$ and the remaining 1/3 the strict weak order preference $\{(b,c),(c,a),(b,a)\}$. Using Definition 2.1.3, the strict majority preference relation, with the indifference relationships at the level of individual preferences excluded, is $a \succ b \succ c$ (and thus the weak majority relation is $a \succsim b \succsim c$), which, we believe, is also the only reasonable definition of the majority relation for the original distribution (with the indifferences included). In other words, the indifference (and, similarly, the incomparability) relationships cancel out in majority rule calculations.

probability distribution $\mathbf{NP}^B$, define *majority rule preference relations* $\succsim$ and $\succ$ through, $\forall c, d \in C$,

$$c \succsim d \;\Leftrightarrow\; \mathbf{NP}^B_{cd} \geq 0, \tag{2.4}$$
$$c \succ d \;\Leftrightarrow\; \mathbf{NP}^B_{cd} > 0. \tag{2.5}$$

We say that c has a *weak majority* over d (including the possibility of a tie) whenever $c \succsim d$. We also say that c has a *strict majority* over d (excluding the possibility of a tie) whenever $c \succ d$.

   In words, a has a strict majority over b if a is (strictly) preferred to b strictly more often (or with more total probability mass) than b is (strictly) preferred to a.

   Because the conditions involved in the study of social orders, namely transitivity and negative transitivity, are conditions on triples, we now investigate various properties for triples of choice alternatives. Some abbreviating and mnemonic notation for various individual preference relations is useful for what follows. Suppose for a moment that $C = \{a, b, c\}$. We write $\begin{smallmatrix} a \\ b \\ c \end{smallmatrix}$ for the binary relation $\{(a, b), (a, c), (b, c)\}$, a linear order. We write $\begin{smallmatrix} a \\ b \;\; c \end{smallmatrix}$ for the binary relation $\{(a, b), (a, c)\}$, a strict weak order in which b and c are tied and both are dominated by a. Similarly we write $\begin{smallmatrix} b \;\; c \\ a \end{smallmatrix}$ for the binary relation $\{(b, a), (c, a)\}$, a strict weak order in which b and c are tied and both dominate a. The symbol $\begin{smallmatrix} a \\ b \end{smallmatrix}$ stands for the binary relation $\{(a, b)\}$, a strict partial order (which is also an interval order, and in fact, a semiorder) where a and c are tied, and also b and c are tied, while a is strictly preferred to b. The symbol $\begin{smallmatrix} a \\ c \quad b \end{smallmatrix} \circlearrowright$ stands for a (forward, clockwise) cycle $\{(a, b), (b, c), (c, a)\}$. The symbol $\begin{smallmatrix} a \\ > b \\ c \end{smallmatrix}$ denotes the nontransitive binary relation (read clockwise) $\{(a, b), (b, c)\}$. Finally, ϕ denotes the state of total indifference between the three choice alternatives, i.e., the empty relation.

   Up to relabeling of the choice alternatives, the above 6 relations are all possible asymmetric binary relations on three choice alternatives, which makes a total of 27 different relations. There are eight different nontransitive binary relations on three objects, 19 different strict partial orders on three choice alternatives, 13 of which are strict weak orders, of which in turn 6 are linear orders. Note that every strict partial order on three choice alternatives is in fact also a semiorder and an interval order. Notice also that we always have $N\!P(\phi) = 0$. Thus, going from the most general to the most specific binary relations, the net preference probability distribution is positive on at most 13 binary relations, 9 of which are semiorders, 6 of which are, in turn, strict weak orders, 3 of which are, in turn, linear orders.

We now generalize Definition 1.2.8 from linear orders to arbitrary binary relations.

Definition 2.1.4 Consider a net preference probability distribution $N\!P^{\mathcal{B}}$ (associated with some probability distribution P) on a set $\mathcal{B}$ of binary relations over a finite set $\mathcal{C}$, if $|\mathcal{C}| \geq 3$ and $\{a, b, c\} \subseteq \mathcal{C}$. Then the *marginal net preference probabilities* over $\{a, b, c\}$ are defined as follows:[6] For $B' \subseteq \{a, b, c\}$,[2]

$$N\!P^{\mathcal{B}}(B') = \sum_{\substack{B \in \mathcal{B} \\ B \cap \{a,b,c\}^2 = B'}} N\!P^{\mathcal{B}}(B).$$

The next theorem and its corollaries show how the general case of majority rule tallies on binary relations, strict partial orders, semiorders, interval orders, and strict weak orders can be translated into equivalent majority rule tallies on linear orders. We use the fact that, for any strict partial order B over a set $\mathcal{C}$ and for any triple $\{x, y, z\} \subseteq \mathcal{C}$, the binary relation $B \cap \{x, y, z\}^2$ is a semiorder. We also continue to use the convention (of Definition 2.1.2) that net probabilities $N\!P(B)$ are defined only on asymmetric binary relations B.

Theorem 2.1.5 *Let $N\!P$ be a net probability distribution (associated with some probability distribution P) on the set of all asymmetric binary relations over $\mathcal{C}$. Let $N\!P^{\Pi}$ be a net probability distribution (associated with some probability distribution P^{Π}) on the set Π of all linear orders over $\mathcal{C}$ and let $\mathcal{C}' \subseteq \mathcal{C}$ with $|\mathcal{C}'| = 3$. Then the identity*

$$N\!P^{\Pi}_{xy} = N\!P_{xy}, \qquad \forall x, y \in \mathcal{C}', x \neq y, \tag{2.6}$$

---

[6] While we could also study net probabilities and majority preferences for the case of two candidates, we leave out this trivial case in order to simplify the exposition of the case where $|\mathcal{C}| \geq 3$.

holds if and only if

$$
\mathbf{NP}^\Pi \begin{pmatrix} a \\ b \\ c \end{pmatrix} = \mathbf{NP} \begin{pmatrix} a \\ b \\ c \end{pmatrix} + 1/2 \left[\mathbf{NP} \begin{pmatrix} a \\ b\ c \end{pmatrix} + \mathbf{NP} \begin{pmatrix} a\ b \\ c \end{pmatrix} + \mathbf{NP} \begin{pmatrix} a \\ b \end{pmatrix} \right.
$$

$$
\left. + \mathbf{NP} \begin{pmatrix} b \\ c \end{pmatrix} - \mathbf{NP} \begin{pmatrix} a \\ > c \\ b \end{pmatrix} - \mathbf{NP} \begin{pmatrix} b \\ > a \\ c \end{pmatrix} \right] + \mathbf{NP} \begin{pmatrix} a \\ > b \\ c \end{pmatrix}
$$

$$
+ \mathbf{NP} \begin{pmatrix} a \\ \bigcirc \\ c\ b \end{pmatrix}, \quad \text{for all relabelings } \{a, b, c\} = C'. \quad (2.7)
$$

Suppose that (2.7) holds for all three-element subsets $C' \subseteq C$. Then $\succsim$, as defined in Definition 2.1.3, is the same, regardless of whether we substitute $\mathbf{NP}$ or $\mathbf{NP}^\Pi$ for $\mathbf{NP}^B$. The same holds for $\succ$.

The proof is in Appendix C.

Important special cases occur when individual preferences are all strict partial orders (semiorders, interval orders) or all strict weak orders. We present the cases for strict partial orders (Corollary 2.1.6) and strict weak orders (Corollary 2.1.7).

Corollary 2.1.6 *Let $\mathbf{NP}^{SPO}$ be a net probability distribution (associated with some probability distribution P^{SPO}) on the set SPO of all strict partial orders over C and let $\mathbf{NP}^\Pi$ be a net probability distribution (associated with some probability distribution P^Π) on the set Π of all linear orders over C. Let $C' \subseteq C$ with $|C'| = 3$. Then the identity*

$$
\mathbf{NP}^\Pi_{xy} = \mathbf{NP}^{SPO}_{xy}, \qquad \forall x, y \in C', x \neq y, \quad (2.8)
$$

holds if and only if, for all relabelings $\{a, b, c\} = C'$,

$$
\mathbf{NP}^\Pi \begin{pmatrix} a \\ b \\ c \end{pmatrix} = \mathbf{NP}^{SPO} \begin{pmatrix} a \\ b \\ c \end{pmatrix} + 1/2 \left[\mathbf{NP}^{SPO} \begin{pmatrix} a \\ b\ c \end{pmatrix} \right.
$$

$$
\left. + \mathbf{NP}^{SPO} \begin{pmatrix} a\ b \\ c \end{pmatrix} + \mathbf{NP}^{SPO} \begin{pmatrix} a \\ b \end{pmatrix} + \mathbf{NP}^{SPO} \begin{pmatrix} b \\ c \end{pmatrix} \right]. \quad (2.9)
$$

Suppose that (2.9) holds for all three element subsets $C' \subseteq C$. Then $\succsim$, as defined in Definition 2.1.3, is the same, regardless of whether $B = \Pi$ or $B = SPO$. The same holds for $\succ$.

A parallel corollary holds with $\mathcal{SPO}$ replaced by the set $\mathcal{SWO}$ of strict weak orders on $\mathcal{C}$.

Corollary 2.1.7 *Let* $\mathbf{N}\mathbf{P}^{\mathcal{SWO}}$ *be a net probability distribution (associated with some probability distribution* $\mathbf{P}^{\mathcal{SWO}}$*) on the set* $\mathcal{SWO}$ *of all strict weak orders over* C *and let* $\mathbf{N}\mathbf{P}^{\Pi}$ *be a net probability distribution (associated with some probability distribution* $\mathbf{P}^{\Pi}$*) on the set* Π *of all linear orders over* C*. Let* $C' \subseteq C$ *with* $|C'| = 3$*. Then the identity*

$$\mathbf{N}\mathbf{P}^{\Pi}_{xy} = \mathbf{N}\mathbf{P}^{\mathcal{SWO}}_{xy}, \qquad \forall x, y \in C', x \neq y, \tag{2.10}$$

holds if and only if, for all relabelings $\{a, b, c\} = C'$,

$$\mathbf{N}\mathbf{P}^{\Pi}\begin{pmatrix} a \\ b \\ c \end{pmatrix} = \mathbf{N}\mathbf{P}^{\mathcal{SWO}}\begin{pmatrix} a \\ b \\ c \end{pmatrix} + 1/2\left[\mathbf{N}\mathbf{P}^{\mathcal{SWO}}\begin{pmatrix} a \\ b\ c \end{pmatrix} + \mathbf{N}\mathbf{P}^{\mathcal{SWO}}\begin{pmatrix} a\ b \\ c \end{pmatrix}\right].$$
$$\tag{2.11}$$

Suppose that (2.11) holds for all three element subsets $C' \subseteq C$*. Then* $\succsim$*, as defined in Definition 2.1.3, is the same, regardless of whether* $\mathcal{B} = \Pi$ *or* $\mathcal{B} = \mathcal{SWO}$*. The same holds for* $\succ$*.*

The proofs of these two corollaries are straightforward, and thus omitted.

2.1.2 Majority Rule Based on Utility Functions or Random Utility Representations

We now move from preference relations to utility functions. We first discuss the relationship between preference representations and utility representations, both deterministic and probabilistic. Then we define a general concept of majority rule in terms of utility functions and random utility representations. We subsequently show how majority rule defined in terms of preference representations relates to majority rule defined in terms of utility representations.

Most mathematical representations of utility (as opposed to preference) rely on real-valued functions that map objects into their (utility) values. A very general conceptual framework to represent and quantify the variability of utilities is provided by random utility theory. Here, the utility of an object is (the value of) a random variable (or a random vector). Just as preference relations are in close correspondence with utility functions from C into $\mathbb{R}^n$ (for some n), so are probability distributions over preference relations in close correspondence with utility random variables, i.e., random utility models. Just as probability distributions over preference relations generalize and include deterministic preference relations, so do random utilities generalize and include real-valued deterministic utility functions.

Note that we make no assumptions about where the randomness comes from. Probabilities may capture random error, random sampling, probabilistic mechanisms inside the decision maker's head, or they may simply quantify the 'proportion' of the population that satisfies some property. In particular, we require no independence assumptions. Since people interact and communicate, we allow individual preferences to be interdependent and/or systematically biased in the following sense: In a probability distribution over preference relations, interdependencies can simply be quantified through setting the probabilities of certain preference orders very high or very low; in the random utility framework, the interdependent nature of utilities is captured and quantified through the joint distribution of the utility random variables. We also make no assumptions about that joint distribution. In particular, while we do not rule out an impartial culture, we do not require one, and indeed in Chapter 1 we already demonstrate that the impartial culture is unrealistic. Similarly, Chapter 5 focuses on sampling and inference for realistic distributions.

We now review deterministic representations and then move on to discuss random utility representations.

There is a close relationship between preference orders and real-valued utility functions. This wellknown relationship (in the deterministic realm) has been spelled out in representation theorems like the one that follows (for references see, for instance, Fishburn, 1985; Krantz et al., 1971; Roberts, 1979). (Note that the formulation below holds only for finite C. The infinite case is more complex.)

Theorem 2.1.8 *Let B be a binary relation on a finite set C. B is a strict weak order if and only if it has a real representation $u : C \to \mathbb{R}$ of the following form:*

$$a\,Bb \Leftrightarrow u(a) > u(b).$$

If B is a linear order, then it has the above representation, but the converse holds only if u is a one-to-one mapping.

B is a semiorder if and only if it has a real representation $u : C \to \mathbb{R}$ of the following form:

$$a\,B\,b \Leftrightarrow u(a) > u(b) + \epsilon,$$

where $\epsilon \in \mathbb{R}^{++}$ is a fixed strictly positive real-valued (utility) threshold.

B is an interval order if and only if it has a real representation $l, u : C \to \mathbb{R}$, with $l(x) < u(x)$ (for all x), of the following form:

$$a\,B\,b \Leftrightarrow l(a) > u(b).$$

In the interval order representation, the utility functions u and l can be interpreted as upper and lower utility respectively, and thus the function $(u - l)$ can be interpreted as an object-dependent utility threshold.

Later, we also make use of the wellknown fact that each strict partial order can be written as an intersection of linear orders. The *dimension* of a strict partial order is the smallest number k such that the strict partial order is the intersection of k many linear orders.[7]

We now move on to variable preferences and utilities. There is no particular reason why individual preference orders should not vary and why the utility of a commodity should not differ for different observers. A natural and general way to account for and quantify variability is through probability measures. We can simply introduce a probability distribution over binary preference relations of a given type. Alternatively, we can define the utility of an object to be a random variable. (For ease in interpreting notation, random variables are written in boldface.)

Definition 2.1.9 A *(real) random utility representation* on a finite set C of choice alternatives is a collection of jointly distributed real-valued random variables $\mathbf{U} = (\mathbf{U}_{i,c})_{\substack{i=1,\dots,k \\ c \in C}}$ (with a finite k) on some sample space with probability measure $\mathbb{P}$. Given a measurable set $X \subseteq \mathbb{R}^{|C|}$, we write $\mathbb{P}(\mathbf{U} \in X)$ for the probability of the event that the joint utility takes a value in X.

When $k = 1$, we usually write $\mathbf{U}_c$ as a shorthand for $\mathbf{U}_{1,c}$, since the first index does not carry any useful information in that case. We always use the same symbol $\mathbb{P}$ for the probability measure on the sample space underlying a random utility representation, since this does not lead to any ambiguities. For instance, we can interpret the probability $\mathbb{P}(\mathbf{U} \in X)$ as

---

[7] Dimension theory is an active research domain. For instance, Trotter (1992) provides a detailed analysis.

the proportion of people in the population who give the candidates joint utilities in X. In particular, if $X = \{(x_c)_{c \in C} \in \mathbb{R}^C | x_d = x_e; \ \forall d, e \in C\}$, and $k = 1$, then $\mathbb{P}(U \in X)$ can, for instance, be interpreted as the proportion of voters who are completely indifferent between all candidates, in the sense that they assign equal utilities to all of them. Another interpretation, in a sampling framework, would be that $\mathbb{P}(U \in X)$, with the above choice of X, is the probability that a randomly selected voter is completely indifferent between all candidates. A third interpretation of these probabilities is in terms of degree of certainty or uncertainty. Thus, $\mathbb{P}(U \in X)$ could quantify our degree of uncertainty as to whether or not the joint utility of the candidates (possibly to a fixed, given observer) is constrained to the real measurable subspace X.

In order to situate our approach to probabilistic preferences and random utility representations with respect to existing work on probabilistic representations of preference and utility, several remarks are in order.[8]

1. Much traditional research in random utility modeling (Ben-Akiva and Lerman, 1985; McFadden, 1991, 1998; Thurstone, 1927a,b) places all randomness in an 'error' term by assuming the following form:

   $$U = U + E,$$

   where U is a (deterministic) real vector (interpreted as the 'true utility' of the objects in C) and E is a family of jointly distributed random variables (interpreted as a vector of random errors or exogenous shocks). Furthermore, random utility models often assume that the mean of E is zero, and/or that E belongs to a particular parametric family, typically either the multivariate normal (Böckenholt, 1992; Thurstone, 1927a,b) or the multivariate extreme value family (Dagsvik, 1995; Joe, 1997; McFadden, 1998). Marley (1989a,b) presents an integrative framework that includes various of these models as special cases. While this scenario is a special case of our framework, we generally do not make any assumptions about the joint distribution of the family U.

   Furthermore, we emphasize that randomness has many substantive interpretations, including error only as a special case. To the extent that social choice procedures are used as methods to aggregate

---

[8] See Fishburn (1998) for an excellent general overview of the related literature.

imperfect judgments, this interpretation of random utilities is useful here too (for examples of work on social choice as a judgment aggregation process, see Grofman, 1975, 1981; Grofman and Feld, 1988; Grofman and Owen, 1986a; Grofman et al., 1983; Owen et al., 1989; Shapley and Grofman, 1984). However, for the study of social choice as an aggregation method of truly variable preferences (typically across individuals), the interpretation of random utility as 'true value plus noise' is not very interesting or realistic.

2. The research on nonparametric (i.e., distribution free) random utility models is quite extensive and has focused mainly on the characterization problems of probabilistic binary choice (Fishburn, 1992; Koppen, 1995; Marley, 1991b; Marschak, 1960; Suck, 1992, 1995) and of probabilistic multiple choice (Barberá, 1979; Barberá and Pattanaik, 1986; Falmagne, 1978). The interpretation of our family U of jointly distributed utility random variables is simply that utilities of objects vary and co-vary. The distribution of utility values together with their interdependencies is formally captured by the joint distribution of the relevant random variables.

3. There also exists a literature on parametric models for probabilistic (preference) relations (Critchlow et al., 1991, 1993; Mallows, 1957; Marley, 1991a).

In sum, we argue that variable preferences can be represented appropriately by a probability distribution over a set of binary preference relations, and variable utilities can be represented appropriately through jointly distributed real-valued random variables. The relationship between these two frameworks is reasonably well understood. For instance, Block and Marschak (1960) show that most families of jointly distributed random variables induce a probability distribution over linear orders (i.e., rankings without ties), and that, conversely, each probability distribution over linear orders can be associated with a (highly nonunique) family of jointly distributed utility random variables. In other words, it is equivalent, for instance, to assume that a randomly sampled individual has a strict linear order preference over all choice alternatives or that s/he assigns utilities to objects according to a joint outcome of a family of random variables (satisfying certain properties). Recent developments in mathematical psychology (Niederée and Heyer, 1997; Regenwetter, 1996, 1997; Regenwetter and Marley, 2001; Regenwetter et al., 2002c; Suck, 1995) have extended this type of result to arbitrary relations, including the important special cases where the individual preferences are transitive binary relations, strict weak orders, semiorders, interval orders, and partial orders of dimension $\leq k$ (for some k).

The most general framework for discussing random utility representations is distribution free in that it makes no assumptions about particular parametric families for the underlying distributions. The following theorem (which we state without proof) summarizes various known results concerning the intimate link between (distribution free) random utilities and (distribution free) probabilistic preference relations. (Detailed citations to the original papers are provided after the theorem statement.) This theorem allows us to have a unified definition of majority rule that applies to (probabilistic) preference representations and (random) utility representations simultaneously. In this theorem, we denote $|\mathcal{C}|$ by N.

Theorem 2.1.10 *A family of jointly distributed real-valued utility random variables* $\mathbf{U} = (\mathbf{U}_{i,c})_{i=1,\ldots,k;c\in\mathcal{C}}$ *satisfies the following properties:*

RANDOM UTILITY REPRESENTATIONS OF LINEAR ORDERS: *If $k = 1$ and noncoincidence holds, that is,* $\mathbb{P}(\mathbf{U}_c = \mathbf{U}_d) = 0, \forall c, d \in \mathcal{C}$, *then $\mathbb{P}$ induces a probability distribution $\pi \mapsto P(\pi)$ on the set Π of linear orders over $\mathcal{C}$ through, for any linear order $\pi = c_1 c_2 \ldots c_N$ (c_1 is best, $\ldots$, c_N is worst),*

$$P(\pi) = \mathbb{P}(\mathbf{U}_{c_1} > \mathbf{U}_{c_2} \cdots > \mathbf{U}_{c_N}). \tag{2.12}$$

RANDOM UTILITY REPRESENTATIONS OF WEAK ORDERS: *If $k = 1$, then, regardless of the joint distribution of $\mathbf{U}$, $\mathbb{P}$ induces a probability distribution $B \mapsto P(B)$ on the set $\mathcal{SWO}$ of strict weak orders over $\mathcal{C}$ through*

$$P(B) = \mathbb{P}\left(\left[\bigcap_{(a,b)\in B} (\mathbf{U}_a > \mathbf{U}_b)\right] \cap \left[\bigcap_{(c,d)\in\mathcal{C}^2 - B} (\mathbf{U}_c \leq \mathbf{U}_d)\right]\right). \tag{2.13}$$

RANDOM UTILITY REPRESENTATIONS OF SEMIORDERS: *If $k = 1$, then, regardless of the joint distribution of $\mathbf{U}$, $\mathbb{P}$ induces a probability distribution $B \mapsto P(B)$ on the set $\mathcal{SO}$ of semiorders over $\mathcal{C}$ through, given a strictly positive threshold $\epsilon \in \mathbb{R}^{++}$,*

$$P(B) = \mathbb{P}\left(\left[\bigcap_{(a,b)\in B} (\mathbf{U}_a > \mathbf{U}_b + \epsilon)\right] \cap \left[\bigcap_{(c,d)\in\mathcal{C}^2 - B} (\mathbf{U}_c - \mathbf{U}_d \leq \epsilon)\right]\right). \tag{2.14}$$

RANDOM UTILITY REPRESENTATIONS OF INTERVAL ORDERS: *If $k = 2$ and $\mathbb{P}(\mathbf{U}_{1,c} \leq \mathbf{U}_{2,c}) = 1$ for all choices of c, then, writing $\mathbf{L}_c$ for $\mathbf{U}_{1,c}$ (lower* *utility) and* $\mathbf{U}_c$ *for* $\mathbf{U}_{2,c}$ *(upper utility) we have the following result. In this case,* $\mathbb{P}$ *induces a probability distribution* $B \mapsto P(B)$ *on the set* $\mathcal{IO}$ *of interval orders over* $\mathcal{C}$ *through*

$$P(B) = \mathbb{P}\left(\left[\bigcap_{(a,b)\in B}(\mathbf{L}_a > \mathbf{U}_b)\right] \cap \left[\bigcap_{(c,d)\in \mathcal{C}^2 - B}(\mathbf{L}_c \leq \mathbf{U}_d)\right]\right). \quad (2.15)$$

RANDOM UTILITY REPRESENTATIONS OF PARTIAL ORDERS OF DIMENSION $\leq k$: *For any value of* k, *let* $\mathcal{SPO}(k)$ *be the collection of all strict partial orders of dimension* $\leq k$ *over* $\mathcal{C}$, *and, as before, let* Π *denote the set of all strict linear orders over* $\mathcal{C}$. *Furthermore, for any strict partial order* $B \in \mathcal{SPO}(k)$, *write*

$$\Pi^k(B) = \left\{(\pi_1, \pi_2, \dots, \pi_k) \in \Pi^k \mid B = \bigcap_{m=1}^{k} \pi_m\right\}.$$

Then $\mathbf{U}$ *induces a probability distribution* $B \mapsto P(B)$ *over* $\mathcal{SPO}(k)$ *through*

$$P(B) = \mathbb{P}\left(\bigcup_{(\pi_1, \pi_2, \dots, \pi_k)\in \Pi^k(B)} \bigcap_{i=1}^{k} \bigcap_{(c,d)\in \pi_i}(\mathbf{U}_{i,c} > \mathbf{U}_{i,d})\right) \quad (2.16)$$

if and only if noncoincidence holds on each component (or dimension) i, *that is, if and only if*

$$\mathbb{P}(\mathbf{U}_{i,c} = \mathbf{U}_{i,d}) = 0$$

for $i = 1, \dots, k$, *and for* $(c, d) \in \mathcal{C}^2 - I$.

Conversely, each probability distribution on linear orders, strict weak orders, semiorders, interval orders, or partial orders of dimension $\leq k$ *over* $\mathcal{C}$ *can be represented in the above fashion (nonuniquely) by an appropriately chosen family of jointly distributed random variables.*

The random utility representation of linear orders is the classical result of Block and Marschak (1960). The generalizations to strict weak orders and semiorders were pointed out by Regenwetter (1996), and the interval order case by Suck (1995) and Regenwetter (1997). The partial order case was shown by Regenwetter et al. (2002c). Furthermore, various researchers provide general abstract results including binary relations as very special cases (Heyer and Niederée, 1989, 1992; Niederée and Heyer, 1997; Regenwetter, 1996; Regenwetter and Marley, 2001). We now move on to define pairwise net probabilities for (random) utilities. We start with the situation where we believe that each respondent evaluates the alternatives according to k many different dimensions simultaneously by taking the intersection of k linear orders. (While k is the same for all observers, the actual dimensions may differ across observers.) In other words, we first consider a random utility version of net preference probabilities based on strict partial orders of dimension $\leq k$.

Definition 2.1.11 Given jointly distributed random variables $(U_{i,c})_{i=1,\dots,k;c\in\mathcal{C}}$, the *k-dimensional binary net (preference) probability* of a over b is given by

$$NP_{ab} = \mathbb{P}\left(\bigcap_{i=1}^{k}[U_{i,a} > U_{i,b}]\right) - \mathbb{P}\left(\bigcap_{i=1}^{k}[U_{i,b} > U_{i,a}]\right). \qquad (2.17)$$

As the following observation (which we state without formal proof) spells out in detail, Definition 2.1.1 and Definition 2.1.11 yield identical binary net probabilities when the pertinent conditions in Theorem 2.1.10 hold, and thus the resulting relationship given in (2.16) applies.

Observation 2.1.12 *Let P be a probability distribution over $\mathcal{SPO}(k)$ and let $NP_{ab}^{\mathcal{SPO}(k)}$ be the pairwise net preference probabilities resulting from Equation (2.1) of Definition 2.1.1 for that P and for all choices of $a \neq b$ in C. Consider a family $(U_{i,c})_{i=1,\dots,k;c\in\mathcal{C}}$ of jointly distributed random variables, such that the equalities (2.16) hold (with the random variables being noncoincident on each dimension). Then, for all choices of $a \neq b$ in C, NP_{ab} of Equation (2.17) in Definition 2.1.11 is identical to $NP_{ab}^{\mathcal{SPO}(k)}$ of Equation (2.1) in Definition 2.1.1. If $k = 1$ and we do not assume noncoincidence, then we get the case where only strict weak orders have nonzero probabilities. Furthermore, the special case of $k = 1$, and where noncoincidence holds, yields a result in which only linear orders have nonzero probabilities.*

Further special cases of interest are when only semiorders or interval orders (in $\mathcal{SPO}(k)$) have nonzero probabilities.

Besides the construction in (2.17), there is an alternative route for interval orders and semiorders, based on the representation in Equations (2.14) and (2.15) of Theorem 2.1.10, which again includes the strict weak orders and linear orders as special cases. Using the random utility representation (2.15) of interval orders, we can define the net preference probability of a over b in random utility terms as follows.

Definition 2.1.13 Given $(U_c)_{c \in C}, (L_c)_{c \in C}$, jointly distributed random variables with the property that $\mathbb{P}(U_c \geq L_c) = 1$, the *binary net probability* (derived from U, L) of a over b is given by

$$NP_{ab} = \mathbb{P}(L_a > U_b) - \mathbb{P}(L_b > U_a). \tag{2.18}$$

The following Observation is also stated without proof.[9]

Observation 2.1.14 *Let P be a probability distribution over the set $\mathcal{IO}$ of all interval orders on C and let $NP_{ab}^{\mathcal{IO}}$ be the pairwise net preference probabilities resulting from Equation (2.1) of Definition 2.1.1 for that P and for all choices of $a \neq b$ in C.*

Let $(U_c)_{c \in C}, (L_c)_{c \in C}$ be a family of jointly distributed random variables with the property that $\mathbb{P}(U_c \geq L_c) = 1$ and such that Equation (2.15) holds. Then NP_{ab} of Equation (2.18) in Definition 2.1.13 is identical to $NP_{ab}^{\mathcal{IO}}$ of Equation (2.1) in Definition 2.1.1 for all choices of $a \neq b$ in C.

Consider the special case where P is a probability distribution over the set $\mathcal{SO}$ of all semiorders, and where $L_c = U_c - \epsilon > 0$ (everywhere and $\forall c$), with $\epsilon \in \mathbb{R}^{++}$ being a constant. Then (2.18) becomes

$$NP_{ab} = \mathbb{P}(U_a > U_b + \epsilon) - \mathbb{P}(U_b > U_a + \epsilon). \tag{2.19}$$

If the relation between P and $\mathbb{P}$ given in Equation (2.14) holds, then NP_{ab} of Equation (2.19) is identical to $NP_{ab}^{\mathcal{SO}}$ of Equation (2.1) in Definition 2.1.1 for all choices of $a \neq b$ in C.

Consider the next special case where P is a probability distribution over the set $\mathcal{SWO}$ of all strict weak orders, and where $\epsilon = 0$ in (2.19), i.e., $U_c = L_c$ in (2.18). Then Equation (2.19) becomes

$$NP_{ab} = \mathbb{P}(U_a > U_b) - \mathbb{P}(U_b > U_a). \tag{2.20}$$

If the relation between P and $\mathbb{P}$ given in Equation (2.13) holds, then NP_{ab} of Equation (2.20) is identical to $NP_{ab}^{\mathcal{SWO}}$ of Equation (2.1) in Definition 2.1.1 for all choices of $a \neq b$ in C.

Finally, consider the case where P is a probability distribution over the set Π of all linear orders, and where noncoincidence is satisfied, that is, $\mathbb{P}(U_c = U_d) = 0$ $(\forall c \neq d)$. If the relation between P and $\mathbb{P}$ given in Equation (2.12) holds, then NP_{ab} of Equation (2.20) is identical to NP_{ab}^{Π} of Equation (2.1) in Definition 2.1.1 for all choices of $a \neq b$ in C.

---

[9] The proofs of this and the previous observation are straightforward by substitution of the relevant quantities in the relevant equations.

Now that we have defined and discussed binary net preference probabilities in terms of random utilities, we can define majority rule in terms of random utilities as well, in a way that is consistent with Definition 2.1.3 as stated in terms of probabilities on preference relations. To emphasize the similarity and close relationship with Definition 2.1.3, we label this new definition as Definition 2.1.3'.

Definition 2.1.3' Given binary net probabilities NP (derived from a family of jointly distributed random variables), define *majority rule preference relations* $\succsim$ and $\succ$ through, $\forall c, d \in C$,

$$c \succsim d \;\Leftrightarrow\; NP_{cd} \geq 0, \tag{2.21}$$

$$c \succ d \;\Leftrightarrow\; NP_{cd} > 0. \tag{2.22}$$

We say that c has a *weak majority* over d (including the possibility of a tie) whenever $c \succsim d$. We also say that c has a *strict majority* over d (excluding the possibility of a tie) whenever $c \succ d$.

Whenever Observation 2.1.12 or Observation 2.1.14 applies, we can see that Definition 2.1.3' is the random utility counterpart of Definition 2.1.3 for probabilistic preferences, and the two definitions yield identical majority preference relations $\succ$ and $\succsim$. This reconciles the concept of net preference probability distributions with the general framework of random utility representations. Note that the very way we derive pairwise majorities from random utilities implicitly chooses a family of binary relations for the representation of preferences. We cover the most natural cases, which correspond to linear, strict weak, semi-, interval, and strict partial orders, respectively. As a result of Observations 2.1.12 and 2.1.14 we can, without much loss of generality, from now on state our results only in terms of probabilities over (asymmetric) binary relations.

REMARK. Note that the interval order and semiorder net preference probabilities in (2.18) and (2.19) cannot be obtained by simple substitution in (2.17) and, in that sense, are <u>not</u> special cases of (2.17). Rather, the concept of a (possibly variable) threshold is distinct from the concept of dimension of a strict partial order.[10] In other words, there exist two fundamentally different random utility representations that yield the identical probability

---

[10] Incidentally, Bogart, Rabinovitch, and Trotter (1976) have shown that a finite interval order can have arbitrarily high dimension, whereas Rabinovitch (1978) has shown that finite semiorders have dimension ≤ 3, a result which was extended to arbitrary semiorders by Fishburn (1985) and Duggan (1999).

distribution over semiorders or interval orders (and consequently the same net preference probability distribution and majority rule preference relations), depending on whether we view a semiorder or interval order (of dimension > 1) as a ranking with a threshold of discrimination or as an intersection of two or more rankings (on separate dimensions). While this double interpretation may appear mathematically awkward, it is psychologically intuitive, because the two random utility representations have fundamentally different interpretations as psychological processes: In the first case, the respondent is unable to perfectly discriminate between every pair of alternatives; in the second case, the respondent is able to discriminate perfectly between every pair of alternatives, and does that even on two (or more) distinct dimensions. This double interpretation has been there all along, including in the deterministic domain: It has not been caused by the probabilistic framework.

Thus, we can use random utility formulations and probabilistic preference formulations more or less interchangeably as long as we specify which set of binary relations we are referring to. However, because of the above remark, in some circumstances we may need to keep track of how we translate certain strict partial orders into real representations and vice versa.

In this section, by defining majority preference relations in terms of the theoretical primitives that are common to virtually all models of choice, rating or rankings, we provide a common ground for the theoretical and empirical analysis of majority rule within a panoply of basic and applied research paradigms.

Because the impartial culture and other cultures of indifference play an important role in the literature and in Chapter 1, we now briefly discuss conditions on net probabilities that characterize cultures of indifference on arbitrary (asymmetric) binary relations.

2.2 GENERALIZATIONS OF THE IMPARTIAL CULTURE AND OTHER CULTURES OF INDIFFERENCE

As we discuss in Chapter 1 and in Appendix A, the impartial culture is usually defined as a uniform distribution over all linear orders (DeMeyer and Plott, 1970; Gehrlein and Fishburn, 1976b) and occasionally defined as a uniform distribution over weak orders (Jones et al., 1995; Van Deemen, 1999). The most canonical generalization of the impartial culture to an arbitrary set of binary relations is therefore a uniform distribution over that set of relations. If all preference relations have equal probability, and if $B \in \mathcal{R} \Rightarrow B^{-1} \in \mathcal{R}$, then the probability that aBb is equal to the probability that bBa, and thus the net probability NP_{ab} is zero for all distinct $a, b \in C$. The impartial culture is therefore a special case of a culture of indifference, as introduced in Chapter 1 and formally defined for linear order preferences in Appendix A, by which we mean a culture in which all pairwise majority relationships are complete ties.

As the following simple observation spells out, a culture of indifference (i.e., a completely tied majority preference relation) on asymmetric binary relations requires very strong but also simple conditions.

Observation 2.2.1 *i) Given a net probability distribution NP (associated with some probability P) over asymmetric binary relations on any finite set C, the majority preference relation is a total tie if and only if, $\forall a, b, c$ distinct in C,*

$$NP \begin{pmatrix} a \\ b \\ c \end{pmatrix} + 1/2 \left[NP \begin{pmatrix} a \\ b & c \end{pmatrix} + NP \begin{pmatrix} a & b \\ c \end{pmatrix} + NP \begin{pmatrix} a \\ b \end{pmatrix} + NP \begin{pmatrix} b \\ c \end{pmatrix} \right]$$

$$= 1/2 \left[NP \begin{pmatrix} a \\ > c \\ b \end{pmatrix} + NP \begin{pmatrix} b \\ > a \\ c \end{pmatrix} \right] - NP \begin{pmatrix} a \\ > b \\ c \end{pmatrix} - NP \begin{pmatrix} a \\ \bigcirc \\ c & b \end{pmatrix}.$$

$$(2.23)$$

ii) Given a net probability distribution NP^{SPO} (associated with some probability P^{SPO}) over strict partial orders on any finite set C, the majority preference relation is a total tie if and only if, $\forall a, b, c$ distinct in C,

$$NP^{SPO} \begin{pmatrix} a \\ b \\ c \end{pmatrix}$$

$$= -1/2 \left[NP^{SPO} \begin{pmatrix} a \\ b & c \end{pmatrix} + NP^{SPO} \begin{pmatrix} a & b \\ c \end{pmatrix} + NP^{SPO} \begin{pmatrix} a \\ b \end{pmatrix} + NP^{SPO} \begin{pmatrix} b \\ c \end{pmatrix} \right].$$

$$(2.24)$$

iii) Given a net probability distribution NP^{SWO} (associated with some probability P^{SWO}) over strict weak orders on any finite set C, the majority preference relation is a total tie if and only if, $\forall m, n, k$ distinct in C,

$$NP^{SWO} \begin{pmatrix} m \\ n \\ k \end{pmatrix} = -1/2 \left[NP^{SWO} \begin{pmatrix} m \\ n & k \end{pmatrix} + NP^{SWO} \begin{pmatrix} m & n \\ k \end{pmatrix} \right]. \qquad (2.25)$$

In particular, the following property has to consequently hold for any choice of distinct a, b, c:

$$
\mathrm{NP}^{SWO} \begin{pmatrix} a \\ b \\ c \end{pmatrix} + \mathrm{NP}^{SWO} \begin{pmatrix} b \\ c \\ a \end{pmatrix} + \mathrm{NP}^{SWO} \begin{pmatrix} c \\ a \\ b \end{pmatrix} = 0. \tag{2.26}
$$

iv) Given a net probability distribution NP^{Π} (associated with some probability P^{Π}) over linear order preferences, the majority preference relation is a total tie if and only if, $\forall m, n, k$ distinct in C,

$$
\mathrm{NP}^{\Pi} \begin{pmatrix} m \\ n \\ k \end{pmatrix} = 0. \tag{2.27}
$$

In particular, Equation (2.27) states that the only culture of indifference over linear orders is a dual culture, while the previous equations show how cultures of indifference over general binary preference relations allow for more flexible distributions with less symmetry. The much broader domain of preference representations in this chapter thus relaxes the constraints placed on preference distributions that constitute cultures of indifference. Nonetheless, we believe that none of Equations (2.23–2.27) is a realistic description of preference distributions in real world populations. Thus, even in view of the fact that Equations (2.23–2.27) are more flexible than the impartial culture over linear or weak orders, we still consider cultures of indifference to be highly unrealistic (and worst case scenarios vis-à-vis cycles). This viewpoint is supported by all our empirical analyses in this book.

We now move on to generalizing Sen's value restriction condition, as well as our own probabilistic generalization in Chapter 1, to the same broad array of mathematical representations of preference or utility.

2.3 GENERAL CONCEPTS OF VALUE RESTRICTION AND PREFERENCE MAJORITY

As we discuss in Chapter 1, Sen (1966, 1970) introduced the *value restriction* condition. Sen's definition of value restriction incorporates the concepts of *never worst* (NW), *never middle* (NM), and *never best* (NB). The NW condition on a triple means that, among the members of that triple, there is one alternative that is not ranked worst (i.e., last) among the three by any of the voters. Similarly, for NB and NM. Value restriction, which incorporates Black's (1958) concept of single-peakedness as a special case, is the best known constraint on feasible preference profiles in the social choice literature (see Gärtner, 2001, for a nice overview of domain restriction conditions).

Gärtner and Heinecke (1978) and, independently, Feld and Grofman (1986b) developed natural extensions of value restriction, labeled by Feld and Grofman as "net value restriction." This condition is based on cancellation of reverse orderings, a concept already discussed in Sen (1970). Feld and Grofman (1986b) also defined the concept of *net preference majority,* which is simply one ranking having a strict majority among all the remaining rankings after canceling out all reverse rankings. In Section 1.2 above, we extend these concepts to a probabilistic context, with the main result being stated in Theorem 1.2.15. That result essentially shows that net value restriction and net preference majority are necessary and sufficient conditions for majority preferences to be transitive in the case where individual preferences are captured by a probability distribution over linear orders.[11]

Here, we investigate the extent to which Sen's conditions can be generalized beyond probability distributions over linear orders to provide necessary and/or sufficient conditions for transitivity of majority rule. In this investigation we draw on our general concept of majority rule (for a finite number of choice alternatives) developed in Section 2.1. Again, it should be noted that, quite contrary to Sen's original value restriction condition on the domain of permissible preferences, we continue to allow for an extremely broad domain of preference representations and study restrictions on the (net) preference distributions over that full domain.

The structure of this section is as follows: Subsection 2.3.1 considers conditions for transitive majority rule for arbitrary (asymmetric) binary relations. We do so first without defining net value restriction or net majority beyond linear orders. Rather, we combine Theorems 1.2.15 and 2.1.5 to derive new results on necessary and sufficient conditions for transitive majorities on arbitrary binary relations (Corollary 2.3.2). Subsection 2.3.2 generalizes the concepts of (marginal) net value restriction and net preference majority, from linear orders (as defined in Definitions 1.2.13 and 1.2.14), to arbitrary binary relations (Definitions 2.3.4

---

[11] It should be noted that Sen's original condition was stated for deterministic (nonstrict) <u>weak</u> order preferences, whereas our Theorem 1.2.15 deals with probabilities over (strict) <u>linear</u> orders.

and 2.3.7). Then we state our key new results in terms of these generalizations. Theorem 2.3.8 shows that neither net value restriction nor net majority is necessary for transitive majority preferences to exist when preferences are allowed to be weak orders or more general binary relations. Theorem 2.3.9 shows that net value restriction on binary relations is sufficient for transitive strict majorities (but not sufficient for transitive weak majorities, i.e., majority ties need not be transitive). Finally, Theorem 2.3.10 shows that, if individual preferences are asymmetric binary relations, then a sufficient condition for transitive majority preferences is that a given strict weak order has a net majority (on a given triple). We provide a counterexample showing that a given semiorder or more general binary relation having a net majority is not sufficient for the existence of a transitive majority ordering.

Note that in Chapter 1 we show that net value restriction and net preference majority provide a set of jointly necessary and sufficient conditions for (strict) transitive majorities on linear orders. However, here we show that, in the cases of either strict weak order, strict partial order, or more general binary preferences, it is possible to have a transitive strict majority order without either net value restriction or a net preference majority.

2.3.1 A Generalization of Theorem 1.2.15 Beyond Linear Orders

Theorem 1.2.15 of Chapter 1 shows that if individual preferences are linear orders then net value restriction and net preference majority are (up to additional conditions eliminating knife-edge situations) necessary and sufficient to eliminate majority cycles. We now look into conditions that also give transitive majority preference relations when individual preferences can take the form of arbitrary binary relations, as in Section 2.1.

Regardless of the representation of preferences from which the net probability distribution NP in Definitions 2.1.1–2.1.3 is derived, we can state several properties that hold in general for $\succsim$ and $\succ$ of Definition 2.1.3 (and Definition 2.1.3$'$). The following observation regarding such properties is a direct generalization of Observation 1.2.6.

Observation 2.3.1 *The weak majority preference relation $\succsim$, as defined in Definition 2.1.3 and in Definition 2.1.3$'$, is reflexive and strongly complete (and thus complete). Therefore, $\succsim$ is a weak order if and only if it is transitive. The strict majority preference relation $\succ$, as defined in*

Definition 2.1.3 and Definition 2.1.3′, is asymmetric (and thus antisymmetric). Therefore, $\succ$ is a strict weak order if and only if it is negatively transitive. More generally, $\succ$ is a strict partial order if and only if it is transitive. Furthermore, $\succsim$ is a weak order if and only if $\succ$ is a strict weak order.[12]

The proof is identical to the proof of Observation 1.2.6 provided in Appendix C. Also, recall the comments following Observation 1.2.6 that $\succ$ can be transitive even when $\succsim$ is not.

Theorem 2.1.5 provides an accounting method that reduces the problem of characterizing majority preference relations over a set of asymmetric binary relations (possibly obtained from other binary relations via Definition 2.1.2) to a problem of characterizing majority preference relations over a set of linear orders. We now use Theorem 2.1.5 together with Theorem 1.2.15 to fully characterize the conditions under which we obtain a transitive majority preference relation when individual preferences are general (asymmetric) binary relations.

Corollary 2.3.2 *Given net probabilities NP on asymmetric binary relations, the weak majority preference relation $\succsim$, as defined in Definitions 2.1.3 and 2.1.3′ with respect to NP, is a weak order if and only if for all triples x, y, z of distinct elements in C at least one of the following two conditions holds for NP^{Π} on the linear orders derived from NP via (2.7):*

i) *There exists a relabeling $\{a, b, c\} = \{x, y, z\}$ such that b has a net preference majority for NP^{Π};*

ii) *NP^{Π} satisfies marginal net value restriction on $\{x, y, z\}$ and, if at least one net preference probability is nonzero, then the following implication is true: For every relabeling $\{a, b, c\} = \{x, y, z\}$,*

$$NP^{\Pi}\begin{pmatrix} a \\ b \\ c \end{pmatrix} = 0 \Rightarrow NP^{\Pi}\begin{pmatrix} b \\ a \\ c \end{pmatrix} \neq NP^{\Pi}\begin{pmatrix} a \\ c \\ b \end{pmatrix}.$$

Given net probabilities NP on asymmetric binary relations, the strict majority preference relation $\succ$, as defined in Definitions 2.1.3 and 2.1.3′ with respect to NP, is a strict partial order if and only if for all triples x, y, z of

---

[12] Here, the distinction between *weak order* and *strict weak order* matters.

distinct elements in C at least one of the following two conditions holds for $\mathbf{NP}^\Pi$ *derived from* $\mathbf{NP}$ *via (2.7):*

i) *There exists a relabeling* $\{a, b, c\} = \{x, y, z\}$ *such that* $\begin{smallmatrix} a \\ b \\ c \end{smallmatrix}$ *has a net preference majority for* $\mathbf{NP}^\Pi$;

ii) $\mathbf{NP}^\Pi$ *satisfies marginal net value restriction.*

When only linear order preferences are possible, i.e., if we substitute Π for $\mathcal{B}$ in Definition 2.1.2, then Corollary 2.3.2 is identical to Theorem 1.2.15. The proof of the Corollary is trivial because, by Theorem 2.1.5, Equation (2.7) preserves the pairwise net probabilities, i.e., (2.6) holds.

Corollary 2.3.3 *Let* $\mathbf{NP}$ *be a net probability distribution over asymmetric binary relations on* $\{a, b, c\}$ *and let* $\mathbf{NP}^\Pi$ *be defined as in (2.7).* $\mathbf{NP}^\Pi$ *satisfies* $NB(a)$ *on linear orders as defined in Definition 1.2.12, if and only if the following inequalities hold:*

$$\mathbf{NP}\begin{pmatrix} a \\ b \\ c \end{pmatrix} + 1/2 \left[\mathbf{NP}\begin{pmatrix} a \\ b \ c \end{pmatrix} + \mathbf{NP}\begin{pmatrix} a \ b \\ c \end{pmatrix} + \mathbf{NP}\begin{pmatrix} a \\ b \end{pmatrix} + \mathbf{NP}\begin{pmatrix} b \\ c \end{pmatrix} \right]$$
$$\leq 1/2 \left[\mathbf{NP}\begin{pmatrix} a \\ > c \\ b \end{pmatrix} + \mathbf{NP}\begin{pmatrix} b \\ > a \\ c \end{pmatrix} \right] - \mathbf{NP}\begin{pmatrix} a \\ > b \\ c \end{pmatrix} - \mathbf{NP}\begin{pmatrix} a \\ c \ b \end{pmatrix}.$$
$$(2.28)$$

$$\mathbf{NP}\begin{pmatrix} a \\ c \\ b \end{pmatrix} + 1/2 \left[\mathbf{NP}\begin{pmatrix} a \\ b \ c \end{pmatrix} + \mathbf{NP}\begin{pmatrix} a \ c \\ b \end{pmatrix} + \mathbf{NP}\begin{pmatrix} a \\ c \end{pmatrix} + \mathbf{NP}\begin{pmatrix} c \\ b \end{pmatrix} \right]$$
$$\leq 1/2 \left[\mathbf{NP}\begin{pmatrix} a \\ > b \\ c \end{pmatrix} - \mathbf{NP}\begin{pmatrix} b \\ > a \\ c \end{pmatrix} \right] - \mathbf{NP}\begin{pmatrix} a \\ > c \\ b \end{pmatrix} + \mathbf{NP}\begin{pmatrix} a \\ c \ b \end{pmatrix}.$$
$$(2.29)$$

Consequently, (2.28) and (2.29) together are sufficient for $\succ$ *to be a strict weak order and sufficient for* $\succsim$ *to be a weak order when the usual additional condition, ruling out knife-edge situations, holds.*

For brevity, we omit the corresponding results for $NM(a)$ *and* $NW(a)$.

The proof is immediate.

Note that we have not yet defined net value restriction or net preference majority for anything other than linear orders. While Corollaries 2.3.2 and 2.3.3 give necessary and sufficient conditions on asymmetric binary relations for transitivity of majority rule, and while Corollary 2.3.3 might appear to suggest a definition of $NW(a)$ for general asymmetric binary relations, this would not be a very natural way to generalize (net) value restriction. A more natural generalization requires the net probabilities of some individual preference relations to be nonpositive, instead of imposing inequalities between sums of multiple net probabilities. Our next step in Subsection 2.3.2 is therefore to investigate a plausible generalization beyond linear order preferences of the net value restriction and net preference majority definitions (Definitions 1.2.13 and 1.2.14) themselves. We then also study whether or not the (generalized) conditions remain necessary and/or sufficient for transitivity. However, before we get to Subsection 2.3.2, a remark is in order.

It is tempting to try to define net value restriction on general asymmetric binary relations by constraining the net probabilities of net linear orders only. However, the following example shows that this is not enough to make net value restriction a sufficient condition for the existence of a transitive majority preference relation. We provide a counterexample for strict weak orders, which also suffices for more general asymmetric binary relations. Suppose that

$$NP\begin{pmatrix} a \\ b \\ c \end{pmatrix} = NP\begin{pmatrix} a \\ c \\ b \end{pmatrix} = NP\begin{pmatrix} c \\ a \\ b \end{pmatrix} = .01,$$

$$NP\begin{pmatrix} a \\ b \ c \end{pmatrix} = .1, \qquad NP\begin{pmatrix} b \\ a \ c \end{pmatrix} = .122, \qquad NP\begin{pmatrix} c \\ a \ b \end{pmatrix} = .111.$$

Then 'net value restriction' holds on the linear orders. Nevertheless, there is a majority cycle $\succ = \begin{matrix} a \\ \bigcirc \\ c \ \ b \end{matrix}$, with $NP_{ab} = .008 > 0$, $NP_{bc} = .001 > 0$, $NP_{ca} = .001 > 0$.

2.3.2 Generalizations of Net Value Restriction and Net Preference Majority to Arbitrary (Asymmetric) Binary Relations

We now further generalize the concepts of net value restriction and net preference majority of Definitions 1.2.13 and 1.2.14 to general (asymmetric) binary relations on a finite set, including strict weak orders, interval orders, semiorders, partial orders, and even nontransitive binary relations. We begin with net value restriction, by generalizing Sen's value restriction to binary relations on a finite set.

Definition 2.3.4 Given a net probability distribution $NP^\mathcal{B}$ over any set of (not necessarily asymmetric) binary relations over a finite set C and NP defined on all asymmetric binary relations as in Definition 2.1.2, the marginal net preference probabilities derived on a triple $\{a, b, c\} \subseteq C$ satisfy *net never worst of a*, denoted as $NW(a)$, if the following inequalities hold:

$$NP\begin{pmatrix} b \\ c \\ a \end{pmatrix} \le 0, \quad NP\begin{pmatrix} c \\ b \\ a \end{pmatrix} \le 0, \quad NP\begin{pmatrix} b \\ a\ c \end{pmatrix} \le 0, \quad NP\begin{pmatrix} b\ c \\ a \end{pmatrix} \le 0,$$

$$NP\begin{pmatrix} c \\ a\ b \end{pmatrix} \le 0, \quad NP\begin{pmatrix} b \\ a \end{pmatrix} \le 0, \quad NP\begin{pmatrix} c \\ a \end{pmatrix} \le 0, \quad NP\begin{pmatrix} b \\ c \end{pmatrix} = 0,$$

$$NP\begin{pmatrix} a \\ > b \\ c \end{pmatrix} = NP\begin{pmatrix} a \\ > c \\ b \end{pmatrix} = NP\begin{pmatrix} b \\ > a \\ c \end{pmatrix} = NP\begin{pmatrix} a \\ \bigcirc \\ c\ b \end{pmatrix} = 0.$$

The marginal net preference probabilities derived on a triple $\{a, b, c\} \subseteq C$ satisfy *net never middle of a*, denoted as $NM(a)$, if the following equalities hold:

$$NP\begin{pmatrix} b \\ a \\ c \end{pmatrix} = NP\begin{pmatrix} b \\ a\ c \end{pmatrix} = NP\begin{pmatrix} c \\ a\ b \end{pmatrix} = NP\begin{pmatrix} a \\ b \end{pmatrix} = NP\begin{pmatrix} a \\ c \end{pmatrix}$$

$$= NP\begin{pmatrix} a \\ > b \\ c \end{pmatrix} = NP\begin{pmatrix} a \\ > c \\ b \end{pmatrix} = NP\begin{pmatrix} b \\ > a \\ c \end{pmatrix} = NP\begin{pmatrix} a \\ \bigcirc \\ c\ b \end{pmatrix} = 0.$$

The marginal net preference probabilities derived on a triple $\{a, b, c\} \subseteq C$ satisfy *net never best of a*, denoted as $NB(a)$, if the following inequalities hold:

$$NP\begin{pmatrix} a \\ c \\ b \end{pmatrix} \le 0, \quad NP\begin{pmatrix} a \\ b \\ c \end{pmatrix} \le 0, \quad NP\begin{pmatrix} a\ c \\ b \end{pmatrix} \le 0, \quad NP\begin{pmatrix} a \\ b\ c \end{pmatrix} \le 0,$$

$$NP\begin{pmatrix} a\ b \\ c \end{pmatrix} \le 0, \quad NP\begin{pmatrix} a \\ b \end{pmatrix} \le 0, \quad NP\begin{pmatrix} a \\ c \end{pmatrix} \le 0, \quad NP\begin{pmatrix} b \\ c \end{pmatrix} = 0$$

$$NP\begin{pmatrix} a \\ > b \\ c \end{pmatrix} = NP\begin{pmatrix} a \\ > c \\ b \end{pmatrix} = NP\begin{pmatrix} b \\ > a \\ c \end{pmatrix} = NP\begin{pmatrix} a \\ \bigcirc \\ c\ b \end{pmatrix} = 0.$$

(Generalized) net value restriction holds for N^P if and only if, for each triple $\{a, b, c\} \subseteq C$, there exists $x \in \{a, b, c\}$ such that either $NW(x)$, or $NM(x)$, or $NB(x)$ holds.

Notice that, quite contrary to Sen's original value restriction condition, we do not restrict the domain of possible preference states at all. Rather, the main purpose of this definition, and this chapter, is to enlarge the domain in a fashion that incorporates a broad range of descriptively and behaviorally adequate characterizations of individual preference. Our generalized net value restriction conditions allow for a large proportion of the population to hold any conceivable preference state (within the scope of this chapter) as long as the net distributions satisfy certain inequality constraints.

Notice further that each equality sign in Definition 2.3.4 is really the joint occurrence of a binary relation B and its reverse B^{-1} simultaneously having a nonpositive net probability. Because each equality is a conjunction of two inequalities (that are each other's mirror images), the equalities put much stronger constraints on data than mere inequalities. Equality constraints on probabilities also have a certain resemblence to domain restrictions and, in particular, may be descriptively too strong. If weak orders are the only binary relations (that have nonzero probability), then the equality constraints in Definition 2.3.4 are vacuously satisfied. Therefore, from a statistical point of view, it is easier to satisfy net value restriction when preferences are restricted to weak orders than when they are allowed to be more general partial orders. Our empirical illustrations in this and the next chapter support this intuition.

When N^P satisfies, say, $NB(a)$, we also say in short that $Net NB(a)$ holds. We use the same shortcut for the other conditions and choice alternatives. We give a graphical display of the $Net NB(a)$ and $Net NM(a)$ conditions[13] for linear orders in Figures 2.2 and 2.5, and for partial orders in Figures 2.3 and 2.6.

This generalized concept of net value restriction is related to the one in Definition 1.2.13 in a straightforward manner. We believe that any natural

---

[13] Notice that in Figures 2.2, 2.3, and subsequent similar figures, we shade (and frame) those partial orders whose net probabilities are required to be nonnegative. The $Net NB(a)$ condition is stated in terms of their reverses, i.e., the partial orders whose net probabilities must be nonpositive. This choice of shading makes these figures consistent with other related figures throughout the book.

generalization of net value restriction to general (asymmetric) binary relations needs to satisfy the properties stated in the next observation.

Observation 2.3.5 *Given* NP *on asymmetric binary relations as above, we can deduce the following properties for* NP^Π *derived from* NP *as in* (2.7). *For any triple* $\{a, b, c\} \subseteq C$,

    i) $NW(a)$ *for* $NP \Rightarrow NW(a)$ *for* NP^Π *but the converse does not hold.*
    ii) $NM(a)$ *for* $NP \Rightarrow NM(a)$ *for* NP^Π *but the converse does not hold.*
    iii) $NB(a)$ *for* $NP \Rightarrow NB(a)$ *for* NP^Π *but the converse does not hold.*
    iv) *(generalized) net value restriction for* $NP \Rightarrow$ *net value restriction for* NP^Π *but the converse does not hold.*

The proof is straightforward. Note also that one obtains obvious special cases if one replaces NP in Observation 2.3.5 by, for example, a net probability distribution NP^{SPO} (on strict partial orders) or by NP^{SWO} (on strict weak orders).

Before we turn to a generalization of the net majority condition, we point out that net value restriction on binary relations can fail to satisfy some of the properties satisfied by net value restriction on linear orders.

Observation 2.3.6 *Recall from the remarks following Definition 1.2.13 that if* $NP \neq 0$ *only on linear orders,* $NW(a)$ *implies that either* $NB(b)$ *or* $NB(c)$ *holds. Similarly,* $NM(a)$ *implies that either* $NB(b)$ *or* $NB(c)$ *holds, and* $NB(a)$ *implies that either* $NW(b)$ *or* $NW(c)$ *holds. These implications do not hold for net value restriction on binary relations such as strict partial orders (or strict weak orders), i.e., without the restriction that* $NP \neq 0$ *only on linear orders.*

The proof is in Appendix C.

Next, we turn to generalizations of net preference majority to arbitrary binary relations.

Definition 2.3.7 *Given net preference probabilities* NP^B *as before, a binary (preference) relation* B *over* $\{x, y, z\}$ *has a net preference majority (among all members of a set* $\mathcal{B}$ *of binary relations) on* $\{x, y, z\}$ *if and only if*

$$NP^B(B) > \sum_{\substack{B' \in \mathcal{B} - \{B\} \\ NP^B(B') > 0}} NP^B(B'). \tag{2.30}$$

We show now that Corollary 2.3.2 does not generalize naturally to our general setting defined directly on strict partial orders.

Theorem 2.3.8 *Given a net probability distribution NP over all asymmetric binary relations over $\{a, b, c\}$, neither net value restriction of NP nor net majority of a binary relation is necessary for $\succsim$ and/or $\succ$ to be transitive.*

The proof is in Appendix C. (Examples based on real data are also discussed in Section 4.3.)

While Theorem 2.3.8 demonstrates that neither net value restriction nor net majority is necessary for transitivity of majority rule, our next theorem shows that net value restriction is a sufficient condition for strict majority rule to be transitive. Moreover, similarly to net value restriction for linear orders of Chapter 1, net value restriction alone is not a sufficient condition for transitive weak majority preferences, because majority ties need not be transitive.

Theorem 2.3.9 *Let NP be a net preference probability over asymmetric binary relations, as before.*

  i) SUFFICIENCY OF NET VALUE RESTRICTION FOR TRANSITIVE STRICT MAJORITY: *If net value restriction of NP holds then the strict majority preference relation $\succ$, as defined in Definition 2.1.3, is transitive. However,*

  ii) INSUFFICIENCY OF NET VALUE RESTRICTION FOR TRANSITIVE WEAK MAJORITY: *If net value restriction of NP holds then the weak majority preference relation $\succsim$, as defined in Definition 2.1.3, need not be transitive.*

The proof is in Appendix C.

We provide successful applications of Theorem 2.3.9 to empirical data (strict weak orders) in Section 2.4.

Theorem 2.3.10 below shows that the net preference majority condition retains the ability of Corollary 2.3.2 to guarantee transitive majority preferences when individual preferences are generalized to weak orders, but it loses most of its power when we move to relations more general than weak orders. Without loss of generality, we state the theorem for asymmetric binary relations, following the convention of Definition 2.1.2.

Theorem 2.3.10 *Let* NP *be a net preference probability over asymmetric binary relations on three elements.*

  i) SUFFICIENCY OF NET MAJORITY OF A STRICT WEAK ORDER: *If a strict weak order B has a net majority then* $\succsim$ *and* $\succ$ *are transitive. However,*

  ii) INSUFFICIENCY OF NET MAJORITY OF AN ASYMMETRIC BINARY RELATION MORE GENERAL THAN A STRICT WEAK ORDER: *If a semiorder, interval order, strict partial order, or more general asymmetric binary relation, B', has a net majority then neither* $\succsim$ *nor* $\succ$ *need be transitive.*

The proof is in Appendix C.

This concludes our discussion of the degree to which Sen's conditions generalize (or fail to generalize) to situations where individual preferences are strict weak orders, semi- or interval orders, strict partial orders, or arbitrary (asymmetric) binary relations. Now we turn to visualizations of these conditions and closely related topics.

2.3.3 Visualizations Using the Partial Order Graph on Three Alternatives

In this subsection, we use the graph of all strict partial orders over three elements to illustrate the conditions we study in Chapter 1 and in this chapter. We also use these graphs to illustrate the definition of majority preference in terms of pairwise net probabilities. For each binary relation in the graph, we use a simplified form of standard Hasse diagrams, commonly used in combinatorics.[14] As shown in Figure 2.1 as a referent, the rectangles provide the six linear orders as in our illustrations of Chapter 1; the empty box in the center is the full indifference relation; the circles provide the additional six strict weak orders; and the pentagons contain the additional six semiorders. These displays match the mnemonic notation we use in most mathematical statements of this chapter.

Visualizations of the Different Value Restriction Conditions. Figures 2.1 through 2.6 provide visualizations of Sen's value restriction condition over weak orders, our net value restriction condition over linear orders of

---

[14] The strict weak order subgraph and the strict partial order graph (which, for three alternatives, is simply the semiorder graph) are rather standard (see, for instance, Kemeny and Snell, 1962). See also Falmagne (1997) and Saari (1994, 1995).

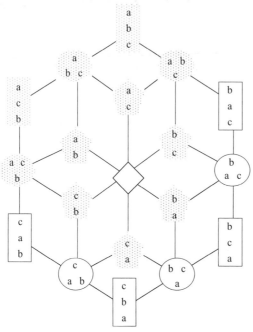

FIGURE 2.1: Graphical display of Sen's $NB(a)$ condition on weak orders shown in the graph of partial orders over three choice alternatives. The lightly shaded frameless partial orders are ruled out of the domain.

Chapter 1, and our generalized net value restriction of this chapter (however, restricted to partial orders).[15] More specifically, Figure 2.1 shows Sen's $NB(a)$ condition of Definition 1.2.7 for weak orders, Figure 2.2 shows our $Net NB(a)$ condition of Definition 1.2.12 for linear orders, and Figure 2.3 shows our generalized $Net NB(a)$ condition of Definition 2.3.4 for partial orders. Similarly, Figure 2.4 shows Sen's $NM(a)$ condition of Definition 1.2.7 for weak orders, Figure 2.5 shows our $Net NM(a)$ condition of Definition 1.2.12 for linear orders, and Figure 2.6 shows our generalized $Net NM(a)$ condition of Definition 2.3.4 for partial orders. These figures can be read as follows. The lightly shaded frameless partial orders are ruled out of the domain, either by a given condition or because they do not belong to the family of relations under consideration. The more darkly shaded frameless partial orders must have net probability zero (i.e., they must have exactly the same probabilities as their reverses), and the shaded framed orderings must have nonnegative net

---

[15] For simplicity of display, the figures do not include intransitive preference relations.

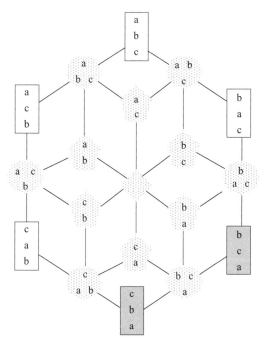

FIGURE 2.2: Graphical display of *NetNB(a)* for linear orders, as introduced in Chapter 1. The condition is shown in the graph of partial orders over three choice alternatives. The lightly shaded frameless partial orders do not belong to the domain. Shaded framed orderings must each have nonnegative net probability.

probabilities (i.e., they must have probabilities at least as large as those of their reverses). As pointed out above, given a probability distribution over (asymmetric) binary relations on three alternatives, there are at most 13 relations with positive net preference probabilities, which include at most 9 semiorders with positive net preference probabilities, which, in turn, include at most 6 strict weak orders with positive net preference probabilities, which, in turn, include at most 3 linear orders with positive net preference probabilities.

We first consider the various versions of *NB(a)* shown in Figures 2.1 through 2.3. To compare Sen's *NB(a)*, our *NetNB(a)* of Chapter 1, and our most general *NetNB(a)* conditions, notice first that Sen's condition is specified for weak order preferences only, and that his *NB(a)* condition completely prohibits all but 8 of 13 weak orders. In Sen's *NB(a)* condition of Figure 2.1, all those partial orders that are lightly shaded and depicted without a frame are ruled out of the domain, either by Sen's condition or because they do not belong to the family of relations under consideration.

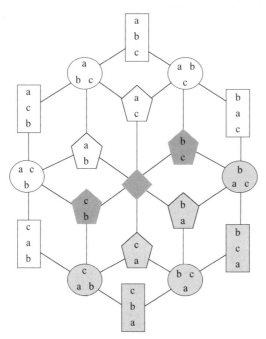

FIGURE 2.3: Graphical display of *NetNB(a)* for partial orders, as introduced in this chapter, depicted in the graph of partial orders over three choice alternatives. The darkly shaded frameless partial orders must each have net probability zero (this is automatically true for the indifference relation). The shaded framed partial orders must each have nonnegative net probability.

Second, notice that when we define the concept of net value restriction in Chapter 1, we only consider linear order preferences. There, our *NB(a)* condition states that, among the six possible linear orders, two occur at least as frequently as their reverses. Accordingly, in the *NetNB(a)* condition depicted in Figure 2.2, all those partial orders that are lightly shaded and depicted without a frame are not included in the domain. Those two linear orders that are shaded and framed are required to have nonnegative net probability.

Finally, in the present chapter we allow for arbitrary binary relations (although Figure 2.3 depicts only the partial orders). For partial orders, our generalized *NB(a)* condition, introduced in this chapter, requires 7 of the 19 partial orders to occur at least as frequently as their reverses; two linear orders and the three-way indifference relation are unconstrained; and one semiorder (and its reverse) has to have net probability zero (i.e., this semiorder has to occur equally often as its reverse). Note that the indifference relation automatically has net probability zero, since it is its

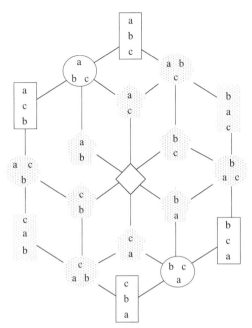

FIGURE 2.4: Graphical display of Sen's *NM(a)* condition on weak orders shown in the graph of partial orders over three choice alternatives. The lightly shaded frameless partial orders are ruled out of the domain.

own reverse. Accordingly, in the generalized *Net NB(a)* condition depicted in Figure 2.3, those seven partial orders that are shaded and framed are required to have nonnegative net probability. Those two semiorders that are darkly shaded and depicted without a frame are required to have net probability zero (i.e., their probabilities must be equal, since they are each other's reverses).

We now consider the various versions of *NM(a)* shown in Figures 2.4 through 2.6. Similar comments apply here as we make for the three *NB(a)* conditions. Sen's condition is specified for weak order preferences only, and his *NM(a)* condition completely prohibits all but 7 of 13 weak orders. Accordingly, in Sen's *NM(a)* condition depicted in Figure 2.4, all those partial orders that are lightly shaded and depicted without a frame are ruled out of the domain, either by Sen's condition or because they do not belong to the family of relations under consideration. In the *Net NM(a)* condition for linear orders of Chapter 1 depicted in Figure 2.5 in the graph of partial orders, all those partial orders that are lightly shaded and depicted without a frame are excluded from the domain. Those two linear orders that are more darkly shaded, but also without a frame,

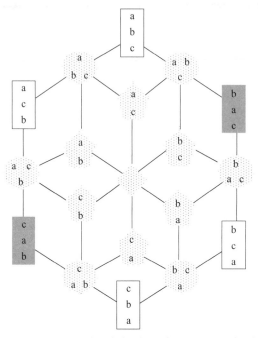

FIGURE 2.5: Graphical display of *NetNM(a)* for linear orders, as introduced in Chapter 1. The condition is shown in the graph of partial orders over three choice alternatives. The lightly shaded frameless partial orders do not belong to the domain. The two darkly shaded frameless orderings must each have net probability zero.

are restricted to occur with net probability zero (i.e., in effect, they are required to have equal probability). Finally, our generalized *NetNM(a)* condition of the present chapter is depicted in Figure 2.6, where those ten partial orders that are darkly shaded and depicted without a frame are required to have net probability zero.

We do not include figures for *NW(a)*, *NetNW(a)*, or generalized *NetNW(a)*, since they are similar to the figures for *NB(a)*, *NetNB(a)*, and generalized *NetNB(a)*. Also, we do not need to draw separate graphs for value or net value restriction on other choice alternatives, since they can be easily obtained from the ones here, e.g., by a simple suitable relabelling of the choice alternatives.

As can easily be seen in Figures 2.1 through 2.6, our developments here move in the opposite direction from Sen's approach (and related work): Sen constraints the domain of possible preference states to a degree where, regardless of the distribution of preferences over that domain, majority preferences are guaranteed to be transitive. We start with the observation that any descriptively adequate theory of social choice behavior

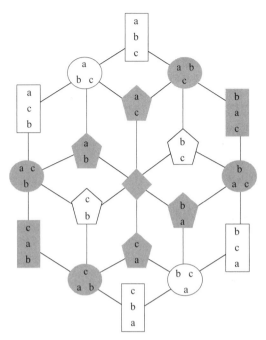

FIGURE 2.6: Graphical display of *NetNM(a)* for partial orders, as introduced in this chapter, depicted in the graph of partial orders over three choice alternatives. The darkly shaded frameless partial orders must each have net probability zero (this is automatically true for the indifference relation).

must expand the domain, not constrain it. Accordingly, we allow for an extremely broad range of deterministic and probabilistic preferences. Instead of constraining the domain to guarantee transitive majority preferences, we constrain the possible distributions of preferences. More specifically, we constrain the net probabilities of the various preference relations in systematic ways. Some of our constraints on net probabilities have a certain resemblence to domain constraints in that we require some net probabilities to be zero. In other words, while we permit all preference states to occur, we do require certain pairs of preference probabilities to perfectly cancel out. Our empirical applications in Chapter 3 show that the latter constraint is, again, descriptively too strong and requires further refinements in the future.

Visualization of Majority Preference in Terms of Pairwise Net Probabilities. Figures 2.7 through 2.9 display the conditions for pairwise majority preference between any two alternatives. The partial order graph shown in Figure 2.7 has those orders shaded in which *a* is preferred to *b*. In order for *a* to be strictly (weakly) majority preferred to *b*, the sum

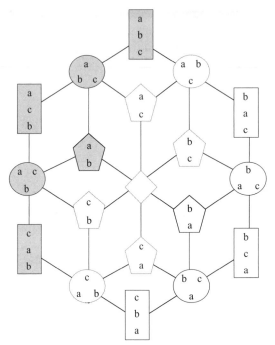

FIGURE 2.7: Graphical display of $a \succ b$ (or $a \succsim b$). The <u>sum</u> of net probabilities over the shaded partial orders needs to be positive (or nonnegative).

of all net probabilities of the shaded partial orders needs to be positive (nonnegative). Equivalently, the sum of net probabilities over all partial orders on white background that have solid frames needs to be negative (nonpositive). The net probabilities of the remaining partial orders (with dotted frames) are unconstrained. Similar comments apply to the majority preferences between b and c, as well as to those between a and c, shown in Figures 2.8 and 2.9, respectively.

It is very important to notice that our visualization in Figures 2.7–2.9 differs from the conventions used in Figures 2.1–2.6 and elsewhere: In Figures 2.7–2.9 we now require the <u>sum of net probabilities</u> over all shaded partial orders to be positive (in the case of $\succ$, and nonnegative in the case of $\succsim$), whereas in other figures the net probability of <u>each</u> shaded (and framed) partial order is required to be nonnegative.

Figures 2.7–2.9, taken together, can be used to visualize transitivity of majority preferences. There are five key scenarios for $\succ$ to be transitive:

1. If we were to have the strict linear majority preference order $a \succ b \succ c$, this would require the shadings in Figures 2.7, 2.8, and 2.9

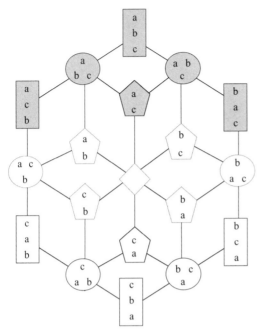

FIGURE 2.8: Graphical display of $a \succ c$ (or $a \succsim c$). The <u>sum</u> of net probabilities over all shaded partial orders needs to be positive (or nonnegative).

      to simultaneously have positive total net probabilities. Again, it is important to note that this involves only the *total* net probability of all shaded states. The individual net probabilities need not all be positive.

2. A strict weak order majority $a \succ b, a \succ c$, where b and c are majority tied, would require the shadings in Figures 2.7 and 2.8 to simultaneously have positive total net probabilities and, in addition, the shaded area in Figure 2.9 would need to have a total net probability of zero.

3. An analogous comment applies to the strict weak order majority $a \succ c, b \succ c$.

4. A three-way tie, $\succ = \phi$, would require the shaded areas in each of the three cases to have a total net probability of zero.

5. A semiorder majority $a \succ b$, where c is majority tied with both a and b, would require the shadings in Figure 2.7 to have a positive total net probability, whereas the total net probabilities of the shaded areas of the other two displays would have to be exactly zero.

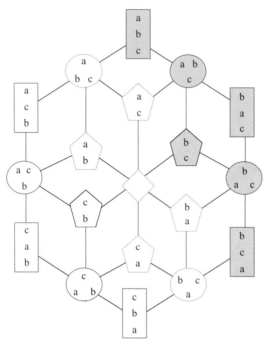

FIGURE 2.9: Graphical display of $b \succ c$ (or $b \succsim c$). The <u>sum</u> of net probabilities over all shaded partial orders needs to be positive (or nonnegative).

These five cases cover all possible scenarios for a transitive majority ordering $\succ$, up to a relabeling of the candidates. In particular, it also follows that a is the unique strict majority (Condorcet) winner if and only if the shaded areas in each of Figures 2.7 and 2.8 have a total positive net probability. Similar constraints and comments apply to the weak majority preference relation $\succsim$.

It is interesting to compare Figures 2.3 and 2.6 for the generalized NB and NM conditions, respectively, with the graphic representations of the following necessary and sufficient conditions for transitive majority rule that can be illustrated using Figures 2.7–2.9. We know, for instance, by Theorems 2.3.9 and 2.3.10, that if net value restriction holds (and thus certain cells each have nonpositive net probability), or if a weak order has a net preference majority, then one of these five scenarios applies (up to relabeling of the candidates), at least for $\succ$.

For instance, if $NW(a)$ holds, which is the mirror image of $NB(a)$ displayed in Figure 2.3, in the sense that each shaded framed state has nonnegative net probability and the darkly shaded unframed states have net probability zero, then either the shaded area in Figure 2.7 or the shaded area in Figure 2.8 must have a total net probability that is nonnegative. Suppose, for example, that $a \succ b$, i.e., the shaded area in Figure 2.7 has positive net probability. Thus, if $a \succ c$, then $\succ$ is transitive. On the other b hand, suppose, for instance, that $c \succ a$. In order for that to be possible, a, c which is the only state with a negative net probability among the shaded states in Figure 2.8, must overwhelm all the other shaded states in order for the total net probability to be negative. But then the shaded area in Figure 2.9 must also have a total net probability which is negative, i.e., $\succ$ is again transitive.

At the same time, one can readily imagine cases where one of the above five scenarios (up to relabeling of the candidates) holds without either net value restriction or net majority holding, as illustrated by the counterexample given in the proof of Theorem 2.3.8. We provide a display of a different counterexample in Figure 2.10. This distribution of weak orders is constructed from "subset choice data" via the "topset voting model" in Chapter 4. The inset table provides the pairwise net preference probabilities NP_{ab}, NP_{ac}, and NP_{bc}. Partial orders with positive net probability are shaded and framed. Lightly shaded frameless partial orders are assumed to have probability (and hence also net probability) zero. The positive pairwise net preference probability NP_{ab} is shaded as well. This example illustrates why we do not have the full generalization of Theorem 1.2.15 as we move from linear orders to arbitrary binary (or even partial order) preference relations. We have transitive majority preferences even though neither Sen's value restriction condition nor any of our sufficient conditions discussed in this chapter are satisfied.

In Section 2.4, we turn to illustrative empirical applications, showing examples where net value restriction is satisfied by empirical preferences that are strict weak orders. In Chapter 3 we show examples for more general binary preference relations where net value restriction is no longer satisfied. The latter is not surprising since it would require equalities among net probabilities whereas net value restriction on weak orders only requires inequalities (see Definition 2.3.4 and the comments following it).

2.4 EMPIRICAL ILLUSTRATIONS

We briefly illustrate our results using 1968, 1980, 1992, and 1996 American National Election Study (ANES) (Sapiro et al., 1998) feeling thermometer data, with each data set involving three major presidential

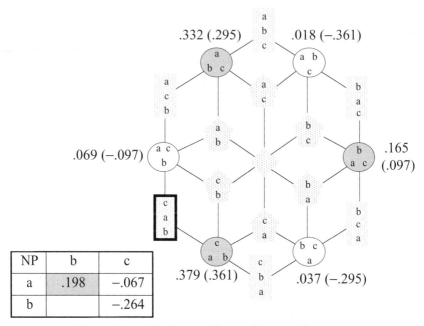

NP	b	c
a	.198	−.067
b		−.264

FIGURE 2.10: Counterexample showing that neither net value restriction nor net majority is needed for transitive majority preferences. The inset table provides the pairwise net preference probabilities NP_{ab}, NP_{ac}, and NP_{bc}. The majority ordering $c \succ a \succ b$ is framed in bold. Lightly shaded frameless partial orders have probability (and here also net probability) zero. (This also holds for the majority ordering despite its boldface frame.) Shaded framed partial orders have positive net probabilities. The positive pairwise net probability is also shaded. These data are obtained from MAA "subset choice" data via the "topset voting model" in Chapter 4.

candidates (Humphrey, Nixon, Wallace in 1968; Anderson, Carter, Reagan in 1980; Bush, Clinton, Perot in 1992; and Clinton, Dole, Perot in 1996); as well as with attitudinal ratings of Barre, Chirac, and Mitterand from the 1988 French National Election Study (FNES) (Pierce, 1996). For the FNES we use only those data that were reported for respondents who identified themselves as being Communists. The first four sets allow us to look at preference distributions from broad national samples, whereas the last (i.e., FNES) data set allows us to study preferences in a highly politically homogeneous subpopulation.

In the figures and in some formulae we use the first letter of the last names as the obvious abbreviation. Also, to keep our illustrations simple, we focus on weak orders only. In Chapter 3 we also investigate semiorder preferences derived from some of these surveys.

Respondents using feeling thermometer ratings assign an integer value between 0 and 100 to each of the candidates. A value of 0 indicates a "very cold feeling" towards a given candidate, a value of 50 indicates a "neutral feeling" towards the candidate, and a value of 100 indicates a "very warm feeling" towards the candidate. We interpret the feeling thermometer data in the survey as outcomes of integer-valued random variables that take values between zero and one hundred. We recode these outcomes as strict weak orders using the random utility representation of strict weak orders reviewed in Theorem 2.1.10. Having derived the strict weak order probabilities in this fashion, we can compute net probabilities and check the various conditions for transitive majority outcomes that we discuss theoretically (above) in this chapter.

For each data set, we first treat the survey as a random sample from an unknown population and briefly consider and quickly reject the null hypothesis that the underlying population, from which the sample originated, is an impartial culture (or other culture of indifference) on weak orders. Similarly, we consider the null hypothesis that the sample originated from a domain restricted population such as one that satisfies Sen's value restriction. Because the sample size is very large, we do not go into much detail regarding the obviously overwhelming significance with which we can reject such null hypotheses.[16] For the analyses of our net value and net majority conditions we circumvent statistical considerations entirely, for the sake of simplicity and because the conclusions would unlikely be affected by such considerations. Here, we identify the relative frequencies of events in the sample with the probabilities of the corresponding events in the underlying population distribution. Chapter 5 is dedicated to a full-blown statistical framework for the analysis of majority outcomes that includes a sampling as well as a Bayesian inference point of view.

The resulting net probabilities over strict weak orders for these five election surveys are reported in Figures 2.11, 2.12, 2.13, 2.14, and 2.15 for the 1968 ANES, 1980 ANES, 1992 ANES, 1996 ANES, and 1988 FNES (Communists) data, respectively. As in Figures 2.1 through 2.6, shaded framed orderings again indicate a nonnegative net probability for each such strict weak order. Note that we largely ignore statistical considerations in these analyses.

Figure 2.11 shows the strict weak order probabilities and net probabilities (in parentheses) for the 1968 United States national election study.

---

[16] Note that there is one interesting data set, the 1988 FNES (Communists), on which we do not reject Sen's value restriction (see also our later discussion of this data set).

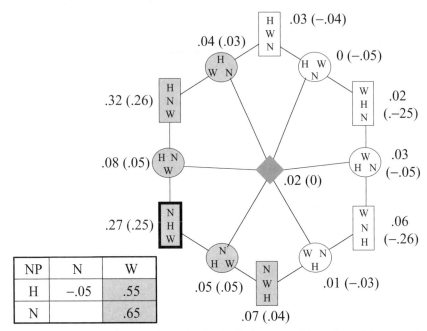

FIGURE 2.11: Net value restriction in the 1968 ANES for Humphrey, Nixon, and Wallace. Weak order probabilities and net probabilities (in parentheses) are reported with the weak order graph. The inset table provides the pairwise net probabilities NP_{HN}, NP_{HW}, and NP_{NW}. Weak orders with positive net probability are shaded and framed. Positive pairwise net probabilities are also shaded. The darkly shaded unframed indifference relation (automatically) has net probability zero. The majority preference relation is the linear order $N \succ H \succ W$ and is shown with a boldface frame.

The inset table provides the pairwise net probabilities NP_{HN}, NP_{HW}, and NP_{NW}. Weak orders with positive net probability are shaded and framed. The complete indifference automatically has net probability zero, and thus is darkly shaded and without a frame. Positive pairwise net probabilities in the inset table are also shaded.

First, referring to our point above about the impartial culture being unrealistic, notice that these weak order probabilities are inconsistent with an impartial culture (i.e., uniform distribution) on weak orders.[17] More generally, the conditions for a culture of indifference on weak orders, given in (2.25) and (2.26), are clearly (significantly) violated by each of these data sets.

[17] Since the ANES, like the GNES in Chapter 1, is a large-scale survey, we do not calculate a p-value for the obviously overwhelming significance with which we can reject the null hypothesis that the survey was drawn from a uniform distribution over weak orders.

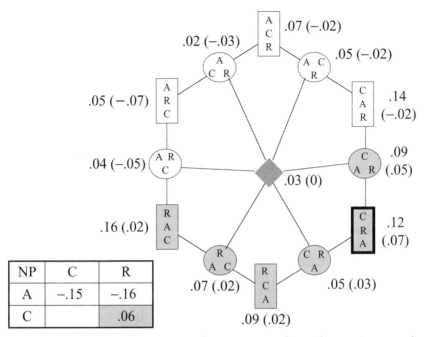

FIGURE 2.12: Net value restriction in the 1980 ANES for Anderson, Carter, and Reagan. Weak order probabilities and net probabilities (in parentheses) are reported with the weak order graph. The inset table provides the pairwise net probabilities NP_{AC}, NP_{AR}, and NP_{CR}. Weak orders with positive net probability are shaded and framed. Positive pairwise net probabilities are also shaded. The darkly shaded unframed indifference relation (automatically) has net probability zero. The majority preference relation is the linear order $C \succ R \succ A$ and is shown with a boldface frame.

Now we turn to issues of transitivity. First, Sen's value restriction condition is violated. In fact, because every weak order is reported by a substantial number of respondents, any other domain constraint on weak orders is equally violated by these data. Second, none of the weak orders has a net preference majority. Nevertheless, the strict majority ordering is a linear order, namely $N \succ H \succ W$ (boldface frame in the figure). An explanation for the transitive majority relation lies in the fact that our generalized net value restriction on weak orders holds, in the form of $Net NB(W)$.[18]

Figure 2.12 shows the strict weak order probabilities and net probabilities (in parentheses) for the 1980 ANES. We display information in the same fashion as in Figure 2.11. As before, the inset table provides the

---

[18] Again, note that this part of the analysis omits statistical considerations and treats the observed relative frequencies like population probabilities.

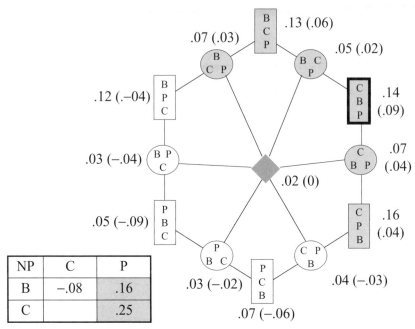

FIGURE 2.13: Net value restriction in the 1992 ANES for Bush, Clinton, and Perot. Weak order probabilities and net probabilities (in parentheses) are reported with the weak order graph. The inset table provides the pairwise net probabilities NP_{BC}, NP_{BP}, and NP_{CP}. Weak orders with positive net probability are shaded and framed. Positive pairwise net probabilities are also shaded. The darkly shaded unframed indifference relation (automatically) has net probability zero. The majority preference relation is the linear order $C \succ B \succ P$ and is shown with a boldface frame.

pairwise net probabilities. In 1980, as in 1968, the weak order probabilities differ strongly from an impartial culture (or other culture of indifference) on weak orders. Furthermore, Sen's value restriction (and any alternative domain constraint) condition is violated once again, because every weak order is held by a substantial number of respondents. None of the weak orders has a net preference majority. Nevertheless, the strict majority ordering is once again a linear order, namely $C \succ R \succ A$ (boldface frame in the figure). The reason for the existence of a transitive majority relation is that our generalized net value restriction on weak orders holds, with $NetNB(A)$.

Figure 2.13 shows, in parallel fashion to the previous two figures, the strict weak order probabilities and net probabilities (in parentheses) for the 1992 ANES. Again, the weak order probabilities differ strongly from an impartial culture (or other culture of indifference) on weak orders.

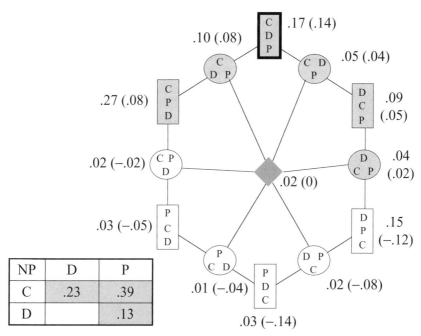

FIGURE 2.14: Net value restriction in the 1996 ANES for Clinton, Dole, and Perot. Weak order probabilities and net probabilities (in parentheses) are reported with the weak order graph. The inset table provides the pairwise net probabilities NP_{CD}, NP_{CP}, and NP_{DP}. Weak orders with positive net probability are shaded and framed. Positive pairwise net probabilities are also shaded. The darkly shaded unframed indifference relation (automatically) has net probability zero. The majority preference relation is the linear order $C \succ D \succ P$ and is shown with a boldface frame.

Again, Sen's value restriction (and any other domain constraint) condition is violated and none of the weak orders has a net preference majority. Nevertheless, the strict majority ordering is a linear order, namely $C \succ B \succ P$ (boldface frame in the figure). The reason for the transitive majority relation is that our generalized net value restriction on weak orders holds, with $Net NB(P)$.

Figure 2.14 shows the strict weak order probabilities and net probabilities (in parentheses) for the 1996 ANES and, in the inset table, it again provides the paired comparison net probabilities. The weak order probabilities again differ strongly from an impartial culture (or other culture of indifference) on weak orders. Sen's value restriction condition is again violated, as would be any other domain restriction. Again, none of the weak orders has a net preference majority. Nevertheless, the

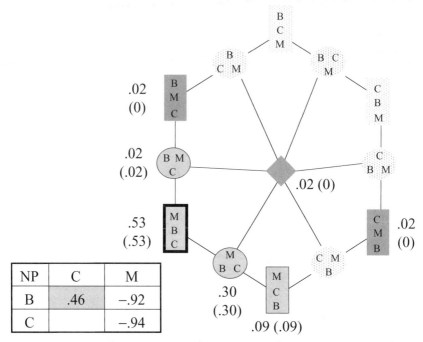

NP	C	M
B	.46	−.92
C		−.94

FIGURE 2.15: Net value restriction in the 1988 FNES for Communist respondents (Barre, Chirac, and Mitterand). Weak order probabilities and net probabilities (in parentheses) are reported with the weak order graph. The inset table provides the pairwise net probabilities NP_{BC}, NP_{BM}, and NP_{CM}. Weak orders with positive net probability are shaded and framed. Positive pairwise net probabilities are also shaded. The three weak orders with net probability zero are darkly shaded and frameless, whereas six weak orders with probability zero (i.e., that were not observed) are lightly shaded and frameless. The majority preference relation is the linear order $M \succ B \succ C$ and is shown with a boldface frame.

strict majority ordering is a linear order, namely $C \succ D \succ P$ (boldface frame in the figure). The reason for the transitive majority relation is that our generalized net value restriction on weak orders holds, again, with $Net NB(P)$.

In summary, the first four surveys yield distributions that are very different from the impartial culture (or other culture of indifference), and that violate both Sen's value restriction (or any other domain restriction) condition and our net preference majority condition. In each distribution, however, the $Net NB$ condition is satisfied for the minor party candidate. As a result, in each case, we find transitive majority preferences.

Now we turn to the 1988 FNES data. Figure 2.15 shows the strict weak order probabilities and net probabilities (in parentheses), for Communist identifiers only. Because we are dealing with a politically cohesive subpopulation, we see in Figure 2.15 a remarkable homogeneity in preference relations, very different from cultures of indifference. For these data, Sen's value restriction is satisfied in the form of $NW(M)$. These data are therefore consistent with the idea that Communist respondents, and possibly other highly homogeneous national subgroups, share a constrained domain of preference states. We also have a net preference majority for the majority ordering $M \succ B \succ C$, but even more strikingly, this specific ordering is held as individual preference by (each of) a strict majority of the Communist respondents (not just a net majority).

Based on these findings, we conjecture that domain restrictions like Sen's value restriction condition are unlikely to successfully describe full national electorates from a behavioral social choice point of view, but they may be very good behavioral models to capture the beliefs and attitudes of extremely homogenous and coherent political or social subgroups like the French Communists. We would like to add, however, that even if one makes the interesting descriptive theoretical claim that a highly homogeneous group operates on a constrained domain, one must be prepared to observe some domain inconsistent data, e.g., due to measurement or response errors, or because the membership in such a group may be probabilistic.

2.5 DISCUSSION

Section 2.1 offers a way to conceptualize majority rule based on a variety of mathematical representations of preference and utility. Moreover, that section provides a method for translating net probabilities from binary relations to linear orders (Theorem 2.1.5). Drawing on the analytical framework of Section 2.1, Section 2.3 gives necessary and sufficient conditions for transitive majority rule on arbitrary binary relations (and corresponding random utilities). The results include full generalizations of Sen's original value restriction condition by specifying extensions of NB, NM, and NW that are applicable in a broad range of contexts. These generalizations stand in contrast to work on domain constraints that is often used to predict transitivity of majority preferences (Gärtner, 2001), because our conditions dramatically expand the domain of permissible preference states.

While we are able to provide a natural generalization of our net value restriction and net preference majority conditions of Chapter 1, the picture of necessary and/or sufficient conditions becomes more complex than it is for linear orders. For strict partial order preferences, we show in this chapter that net value restriction is again sufficient for transitive majority

TABLE 2.1: *Overview of Previous and Current Results About Value Restriction and Related Conditions*

Theoretical Primitives	Basic Quantities	Conditions	Relationship to Transitivity of $\succ$
Weak orders	tallies	*NB, NM, NW* of Gärtner (2001) and Sen (1966, 1970)	sufficient but not necessary
Linear orders	net tallies	*Net NB, Net NM, Net NW,* net preference majority of Gärtner and Heinecke (1978) and Feld and Grofman (1986b)	necessary and sufficient
Probabilities on linear orders	net probabilities	*Net NB, Net NM, Net NW,* net preference majority of Chapter 1	necessary and sufficient
Probabilities on partial orders	net probabilities	generalized *Net NB, Net NM, Net NW,* net majority (weak order)	sufficient but not necessary
		net majority (partial order) of Chapter 2	not sufficient

Note: We use the term "necessary" condition with its usual meaning, not with Sen's unusual meaning.

preferences. Similarly, for strict partial order preferences, net preference majority of a strict weak order is sufficient for transitive (strict or weak) majorities. However, net preference majority of a semiorder is not sufficient for transitive (either strict or weak) majorities. Furthermore, net value restriction and net preference majority, even when taken jointly, are not necessary for a transitive majority preference relation when individual preferences are strict weak orders or more general strict partial orders.

Table 2.1 enumerates important earlier results and summarizes our own new results of Chapter 1 and of Section 2.3 that are related to generalizations of Sen's (1966, 1970) value restriction theorem.[19]

---

[19] There are other conditions in the social choice literature, such as "extremal restriction," for which we could develop probabilistic analogues and generalizations. We do not do so for several reasons, which we illustrate for the case of extremal restriction. First, in our

Turning to the empirical results of Section 2.4, we find that for four mass surveys in the United States, involving presidential candidates, value restriction is violated even though majority preferences are nevertheless transitive. In each of these four surveys, our net value restriction holds. Based on the distributions on weak orders, reported in the data analysis, we conclude that for these mass publics, any domain restriction condition is bound to fail descriptively, because every weak order preference is held by a substantial number of respondents. However, for an extremely cohesive subpopulation, such as the 1988 French Communists, we do find Sen's original value restriction satisfied. Based on these illustrative results, and those of other studies, we do not expect Sen's value restriction (or other domain restriction conditions) to be satisfied in surveys for mass populations. Indeed, we do not expect Sen's condition to be satisfied in any but the most cohesive subpopulations of mass electorates, and we conjecture that the same applies to other domain restriction conditions. For instance, Feld and Grofman (1988) looked at politically cohesive subpopulations within the United States and did not find value restriction satisfied in choice among a set of four potential presidential candidates for any of the subpopulations they studied. On the other hand, based on the 1988 French Communist data, we would expect that extremely cohesive subgroups may satisfy Sen's and other domain restriction conditions, with the additional caveat that, even in that case, very large data sets may still produce 'domain inconsistent' data, due, e.g., to measurement or response errors.[20] We think of national electorates as consisting of multiple constituencies, some of which may satisfy strong domain restrictions. In other words, we expect future work to show that domain restrictions are descriptively adequate to model the social choice behavior of certain (but not all) subnational groups, whereas national electorates may be more adequately modeled via approaches that either avoid domain restrictions or that are based on a probability mixture of domain restricted subpopulations.

Finally, the inspection of the five data sets in this chapter supports our earlier claim that the impartial culture is a completely unrealistic

---

terminology, extremal restriction is sufficient but not necessary for transitive majority as can be demonstrated using the example of Footnote 2 in Chapter 1. (As we note in that footnote, Sen, 1970, uses the word 'necessary' in a special way distinct from customary usage.) Second, by Sen's (1970) Lemma 10*e, if preferences are antisymmetric (i.e., a special case of asymmetric preferences considered here), then extremal restriction implies value restriction.

[20] We leave full-blown statistical considerations for Chapter 5.

preference distribution, even for mass publics. Even more, when we look at a cohesive subpopulation such as the 1988 French Communists, we find a highly skewed distribution of preferences in the sense that a single preference ordering is held by a majority (and not just a net majority) of the respondents.

Chapter 3 makes use of the theoretical and conceptual apparatus of this chapter to study the extent to which majority preferences derived from empirical data may depend on the implicit or explicit model of preferences and/or utilities underlying the analysis. In passing, we also provide evidence that any condition that requires certain net probabilities to equal zero is bound to fail descriptively in a confrontation against empirical data: Just as it is unrealistic to rule out certain preference states entirely, it is also unrealistic to require that certain preference states should have exactly equal probability.

II

APPLICATIONS OF PROBABILISTIC MODELS TO EMPIRICAL DATA

3

On the Model Dependence versus Robustness of Social Choice Results

Chapter Summary

The Condorcet criterion requires a majority winner to be elected whenever it exists. In practice, virtually no social choice procedure or survey research study reports complete pairwise comparisons or a complete linear order of the choice alternatives for each voter, as required by standard majority rule. Thus, classical majority rule can almost never be computed directly from ballots or survey data. Using our general definition of majority rule developed in Chapter 2, we show here and in Chapter 4 that any 'reconstruction' of majority preferences from ballot or survey data can be sensitive to the underlying implicit or explicit model of decision making. In passing we also provide additional empirical evidence that cultures of indifference such as the impartial culture, as well as domain restrictions such as Sen's value restriction, are descriptively invalidated by all data sets and data analysis methods considered in this chapter.

The Condorcet criterion, according to which a majority winner ought to be elected whenever one exists, still enjoys very widespread support as a normative benchmark of rational social choice (however, see, e.g., Saari, 1994, 1995, for a different point of view). At the same time, explicitly collecting all paired comparisons among candidates to directly calculate majority preferences is rather tedious and expensive. Thus, it is generally desirable to find a simpler, cost-effective voting procedure, which, at the same time, carries the benefit of satisfying the Condorcet criterion with high probability. When an argument is made for or against a social choice procedure, it is therefore common practice to examine the procedure's *Condorcet efficiency*, i.e., the likelihood that the procedure satisfies the Condorcet criterion. In this vein, a significant effort has been made in the social choice literature to discuss the Condorcet efficiency of various voting methods (Adams, 1997; Felsenthal and Machover, 1995; Felsenthal et al., 1990, 1993; Gehrlein, 1987, 1992, 1998a,b; Gehrlein and Berg, 1992; Gehrlein and Lepelley, 1998, 1999, 2001; Gehrlein and Valognes, 2001; Lepelley, 1993; Lepelley and Gehrlein, 2000; Lepelley et al., 2000; Lepelley and Valognes, 1999; Tataru and Merlin, 1997). In this mainly theoretical and hypothetical literature, very little effort has been made to empirically check whether a given aggregation procedure satisfies the Condorcet criterion on a given set of real-world ballot or survey data. Furthermore, much of the theoretical work is based on implausible or unrealistic assumptions about the nature or distribution of individual preferences, such as the impartial culture that we criticize in Chapter 1.

Here and in the next chapter, we show that the virtual absence of empirical work is not a surprise. We argue and illustrate that majority rule cannot in practice be calculated without an explicit or implicit model that explains voting behavior or survey responses as a function of underlying preferences or utilities. We also show that the (re)constructed majority preferences can completely depend on the chosen model. Similar caveats apply to theoretical work, say, on the likelihood of obtaining a Condorcet winner. Sometimes, changing the theoretical assumptions even slightly will drastically alter the theoretical conclusions one can derive. Our critique of the impartial culture assumption in Chapter 1 (as well as our related work in Chapter 5) rests fundamentally on this fact: Deviating ever so slightly from a culture of indifference will make majority preferences in samples converge to the majority preferences in the underlying population as sample size increases. This prediction runs contrary to the implications drawn from sampling from cultures of indifference (such as the impartial culture).

This chapter is organized as follows. Section 3.1 introduces our concepts of model dependence and robustness. Section 3.2 provides empirical illustrations on four ANES data sets that illustrate the model dependence and/or robustness of conclusions about (1) the absence of majority cycles, (2) the nature of the majority preference relations, and (3) the satisfaction or violation of our generalized net value restriction and net majority conditions in these data. Section 3.3 discusses the fact that we often find transitive majority preferences despite (albeit only 'slight') violations of net value restriction. Section 3.4 concludes the chapter with a discussion of these and related issues.

3.1 MODEL DEPENDENCE VERSUS ROBUSTNESS

Recall that majority rule for a set of candidates C is usually defined either in terms of comparisons of every pair of candidates in C, or in terms of complete rankings of the candidates in C. In particular, for $a, b \in C$, a is (strictly) majority preferred to b if and only if more than 50% of the voters prefer a to b in their individual strict linear order preferences. A majority rule winner is a candidate $a \in C$ who is majority preferred to each $b \in C - \{a\}$. The *Condorcet criterion*, arguably the most universally accepted normative benchmark for rational social choice, says that a majority winner should be elected whenever it exists.

Quite interestingly, though, virtually no social choice procedure that is actually used in practice explicitly requires or records all pairwise comparisons or complete rankings, and only few social choice procedures record any. For instance, the *single nontransferable vote* and *limited voting* require the voter to choose $k < |C|$ many candidates, *approval voting* requires the voter to choose any subset of the candidates, the *single transferable vote* typically requires the voters to rank order the top $k \leq |C|$ candidates, *cumulative voting* requires that the voters distribute m points among k many alternatives, etc. Polling and experimental data often take the form of Likert scale ratings, feeling thermometer ratings, elicitations of real-valued utility ratings, buying or selling prices, or partial paired comparisons.

In many empirical circumstances, majority rule cannot be uniquely operationalized because the standard definition is stated in terms of hypothetical but unobserved pairwise comparisons (or strict linear orders). Chapter 2 places virtually all empirical paradigms on an equal footing by defining majority rule in terms of theoretical primitives that virtually all choice, rating, and ranking paradigms share. To phrase it loosely, our general concept of majority rule of Chapter 2 states that a is majority preferred to b if the total probability (or frequency) of all preference relations in which a is preferred to b exceeds the total probability (or frequency) of all preference relations in which b is preferred to a. In utility terms, the general concept of majority rule states that a is majority preferred to b if the total probability (or frequency) of all utility functions in which a has sufficiently higher utility than b exceeds the total probability (or frequency) of all utility functions in which b has sufficiently higher utility than a. We refer the reader to Chapter 2 for more precise formulations, references, definitions, theorems, and other theoretical results that we use here. We now turn to applications of that general concept of majority rule.

We say that a theoretical or empirical conclusion (or prediction) is *model dependent* if this conclusion (or prediction) changes as the implicit or explicit model that enters the derivation of the conclusion (or prediction) is changed. For instance, we are interested in the extent to which the absence of majority cycles, the nature of the majority preference relation, the presence or absence of net value restriction, or similar properties are model dependent. In this chapter, we focus on the model dependence of the interpretation of empirical data, for example, of the majority preference relations constructed from empirical survey data. Chapters 1 and 2 already provide some theoretical model dependence results. For instance, the policy suggestion that one should minimize turnout in order to avoid majority cycles is completely reversed when one moves away from cultures of indifference (and stays away from cyclical cultures). We say that a theoretical or empirical conclusion (or prediction) is *robust* if this conclusion (or prediction) remains unchanged as we change our implicit or explicit model that enters into the derivation of this conclusion (or prediction). In other words, the less model dependent social choice findings are, the more robust they are. For instance, in Chapter 2 we show in Theorem 2.3.9 that the sufficiency of net value restriction for transitivity of majority preferences is robust across alternative models of preferences. Theorem 2.3.8 shows that the necessity of net value restriction or a net majority for transitivity of majority preferences, established for linear orders in Chapter 1, no longer holds for more general representations of preference. Similarly, Theorem 2.3.10 establishes that net majority of a preference relation is sufficient for transitive majority preferences only under some, but not all, models of preference. Here we illustrate some of these results, particularly Theorem 2.3.8, on empirical data. We provide evidence in the present chapter that the absence of (constructed) majority cycles in the ANES data sets is highly robust, whereas the exact nature of the majority preferences and the explanations we can provide for the absence of (constructed) majority cycles, are model dependent. In particular, we show that in all our data analyses here, the (constructed) absence of cycles in these data is robust even under widespread violations of our net value restriction and net preference majority conditions.

We revisit, in a random utility framework, four sets of National Election Study feeling thermometer ratings of presidential candidates in certain years in which there were three potentially viable candidates (1968, 1980, 1992, and 1996). The feeling thermometer ratings are treated as outcomes of integer-valued random utilities, which we translate into probabilistic strict weak order and semiorder preference representations. These various translations account for the basic psychological intuition that feeling thermometer ratings cannot be taken as literal reflections of the respondents' preferences. For instance, there are many response biases that can play a role in the data generating process, such as the use of rating values that are multiples of 10 (or 5) and the excessive use of the value 50 on a 100-point scale. Another concern is the fact that respondents' rating values tend to be somewhat unreliable: For example, a respondent who rates candidate A as 50 and candidate B as 55 might, a short time later, rate candidate A as 55 and candidate B as 60. It is psychologically plausible to expect that the more similar the recorded ratings of two candidates are, the less sure we can be that the implied ordering of the choice alternatives is the correct one (or a stable one). This is why we consider different possible thresholds of utility discrimination in our analysis of the thermometer data.[1] Section 2.4 of Chapter 2 provides analyses of these data sets in the case where the thermometer scores are translated into strict weak orders.

In our empirical applications below, we find a mixed bag of results as a function of the underlying model of preferences or utilities. We do not find any majority cycles, regardless of the method by which we analyse any of these data. For some data sets the majority winner is model dependent, while in other data sets the modeling assumptions do not seem to affect the nature of the majority preference relation at all. These results suggest that we need to study in more detail when and why, in practice, the computed majority or other social choice functions tend to be robust under model variations or model violations. In any case, the diversity of our results supports our view that the modeling assumptions, which necessarily enter any analysis of voting data, play an important role in the interpretation of such data.

3.2 EMPIRICAL ILLUSTRATIONS

We revisit the 1968, 1980, 1992, and 1996 American National Election Study (ANES) feeling thermometer data (Sapiro et al., 1998) discussed in Chapter 2. Recall that feeling thermometer ratings assign integer values between 0 and 100 to each of the candidates, where a value of 0 denotes

---

[1] A more appropriate semiorder representation of thermometer data would even allow for different threshold values for different respondents. Such elaborations would only further complicate the picture of results, not simplify it. In particular, we can make our point that different models matter, since they matter even with the simplest possible representations.

a "very cold feeling towards" a given candidate, a value of 50 denotes a "neutral feeling towards" the candidate, and a value of 100 denotes a "very warm feeling towards" the candidate. Feeling thermometer ratings can be viewed as elicitations of integer-valued utility functions that are constrained between 0 and 100.[2] More correctly, since the data form a random sample, we can naturally view the sampled joint values as realizations of integer-valued jointly distributed random variables each taking values between 0 and 100. In turn we can recode the observed data (relative frequencies) as a probability distribution over strict weak orders using Equation (2.13). The resulting probabilities (and net probabilities) on strict weak orders are reported in Figures 2.11–2.14 for the 1968, 1980, 1992, and 1996 ANES data, respectively. Again, to keep our analyses simple, we omit statistical considerations in this chapter.

Recoding feeling thermometer data as strict weak orders discards the strength of preference that may have been expressed by the reported thermometer scores and treats the data in a rather literal fashion. Instead, one may count preference relationships between two candidates as relevant (reliable) only when the utility values indicated by the thermometer scores differ by a 'large enough amount.'

We now use the thermometer scores to illustrate our main point that the method by which we derive majority relationships from utilities (or ratings) makes an implicit or explicit choice of preference representations. By formulating 'large enough amount' as a particular threshold value $\epsilon > 0$ we specify a particular semiorder representation for thermometer data. More precisely, by choosing a threshold of discrimination, we can derive a probability distribution over semiorders using Equation (2.14). By varying the magnitude of the threshold, we can establish how sensitive the results of majority rule analyses are to the possible lack of reliability in respondents' thermometer ratings. Very large threshold values discard thermometer ratings that are very close to each other, and possibly unreliable, whereas small threshold values treat the comparisons of rating values as highly reliable.

For example, a threshold of 10 means that we consider a as being preferred to b if and only if the feeling thermometer score for a exceeds that for b by more than 10 points. Note also that a threshold of zero would lead us back to the strict weak order case that we discuss in Chapter 2.

---

[2] Analogously to Footnote 1, one could complicate matters further by not viewing the thermometer scores as necessarily directly reflecting the utilities in the decision makers' heads. This would again only further emphasize our main point that the underlying model of preferences and utilities can play a key role in the results we obtain.

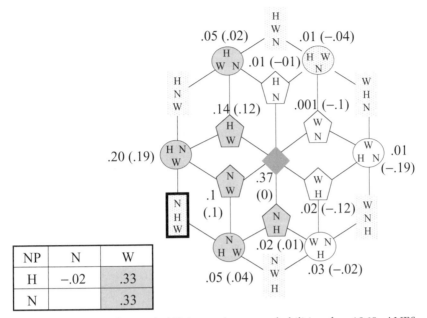

FIGURE 3.1: Semiorder probabilities and net probabilities for 1968 ANES (Humphrey, Nixon, and Wallace) with a utility discrimination threshold of 50. The inset table provides the pairwise net preference probabilities. Semiorders with positive net probabilities are shaded and framed. The darkly shaded frameless indifference relation automatically has net probability zero. Positive pairwise net probabilities are also shaded. The majority ordering is $N \succ H \succ W$ and is framed in boldface. All linear orders have probability zero and are lightly shaded and (with the exception of $\succ$) frameless.

Also, for a threshold of 100, all net probabilities obviously vanish, i.e., the majority preference relation trivially becomes a three-way tie.

1968 ANES. We begin the semiorder based analysis with the 1968 ANES data set. We use the graph of all strict partial orders over three elements to illustrate our results about finding majority rule relations. For instance, as we move from weak orders in Figure 2.11 to semiorders with threshold 50 in Figure 3.1, the distributions change dramatically. Nonetheless, the majority preference relation is $N \succ H \succ W$, no matter which threshold value we use for ϵ in the half-open interval $[0, 97)$.[3] Recall that a threshold of 0 yields the strict weak order distribution of Figure 2.11 that

---

[3] For this data set, the highest value recorded for the thermometer scores was 97, because the values 98 and 99 were used to record other information and only two digits were used to store each rating.

we discuss in Chapter 2. Note also that, for threshold values above 49, the majority ordering $N \succ H \succ W$ holds even though this strict linear order has probability (and net probability) zero as an individual preference in the distribution obtained with such threshold values.

We now consider the model dependence or robustness of our net value restriction and net majority conditions of Chapter 2 for these data. At a threshold of zero (i.e., for a weak order coding of the thermometer scores) we begin with the $NB(W)$ condition satisfied. $NB(W)$ remains satisfied as we increase the threshold until, for $\epsilon = 5$, net value restriction is no longer satisfied (in any of its forms). In the range of $5 \le \epsilon \le 15, 20 \le \epsilon \le 97$ net value restriction is violated, whereas for $16 \le \epsilon \le 19$ the $Net NB(W)$ condition holds. For threshold values from 37 to 44 and from 47 to 49, there is a net preference majority for the weak order $\{(N, W), (H, W)\}$. As Theorem 2.3.10 shows, this is sufficient to guarantee transitivity. Also, for very large values of the threshold, from 85 to 96, we find that the semiorder $\{(H, W)\}$ has a net preference majority. But according to Theorem 2.3.10 this, by itself, is not sufficient for transitivity of majority rule preferences.

Recall that, for this data set, we have the same transitive majority ordering of the candidates for all values of ϵ. Yet, as we state above, there are only few threshold values for which either net value restriction is satisfied or for which the net majority condition holds for a weak or linear order. Thus, while we observe transitivity of majority rule for all threshold values, the sufficient conditions from the social choice literature, as generalized here, do not provide an explanation for why we find that transitivity. We look at the question "why so much transitivity?" in Section 3.3.

1980 ANES. For the 1980 ANES (Anderson, Carter, and Reagan), by varying the possible values of the threshold we obtain two different majority rule orderings. For threshold values of 1–29 we obtain the majority preference relation $C \succ R \succ A$, which is what we also find in Chapter 2 based on weak orders preferences (i.e., for $\epsilon = 0$). For thresholds of 30 to 99, we obtain the majority preference relation $R \succ C \succ A$. Thus, we again find that majorities are transitive for all threshold values and we can conclude that the absence of a majority cycle is a robust finding. Yet, as in the 1968 data, the net value restriction condition and the net majority preference condition are satisfied only for a handful of values. $NB(A)$ is satisfied for threshold values between zero and 9. For $\epsilon > 9$, net value restriction is no longer satisfied. For threshold values between 60 and 69 the semiorder $\{(R, C)\}$ has a net majority, which, by itself, is not sufficient for transitive majorities.

1992 ANES. For Bush, Clinton, and Perot, the majority preference relation is $C \succ B \succ P$, for every value of ϵ, with $0 \leq \epsilon < 100$. Despite there being consistent transitivity of majority preferences across all threshold values, and despite the majority preference relation itself being robust as well, net value restriction holds only for thresholds of zero and 1. Furthermore, there is never any ordering with a net preference majority.

1996 ANES. Here we see two different aggregate preference orderings among Clinton, Dole, and Perot. For threshold values from 0 to 49 and from 85 to 99 the majority order is $C \succ D \succ P$. For threshold values from 50 to 84 the majority ordering is $D \succ C \succ P$. Thus, once again, regardless of threshold, we have transitive majorities, but here the exact nature of the majority preference relation is model dependent. When we look at the net value restriction condition and the net preference majority condition, we find them almost never satisfied. $NB(P)$ only holds for threshold values of 0, 3, and 85–98. No other net value restriction condition ever holds. Only for threshold values from 0 through 9 do we have a net majority for the linear order $C \succ D \succ P$. Only for thresholds from 85 through 99 do we have a net majority, for the semiorder $\{(C, P)\}$. Of course, because the net majority is not held by a weak order, this, by itself, is not sufficient for transitivity.

In conclusion, the absence of majority cycles under all different analyses for each of these four data sets indicates that transitivity is a robust finding. The finding that for the 1968 and 1992 data sets the majority preference relation is the same for all applicable threshold values can be interpreted as an indication that in these two cases the majority preferences are robust under variations of our model of preferences and utilities. This is not an artifact of our method, but rather an empirical finding for these two particular elections, as the other two analyses demonstrate. In contrast, in the 1980 and 1996 cases, the majority rule ordering is sensitive to variations in ϵ. The latter two data sets demonstrate that the majority ordering can change (even back and forth) as we vary the value of the threshold of utility discrimination, and thus, that the majority ordering depends on the modeling assumptions that implicitly or explicitly enter the data analysis.

3.3 NEAR NET VALUE RESTRICTION

It is important to see how the net value restriction condition is violated, say in the 1968 ANES. The only violation for thresholds of 10, 40, and 90 is that the semiorder $\{(N, H)\}$ does not have exactly zero net probability. However, its net probability is always very low: For $\epsilon = 10$ it is $-.001$, for $\epsilon = 40$ it is $.004$, and for $\epsilon = 90$ it is $.01$. In fact, for all values of the threshold from 0 to 56 and from 82 to 99, this semiorder net probability is less than $.01$ in absolute value. Moreover, for all values of the threshold, it is less than $.02$ in absolute value. It can therefore safely be said that, at each threshold value, we either do or we 'nearly' do satisfy $NetNB(W)$.

A similar pattern of nearly satisfying one of the net value restriction conditions also holds for the other three election years that we examine. For instance, in each case, the NB condition applied to the minor party candidate is always approximately satisfied, with the only violation being a nonzero net probability of the semiorder involving the two major candidates. Moreover, the magnitude of the violation is always very small.

In 1980, 6% of the threshold values yield the $NB(W)$ condition, 38% of the threshold values yield a violation by less than $.01$, 84% yield a violation by less than $.02$, 94% yield a violation by less than $.03$, and 100% of the violations are by less than $.04$. In 1992, 2% of the threshold values yield the $NB(P)$ condition, 55% of the threshold values yield a violation by less than $.01$, and 100% of the violations are by less than $.02$. In 1996, only a threshold value of 0 yields the $NB(P)$ condition, 36% of the threshold values yield a violation by less than $.01$, 68% yield a violation by less than $.02$, and 100% of the violations are by less than $.03$.

If a is a candidate with little support, then we would expect the first four terms in the inequalities (2.28) and (2.29) in Corollary 2.3.3 to be negative. Furthermore, for the ANES data, the last four terms in each of these inequalities are automatically zero (because the stated individual preferences are transitive). Below, we restate (2.28) and (2.29) with the zero terms dropped.

$$NP\begin{pmatrix} a \\ b \\ c \end{pmatrix} + 1/2\left[NP\begin{pmatrix} a \\ b\ c \end{pmatrix} + NP\begin{pmatrix} a\ b \\ c \end{pmatrix} + NP\begin{pmatrix} a \\ b \end{pmatrix} + NP\begin{pmatrix} b \\ c \end{pmatrix} \right] \leq 0.$$
$$(3.1)$$

$$NP\begin{pmatrix} a \\ c \\ b \end{pmatrix} + 1/2\left[NP\begin{pmatrix} a \\ b\ c \end{pmatrix} + NP\begin{pmatrix} a\ c \\ b \end{pmatrix} + NP\begin{pmatrix} a \\ c \end{pmatrix} + NP\begin{pmatrix} c \\ b \end{pmatrix} \right] \leq 0.$$
$$(3.2)$$

Recall that these two conditions characterize the situations in which NP^{Π} satisfies $NB(a)$. Thus, if a is a candidate with little support (in the sense that the first four terms are negative in each inequality) then the only way in which these inequalities could be violated is if either $NP\begin{pmatrix} b \\ c \end{pmatrix}$ or $NP\begin{pmatrix} c \\ b \end{pmatrix}$ is positive and sufficiently large to outweigh the other (negative) values. Clearly, if $NP\begin{pmatrix} b \\ c \end{pmatrix} = NP\begin{pmatrix} c \\ b \end{pmatrix} = 0$, which is one of the conditions for $NB(a)$ given in Definition 2.3.4, then we can expect to have no problem. Overall, when a has little support, as long as $NP\begin{pmatrix} b \\ c \end{pmatrix}$ is sufficiently small in absolute value, both inequalities must be satisfied. Therefore, it is very plausible that NP^{Π} satisfies $NB(a)$ even though it is difficult to have NP satisfy $NB(a)$ because of the required zero value for one net probability.

For example, for a threshold of 10, the first four terms of Equation (3.1) are all negative and sum to $-.28$, while the last term is $-.0014/2 = -.0007$. For Equation (3.2) the first four terms are also all negative and sum to $-.29$, while the last term is $.0007$.[4] In fact, for the 1968 ANES data, the first four terms are negative for all threshold values. Furthermore, in absolute value terms their sum is at least an order of magnitude larger than the last term. Thus, the necessary and sufficient condition of Corollary 2.3.3 to get $NB(W)$ for the net probabilities NP^{Π} is always satisfied, which, in turn, explains why we find transitive majority preferences for all threshold values.

Similar results apply to the 1992 and 1996 elections with Perot taking the place of Wallace. For 1992, net value restriction holds only for threshold values of 0 and 1. However, for threshold values from 0 to 92, Equations (3.1) and (3.2) restated from Corollary 2.3.3 hold with $a = P$ (i.e., Perot).[5] For 1996, $NB(P)$ holds for 16% of all threshold values, whereas Equations (3.1) and (3.2) hold for all threshold values.

---

[4] For a threshold of 17, where value restriction is satisfied, the first four terms of Equation (3.1) are all negative and sum to $-.28$, while the last term is 0. For Equation (3.2) the first four terms are also all negative and sum to $-.28$, while the last term is 0. For a threshold of 40, the first four terms of Equation (3.1) are all negative and sum to $-.20$, while the last term is $-.002$. For Equation (3.2) the first four terms are also all negative and sum to $-.20$, while the last term is $.002$. For a threshold of 90, the first four terms of Equation (3.1) are all negative and sum to $-.04$, while the last term is $-.006$. For Equation (3.2) the first four terms are also all negative and sum to $-.03$, while the last term is $.006$.

[5] We do not report the analysis for the remaining threshold values, since more than 95% of all ratings are already recorded as full indifference when $\epsilon = 92$.

When one candidate, say a, has a commanding lead, then we can also find the situation where $NW(a)$ is satisfied except for the net probability of $\begin{pmatrix} b \\ c \end{pmatrix}$ failing to equal zero. This happens in 1980 for Reagan: There is no single threshold value where $NW(R)$ holds for the net probabilities NP. However, when translating back to the net probabilities NP^Π on linear orders using Theorem 2.1.5, $NW(R)$ holds for NP^Π for 80% of all threshold values. In addition, $NB(A)$ holds for NP^Π for 70% of all threshold values, and for those threshold values where neither of these two value restriction conditions (on NP^Π) holds, we have a net majority preference relation $R \succ C \succ A$ (on NP^Π). This net majority for NP^Π on the linear orders also holds for threshold values of $35 - 50$ and $80 - 85$.

3.4 DISCUSSION

The primary motivation of this chapter and of Chapter 4 (as well as much of Chapter 5) is to show a fundamental fact about behavioral social choice theory and analysis, namely that results on majority rule outcomes are hypothetical or circumstantial in many empirical settings: often the empirical data do not provide the full ranking or full paired comparison information that is required for the traditional definition of majority rule to apply. In other words, majority rule can usually be calculated only by making an inference from the available data. Yet many discussions about the virtues and faults of any given voting method center around the *Condorcet efficiency*, namely a given voting method's ability to satisfy the Condorcet criterion, according to which a majority winner ought to be elected whenever one exists. It is thus, in general, not at all straightforward to check an empirically observed set of ballot data against the normative benchmark imposed by the Condorcet criterion. We address this problem by defining majority rule at an abstract level that places all rating, ranking, and choice paradigms on an equal footing. Accordingly, we use the general definition of majority rule for profiles of arbitrary binary relations, probability measures over arbitrary binary preference relations, real-valued utility functions, and real-valued utility random variables that is provided in Chapter 2.

We emphasize that any computation of majority rule for data other than full paired comparisons or rankings implicitly or explicitly involves a model of the underlying preferences or utilities that are assumed to generate these data. Of course, it is conceivable that even elicited paired comparisons do not directly reflect binary preferences. Thus one may want to consider a model even for paired comparison data, if one wants to define majority preferences in terms of the underlying voter preferences, rather than elicited paired comparisons. We conclude from the analyses of four ANES data sets that using different threshold values for thermometer data to create semiorders can affect the majority ordering that we construct. This demonstrates that even the most subtle changes in modeling approaches can affect the outcome of any analysis of voting or ballot data vis-à-vis the Condorcet criterion. While the present chapter emphasizes the model dependence of empirical findings, Chapters 1 and 2 provide important theoretical results on model dependencies in the theoretical realm.

It is thus essential to spell out the preference or utility representation underlying any given method of computing majority preference relations in situations where full ranking or full paired comparison data are unavailable. Similarly, it is essential, when analyzing empirical data, to conduct a sensitivity analysis to find out how robust the conclusions are under variations or violations of the modeling assumptions, in order to guard against the results being an artifact of a particular method of computation.

Our other findings from the ANES data are as follows: First, we find no evidence for majority cycles in the ANES data. Thus, consistent with Tangiane (1991), we conclude from our empirical applications that majority cycles are much less frequent in practice than normative theory suggests they could be in principle. Second, we find in the 1992 and 1968 data sets that the majority preference relation is identical for all values of the threshold. In such a case, we can argue that the majority order is robust under variations and/or violations of our model regarding latent preferences or utilities. Note that there is no mathematical feature of our analysis that would force majority preference relations to be unchanged with changing values of the preference threshold underlying a semiorder representation.

In passing, we also mention that all our analyses here are clear empirical rejections of cultures of indifference as well as rejections of domain restrictions. The latter holds because every possible preference state is held by a substantial number of respondents in every case. Furthermore, we also conclude that equality constraints on probabilities are very similar to domain restrictions in that they are too strong to be empirically valid. In all these cases, we find our conditions to be 'sufficiently nearly' satisfied for majority preferences to still be transitive.

These results, based on our general concept of majority rule, open the stage for the multi-faceted investigation of majority rule social choice via future relaxations of our conditions as well as via the adoption of a statistical perspective:

1. A major open question is how to further generalize our net value restriction conditions in a natural and behaviorally appropriate way that eliminates equality constraints, while still preserving the main idea of obtaining Sen's value restriction conditions after canceling out opposite preferences (and possibly projecting down from arbitrary binary relations to, say, weak orders).

2. Our results lead to the general statistical question for rating, ranking, or choice paradigms: How robust will majority preference relations (or other social choice functions) turn out to be in practice under violations and/or variations of the models used to analyze and/or explain the data? Given available computing power, this question can be addressed easily from situation to situation by running computer simulations that allow the researcher to explore the statistical features of the estimated social choice function for a particular set of empirical data.

3. We treat the data in a literal fashion here in that we identify the observed thermometer scores and their relative frequencies with the sample space of the utility random variables and its probability measure. An obvious extension would be to treat the thermometer scores as the outcome of a random sample from a theoretical population and to be interested in the social choice functions of that theoretical population. In some situations, it is possible to obtain analytical results about the likelihood of a voting cycle or the likelihood of a correct or incorrect Condorcet winner when drawing a random sample from a specified population of reference, or when making an inference about a population based on a sample of data (DeMeyer and Plott, 1970; Regenwetter et al., 2002a; Saari and Tataru, 1999). Chapter 5 is largely dedicated to the development of such results.

4. While our analysis here is in the domain of 'distribution free' random utility or ranking models, a related task is to classify existing parametric families of random utility and ranking models (Critchlow et al., 1991; Fishburn, 1998) according to whether or not they (or random samples generated from them) automatically yield a transitive majority preference relation and how the majority outcomes of different models may relate to each other (for related relevant work on 'optimal scoring rules' for parametric random

utility models in the 'exponential family,' see, e.g., Buhlmann and Huber, 1963; Huber, 1963).

5. Because theoretical and empirical results can fundamentally depend on the modeling assumptions entering such results, it is important for researchers interested in Condorcet efficiency and related issues to check how robust their findings are to model variations or violations, and to combine their theoretical work with empirical analyses aimed at testing the descriptive validity of their modeling assumptions against actual social choice behavior.

4

Constructing Majority Preferences
from Subset Choice Data

Chapter Summary

In an election there are many ways of collecting and tallying votes so as to determine one or more winners (Levin and Nalebuff, 1995; Lijphart and Grofman, 1984). Among them, *approval voting* (AV) is particularly interesting for behavioral social choice research, because it provides exceptionally rich empirical data. Approval voting is an example of a choice paradigm that we call "subset choice." By *subset choice(s)* we mean a voting, polling, or other choice situation, in which each participant is presented with a (fixed) finite set C of alternatives, candidates, products, or brands, and is asked to choose a subset of any size. In approval voting we commonly interpret this subset as containing those alternatives that the voter 'approves' of, i.e., regards as satisfactory. Under AV each candidate that a voter approves of scores a point. If k alternatives are to be elected, then the k candidates with the highest AV scores are the winners.[1]

Although variants of AV have been independently invented by a number of authors, this method is most closely associated with S. Brams and P. Fishburn, who have most extensively contributed to the literature that explores its properties (Brams, 1988, 1993; Brams and Fishburn, 1983,

---

[1] In Falmagne and Regenwetter (1996) subset choice is called approval voting. Here we use the more general term 'subset choice' whenever we wish to abstract from the particular tallying procedure and to allow for broader interpretations of the chosen subsets than sets of 'approved' alternatives. For detailed discussions of the size-independent model, the topset voting model, and a variety of other probabilistic models for subset choice and approval voting, see Falmagne and Regenwetter (1996) and Regenwetter et al. (1998). Here we look at only two such models.

1985, 1988, 1992, 2001; Brams et al., 1988a,b; Brams and Herschbach, 2001; Brams and Nagel, 1991; Chamberlin and Featherston, 1986; Falmagne and Regenwetter, 1996; Felsenthal et al., 1986, 1990, 1993; Felsenthal and Machover, 1995; Fishburn and Little, 1988; Forsythe et al., 1996; Gehrlein and Lepelley, 1998; Garcia-Lapresta and Martinez-Panero, 2002; Laslier, 2002, 2003; Myerson, 1993, 2002; Nagel, 1984; Regenwetter, 1997; Regenwetter and Grofman, 1998a,b; Regenwetter et al., 1998; Regenwetter and Tsetlin, 2004; Saari and Van Newenhizen, 1988a,b; Saari, 2001a; Sonstegaard, 1998; Weber, 1995; Wiseman, 2000).

This chapter further pursues the question of how to compute majority preference relations from incomplete data, i.e., data that do not provide the full rankings or complete paired comparisons technically required as input for majority rule computations. We move beyond the survey data discussed earlier to real and mock election ballots that provide "subset choice" information. The main purpose of the chapter is to present two descriptive models of subset choice behavior, the "size-independent model" and the "topset voting model," and to show how one can use such psychological models as a measurement device to construct the majority preference relation from the subset choice data. Another purpose is to show some of the limitations that are inherent in any attempt to construct preference distributions or aggregate preferences, such as majority preferences, from incomplete data.

Put differently, within the subset choice context, we integrate axiomatic concepts from social choice theory in the Arrowian tradition (Arrow, 1951; Heiner and Pattanaik, 1983; Murakami, 1968; Pattanaik, 1971; Sen, 1966, 1969, 1970) with descriptive probabilistic models of judgment and decision making of a type commonly used in mathematical psychology (e.g., Luce and Suppes, 1965). While there exists a vast literature on computer simulations and analytical results in social choice theory, the present chapter emphasizes how the unobserved majority preference relations can be investigated empirically for real elections in which only subset choice data are available. However, the chapter also lays out some of the limitations and obstacles that arise in the construction of individual or aggregate preferences from incomplete data. This approach follows our fundamental research strategy towards behavioral social choice theories, in which theoretical arguments are systematically linked to the real world via the analysis of empirical data.

We first use a probabilistic choice model, the "size-independent model" proposed by Falmagne and Regenwetter (1996), that is built upon the notion that each individual voter has a (possibly latent) strict linear order (i.e., complete ranking) of the alternatives, and chooses a subset (possibly nondeterministically) at the top of that linear order. Using our extension of Sen's (1966) theorem about value restriction discussed in Section 1.2, we provide necessary and sufficient conditions for this empirically testable choice model to yield a transitive majority preference order. Also, in the framework of the size-independent model, we develop a method to compute Condorcet winners from such subset choice probabilities. In the case of three candidates, we show that the size-independent model yields a unique probability distribution on the latent preference rankings underlying the choices if and only if our probabilistic version of Sen's value restriction of Definition 1.2.8 holds. When there is more than one solution, we can partition the solution space into different areas that correspond to the possible majority preference relations compatible with the data.

Second, we introduce an alternative probabilistic model, the "topset voting model" proposed by Regenwetter (1997), that is built upon the notion that each voter has a strict weak order (or other partial order) preference relation and approves of the 'top' objects in that strict weak order, i.e., the set of those objects to which the voter does not prefer any of the remaining candidates. As we mention above, in approval voting, each candidate in a voter's chosen subset scores a point, and winners are determined by ranking the candidates according to their total approval voting scores. It can readily be shown that majority preferences consistent with (our specific version of) the topset voting model always coincide with the approval voting order associated with the approval voting scores. (Note that, since the approval voting scores are numerical, they always automatically induce a transitive ordering.)

The topset voting model is also always consistent with any possible subset choice data, that is, we can always find parameters for the model that account perfectly for any given set of data. Thus, the model is empirically vacuous, i.e., it is empirically and statistically nontestable. Nonetheless, we still find the topset voting model useful, for example, as a filter through which we can view the subset choice data as though they were, in fact, strict weak order data. Moreover, treating the topset voting model as an alternative to the size-independent model allows us to illustrate one of the ways in which constructing preferences from subset choice data can be model dependent.

We illustrate the size-independent and topset voting models on several real or mock elections conducted under approval voting. As just mentioned, the topset voting model automatically yields transitive majority preferences, and thus does not provide a test of transitivity. Nonetheless, it is interesting to note that, using that model, we find three cases in which majority preferences are transitive without either net value restriction or net majority holding on the strict weak orders. Unlike the topset voting model, the size-independent model does not force transitivity of majority preferences. Yet, in those cases where the size-independent model fits the data, we fail to find convincing evidence for majority cycles. Two of the seven data sets which the size-independent model fits well allow for the possibility of cyclical majority preferences consistent with the size-independent model. However, even in those two cases, the cycles occur only in a relatively small part of the solution space of the model.

By contrasting the results for the topset voting model and the size-independent model, we show that the choice of model used in the evaluation of subset choice data plays an important role in the conclusions we draw about the underlying distribution of preferences, as well as about the induced majority preference relation associated with that distribution. In other words, the constructed majority preference relation is, indeed, model dependent. In fact, the problem of model dependence appears to loom larger than the problem of majority cycles for the models and the data that we have so far investigated.

The chapter is organized as follows: Section 4.1 introduces a method for inferring majority preference relations from subset choice data via the size-independent model, shows how to evaluate net value restriction via that model, and briefly introduces the topset model. Section 4.2 shows that the majority preferences inferred from incomplete data, such as subset choices here, may be model dependent and comments more generally on the issue of model dependence. Section 4.3 provides empirical illustrations. Section 4.4 completes the chapter with a conclusion and discussion.

4.1 MAJORITY RULE PREFERENCES CONSTRUCTED VIA TWO PROBABILISTIC MODELS OF SUBSET CHOICE DATA

In this section we start with the case where individual preferences are conceptualized as strict linear orders and we continue with a second model built on the notion that individual preferences are weak orders. We first briefly introduce a simple (probabilistic) psychological model of subset choice behavior, called the "size-independent model" (Falmagne and Regenwetter, 1996). This model assumes that each voter has a (possibly probabilistic) strict linear preference order on the alternatives and approves (possibly probabilistically) of a subset at the top of that ranking. After summarizing the relevant known properties of the model (Doignon and Regenwetter, 1997; Regenwetter et al., 1998), we discuss how we can evaluate the notions of value restriction and net value restriction introduced in Section 1.2 for probabilistic linear order preferences when the available data are only subset choice data. Subsequently, we briefly introduce the topset voting model.

As before, let Π denote the set of all linear orders on $\mathcal{C} = \{1, 2, \ldots, N\}$ with $N \geq 3$. In some cases, N is explicitly assumed to be equal to three. We denote by $X \subseteq \mathcal{C}$ any subset of $\mathcal{C}$ (including the empty set ø and the full set $\mathcal{C}$) and, for any subset X of $\mathcal{C}$, we write Π_X for the collection of all linear orders in Π which rank the members of X ahead of all other members of $\mathcal{C}$. Clearly, $\Pi_\emptyset = \Pi_\mathcal{C} = \Pi$.

The size-independent model of subset choice (Falmagne and Regenwetter, 1996) assumes that the choice behavior of a randomly chosen voter in the population takes the form of the joint realization of three random variables: V (as in "vote"), R (as in "ranking"), and S (as in "set size"). Accordingly we write $V = X$; $R = \pi$; and $S = s$, respectively, for the events that a randomly drawn voter approves of subset $X \subseteq \mathcal{C}$; has latent linear preference order $\pi \in \Pi$; approves of $s \in \{0, 1, \ldots, N\}$ many elements, respectively.

Because the subset chosen by the voter (and thus also the number of candidates contained in his/her vote) is observable, the realizations of the random variables V and (hence) S are observable. However, since the realizations of R are unobservable, R is a latent variable, the distribution of which we would like to characterize (at least partially) using the observed subset choices. We now formally state Falmagne and Regenwetter's model.

Definition 4.1.1 Given V, R, and S as above, the *size-independent model* assumes that

$$\mathbb{P}(V = X) = \mathbb{P}(S = |X|) \times \mathbb{P}(R \in \Pi_X).$$

Thus, the probability that a randomly selected voter chooses the set X is the product of the probability that s/he votes for as many alternatives as X contains times the probability that s/he likes all candidates in X better than all others. Whenever we view the vote participants as being the entire sample space (endowed with the trivial relative frequency probability measure), the above statements are equivalent to relative frequency statements.

Although the product form suggests a certain degree of independence between the latent preferences and the number of objects chosen,

Regenwetter, Marley, and Joe (1998) have shown that the model can take into account some directionality biases, say, in a case with a single candidate from one party, and two candidates from an opposing party. They have also compared the model with other probabilistic models of subset choice.

In statistical terms this model has more parameters (namely $N! + N - 1$) than the choice probabilities have degrees of freedom (namely $2^N - 1$). Although this might suggest that the model is empirically vacuous, Falmagne and Regenwetter (1996) have given examples of empirical constraints implied by the model. Doignon and Regenwetter (1997) have shown that a simple transformation of the model-compatible choice probabilities produces a $2^N - N - 1$ dimensional convex polytope in $\mathbb{R}^{2^N}$. They have characterized the resulting "approval-voting polytope for linear orders" for $N \leq 5$. A complete charaterization of the AV-polytope has subsequently been obtained by Doignon and Fiorini (2003, 2004).

For the rest of this chapter, we concentrate on the case of three candidates.[2] For three alternatives, Doignon and Regenwetter (1997) have also derived closed form solutions for the possible distributions of R underlying V when the size-independent model holds. Writing $C(X) = \frac{\mathbb{P}(V = X)}{\mathbb{P}(S = |X|)}$, when it is well defined, $C = C(\{c\})$, $DE = C(\{d, e\})$, etc., and cde for the ranking (over $\{c, d, e\}$) in which c is best and e is worst, the following theorem (stated here without proof) summarizes some crucial results from Doignon and Regenwetter (1997). Note that the ratios $C(X)$ can be directly estimated from the data.

Theorem 4.1.2 *Suppose that $C = \{c, d, e\}$ and consider subset choice probabilities over all subsets of C, as well as the derived quantities C just introduced.*

1) The subset choice probabilities are consistent with the size-independent model if and only if for each element $x \in C$ and for each $k \in \{1, 2, 3\}$ the quantity

$$\mathbb{P}_k(x) = \sum_{\substack{Y \subseteq C - \{x\} \\ |Y| = k-1}} C(\{x\} \cup Y) - \sum_{\substack{Z \subseteq C - \{x\} \\ |Z| = k-2}} C(\{x\} \cup Z) \tag{4.1}$$

is nonnegative (where the second sum is set to zero when $k = 1$).

---

[2] While theoretical results are known for more than three candidates, properties that relate to transitivity are always formulated in terms of triples. Furthermore, all our subset choice data sets involve only three candidates.

2) Assuming that the size-independent model holds, the quantity $\mathbb{P}_k(x)$ *is the marginal ranking probability that* R *ranks alternative* x *at position* k *(this holds also when* $|\mathcal{C}| > 3$*).*

3) Given that $\mathbb{P}_k(x) \geq 0$ *for all* x *and* k*, the possible probability distributions on the latent rankings according to the size-independent model can be computed in closed form: Writing* $\mathbb{P}_\pi$ *for* $\mathbb{P}(R = \pi)$,

$$
\begin{pmatrix} \mathbb{P}_{cde} \\ \mathbb{P}_{dec} \\ \mathbb{P}_{ecd} \\ \mathbb{P}_{ced} \\ \mathbb{P}_{dce} \\ \mathbb{P}_{edc} \end{pmatrix} = \begin{pmatrix} C + CD + DE \\ C + D + DE \\ 1 \\ -CD - DE \\ -C - DE \\ -C - D \end{pmatrix} + \lambda \begin{pmatrix} -1 \\ -1 \\ -1 \\ +1 \\ +1 \\ +1 \end{pmatrix}, \tag{4.2}
$$

where

$$
\lambda \in \Big[\max\left(C + D,\ CD + DE,\ C + DE\right),
$$
$$
\min\left(C + CD + DE,\ C + D + DE,\ 1\right) \Big]. \tag{4.3}
$$

Note that the range of λ is not a statistical confidence interval but rather a continuum of possible closed form solutions. As Falmagne and Regenwetter (1996) show, their model can also be stated naturally as a (nonparametric) random utility model of discrete choice like those discussed in Subsection 2.1.2, using Equation (2.12) of Theorem 2.1.10.

We are now ready to derive useful implications from Theorem 4.1.2 by combining it with Theorem 1.2.15, which essentially shows that net value restriction and net preference majority are jointly necessary and sufficient for majority preferences to be transitive (for linear orders).

4.1.1 Evaluating Net Value Restriction and Net Preference Majority from Subset Choices via the Size-Independent Model

Probabilistic subset choice models offer a way to check transitivity of majority preferences even though the only information available from the voters is their choices of subsets. Suppose that, for a given set of ballots with subset choice information, the size-independent model holds, and we have reconstructed a probability distribution on the linear orders from the data using that model. Then, if this probability distribution satisfies weak stochastic transitivity, we can derive a transitive majority preference relation from it. Thus, although majority preference relations and

Condorcet winners are traditionally defined in terms of pairwise choices, we can use the subset choice data to reconstruct voter preferences through a testable choice model such as the size-independent model.

Next, we present an important result for the special case of exactly three candidates that links the size-independent model to Sen's value restriction condition. Illustrative empirical applications of the size-independent model, for the case of three alternatives, are discussed in Section 4.3.

Theorem 1.2.9 above establishes that (a.s.) value restriction of Definition 1.2.8 (our probabilistic version of Sen's value restriction condition) is sufficient (but not necessary) for transitive majority preferences. Together with Theorem 4.1.2 above, it implies the following two results for the special case of three candidates. We state the following theorem of Doignon and Regenwetter (1997) and its corollary without proof.

Theorem 4.1.3 *Suppose that* $C = \{c, d, e\}$ *and that the size-independent model of subset choice holds. Then the following are equivalent (using the notation of Theorem 4.1.2):*

- *The distribution of* **R** *is unique.*
- *At least one of the marginal probabilities* $\mathbb{P}_k(x)$ *in (4.1) is zero.*
- *The probability distribution induced by* **R** *on the linear orders is (a.s.) value restricted.*
- $\max\left(C + D, CD + DE, C + DE\right) = \min\left(C + CD + DE, C + D + DE, 1\right).$

The second and the fourth conditions in Theorem 4.1.3 give us two (equivalent) observable properties on the subset choices to check whether the latent preferences are (a.s.) value restricted. Moreover, when these conditions are observed, we immediately know from the theorem not only that the size-independent model has a solution for the ranking probabilities, but also that this solution is unique. The relationship between value restriction on linear orders and the uniqueness of a solution for the size-independent model is rather surprising. We furthermore have the following immediate implication.

Corollary 4.1.4 *Consider a subset vote with 3 candidates. If the size-independent model holds and the probability distribution of* **R** *is unique, then the weak majority preference relation* $\succsim$ *as defined in (1.3) is a weak order, the strict majority preference relation* $\succ$ *in (1.4) is a strict weak* *order, and, provided that* $\mathbb{P}_{cd} \neq \mathbb{P}_{dc}, \forall c \neq d$, *the strict majority preference relation* $\succ$ *is a strict linear order.*

It is quite unlikely to observe data with exactly one solution for the distribution of R. Nevertheless, we provide an example in the data analysis of Section 4.3, where one of the seven elections, in fact, yields (a.s.) value restriction.[3]

4.1.2 Majority Preferences Constructed from the Topset Voting Model

We now briefly consider another method for computing the majority preference relation from subset choice data, the *topset voting model of subset choice*. This method does not assume that individual preferences are strict linear orders. Instead, it assumes that individual preferences are partial orders. We consider a special case built on two assumptions, namely that (1) a voter is indifferent between any two choice alternatives that are either both included in or both excluded from their chosen subset and (2) that the voter prefers any chosen alternative to any nonchosen alternative.[4] Thus a is counted as preferred to b if and only if a is in the chosen set and b is not.

Definition 4.1.5 Writing $P(X)$ for the probability that the set X is chosen, p_B for the probability of any weak order $B \in \mathcal{SWO}$, and $top(B) = \{c \in \mathcal{C} | \forall d \in \mathcal{C}, [(dBc) \Rightarrow (cBd)]\}$, the *topset voting model* (stated here only for strict weak order preferences) states that, for any nonempty set $X \subseteq \mathcal{C}$,

$$P(X) = \sum_{\substack{B \in \mathcal{SWO} \\ X=top(B)}} p_B = p_{X \times (\mathcal{C}-X)}. \qquad (4.4)$$

Through the lens of this model, there is a one-to-one correspondence between all nonempty subsets X of $\mathcal{C}$ (i.e., the empty set is not accounted for) and the corresponding strict weak orders $X \times (\mathcal{C} - X)$ over $\mathcal{C}$. As a consequence, our general definition of majority rule (Definition 2.1.3) of

---

[3] The one data set in which value restriction is satisfied (when preferences are reconstructed through the size-independent model) comes from an election of the Society for Social Choice and Welfare. It thus appears that this society's members have 'well-behaved,' domain restricted, preferences!

[4] In mathematical terms, this means that each preference relation consists of at most two equivalence classes. If one allows individual voters to be nonindifferent between two candidates that they either both approve or both disapprove of, then one cannot use this method and claim that it generates the majority winner.

Chapter 2 can be directly brought to bear on the subset choice data, treated as elicitations of weak orders. It is straightforward to show that the majority preference relation under this method will automatically match the ordering by approval voting scores, i.e., the ordering by the total number of approval votes that each candidate receives. In contrast to the size-independent model, the topset voting model is statistically nontestable: it can account for any possible subset choice data. In that sense, this model is empirically and statistically vacuous.

4.2 MODEL DEPENDENCE OF MAJORITY PREFERENCE CONSTRUCTED FROM SUBSET CHOICE DATA

We now consider model dependence by way of a hypothetical data set.

Consider a hypothetical example of an approval vote over a set $C = \{a, b, c\}$, where 20 voters approve of candidate a alone, 10 approve of b alone, 10 approve of c alone, 1 voter approves of a and b, 4 voters approve of a and c, and 5 approve of b and c. Also, suppose that 5 voters approve of all candidates. (We ignore how many people voted for none of the candidates.) We ask whether there is a majority rule winner (Condorcet winner), and whether the three candidates can be rank ordered by majority rule.

We now provide the majority preference relations implied by the two methods (namely the topset voting model and the size-independent model, respectively) for this example.

According to the topset voting model, we have

$$NP_{ab} = \sum_{\substack{X \subseteq C \\ a \in X \\ b \notin X}} P(X) - \sum_{\substack{Y \subseteq C \\ a \notin Y \\ b \in Y}} P(Y),$$

with the same computation applying to all other choices of pairs of alternatives from C. Accordingly, we tally the paired comparison a versus b as $20 + 4$ (out of 55) in favor of a because 24 people chose sets that contained a but not b, and $10 + 5$ (out of 55) in favor of b because 15 people chose sets that contained b but not a. With this computation, a has a strict majority over b. Similarly, this method of tallying generates a strict majority of c over b and a strict majority of a over c, i.e., a is the Condorcet winner, and the majority preference relation is the linear order $a \succ c \succ b$.

We develop the details of computations for the size-independent model in Section 4.1, and so we omit the specific computations for this example. We find that the distribution of strict linear orders under the size-independent model is unique, and that the majority preference relation is the semiorder $\succ = \{(c, b)\}$, i.e., the semiorder in which c is majority preferred to b, while a is majority tied with both b and c.

This simple example illustrates that the majority preference relation can, in principle, change dramatically as we change our implicit or explicit model of preferences, that is, as we change our assumptions about the mechanisms generating the observable data. In particular, conclusions about the Condorcet efficiency of approval voting (i.e., about its likelihood of electing a Condorcet winner when one exists) could vary dramatically depending on the model of underlying preferences and of the subset choice mechanism being posited. For example, the majority preference relation generated via the topset voting model automatically coincides with the rank order given by the approval voting scores (irrespective of the distribution of subset choices) because a is majority preferred to b if and only if a and not b is chosen more often than b and not a, which in turn is determined by who has more approval votes. The size-independent model, in contrast, does not force the approval voting ordering and the majority ordering to match.

Given this example, one might be tempted to think that results of any given subset choice model could not be trusted because results under an alternative model might be quite different.[5] However, this conclusion would be premature. First, we find that some results are robust (i.e., remain unchanged) under alternative models. For example, our conclusions in Section 4.3, that majority cycles lack empirical support, are robust under alternative model specifications. Second, not all models provide equally good accounts of empirical data, either because they do not use equally plausible assumptions or because they are not equally testable on empirical data. For example, the topset voting model always finds a transitive majority ordering, regardless of the nature of the approval data.

The same types of model dependence issues arise in theoretical work, such as simulations or theorems. For instance, we discuss in Chapter 1 the fact that commonly cited mathematical results about the expected prevalence of majority cycles are driven by the strong assumption of an impartial culture.[6]

---

[5] One has to expect that model dependence issues occur beyond the models used here: other possible models of subset choice behavior are likely to complicate the picture only further, not to simplify it. For various other models of subset choice see, e.g., Doignon et al. (2004); Laslier (2003, 2002); Marley (1991a); Regenwetter (1997); Regenwetter et al. (1998).

[6] In Chapter 5 we provide a general framework that allows us to evaluate the likelihood of a cycle in samples from virtually any culture. Although we use the methodology in Chapter 5 only for empirical analyses, it applies equally to theoretical distributions.

Having observed the potential for model dependence, it seems obvious that one ought to seek model-robust results, i.e., findings that hold under multiple alternative models, including even models whose assumptions may be mutually inconsistent. For instance, two models may construct mutually incompatible distributions of preferences from the same data and yet they may yield the same majority preference relation (as do the size-independent model and the topset voting model, in many circumstances). In this context, we remind the reader that in Chapter 3 we fail to find any evidence of majority cycles, even after analyzing and reanalyzing the data under a range of different theoretical assumptions. The absence of majority cycles in the survey data studied in Chapter 3 is thus a robust finding that is not driven by the particular way we analyze and interpret those empirical data. Similarly, we can investigate the extent to which theoretical or empirical findings about majority rule preferences, associated, say, with some particular approval voting election, are robust under model variations. In short, the problem of model dependence does not put a halt to theoretical or empirical research. Rather it puts us under the obligation to explore and explain the extent to which our substantive conclusions from empirical data or from theoretical work depend on the assumptions that entered the analysis.

We now illustrate our conceptual and theoretical arguments with empirical data.

4.3 EMPIRICAL ILLUSTRATIONS

We analyze seven sets of subset choice data in terms of both the size-independent model[7] and the topset voting model. The data sets are referred to as TIMS E1, TIMS E2, MAA1, MAA2, IEEE, SJDM, and SSCW. They stem, respectively, from two elections of the Institute of Management Science, two elections of the Mathematical Association of America, a vote by the Institute of Electrical and Electronics Engineers, an election by the Society for Judgment and Decision Making, and an election by the

---

[7] In Regenwetter and Grofman (1998a) there are several minor typographical and/or computation errors. For example, a net probability reported there as .191 in TIMS E1, is corrected here as .190. A number reported there for TIMS E2 as .188 is here correctly reported as .187. A net probability in MAA 2 reported there as .335 is corrected here as being .325. A value reported there for IEEE as .066 is corrected here to be .063. The largest error we found in Regenwetter and Grofman (1998a) was for the upper bound on τ to obtain net value restriction in IEEE, namely .199 instead of the now corrected value of .154. None of these changes affect our substantive interpretations.

TABLE 4.1: *Summary of Data for Seven Real and Mock Approval Voting Elections. The Top Section Reports the Subset Choice Frequency Data. The Central Part Displays the Marginal Probabilities* $\mathbb{P}_k(x)$ *That Any Given Candidate x Is Ranked at Any Given Rank k (for the size-independent model). The Bottom Shows the Approval Voting Scores*

Data Set	TIMS E1	TIMS E2	MAA 1	MAA 2	IEEE	SJDM	SSCW
Subset							
∅	68	78	224	510	6001	0	2
{a}	66	199	1257	413	14365	22	26
{b}	350	248	626	1798	12254	24	11
{c}	290	273	1434	1019	11478	9	26
{a, b}	175	84	68	29	2934	3	2
{a, c}	105	114	260	52	2746	4	2
{b, c}	442	220	141	199	1811	4	0
{a, b, c}	71	161	30	20	4380	1	2
Total	1567	1377	4040	4040	55969	67	71
$\mathbb{P}_1(a)$	.09	.28	.38	.13	.38	.40	.41
$\mathbb{P}_1(b)$	.50	.34	.19	.56	.32	.44	.17
$\mathbb{P}_1(c)$	.41	.38	.43	.32	.30	.16	.41
$\mathbb{P}_2(a)$	.29	.20	.32	.16	.38	.24	.59
$\mathbb{P}_2(b)$	.36	.38	.26	.26	.31	.20	.33
$\mathbb{P}_2(c)$	.35	.42	.42	.58	.31	.56	.09
$\mathbb{P}_3(a)$	.61	.53	.30	.71	.24	.36	0
$\mathbb{P}_3(b)$	.15	.27	.55	.19	.37	.36	.50
$\mathbb{P}_3(c)$	.24	.20	.14	.10	.39	.27	.50
AV score of a	417	558	1615	514	24425	30	32
AV score of b	1038	713	865	2046	21379	32	15
AV score of c	908	768	1865	1290	20415	18	30

Society for Social Choice and Welfare.[8] The raw subset choice frequencies are reported in Table 4.1. As can easily be seen in Table 4.1, some of these data sets are very sparse. In this chapter, we omit any statistical considerations because they would distract from our main conceptual points.

---

[8] TIMS E1 and TIMS E2 were experimental elections, in which approval voting data were gathered at the same time as plurality elections and full candidate rankings. The TIMS elections were reported and first analyzed in Fishburn and Little (1988). The MAA and the SSCW data were kindly provided by S. J. Brams and have also been previously analyzed by others (see, e.g., Brams, 1988; Brams and Fishburn, 2001; Saari, 2001a). The IEEE election was reported in Brams and Nagel (1991). The SJDM data were kindly provided by the Society for Judgment and Decision Making.

Instead, we treat the observed relative frequencies as probabilities (since they satisfy the axioms of probability measures) and directly study those resulting probabilities.[9] The size-independent model can account for each of these seven data sets.[10]

4.3.1 Analyses Using the Size-Independent Model

In addition to the raw data, Table 4.1 reports the marginal rank probabilities $\mathbb{P}_k(x)$ of Equation (4.1) for the seven elections, rounded to the second significant digit. For instance, and as we explain below, by Equation (4.1) we have $\mathbb{P}_1(a) = .09$ for TIMS E1. Each election had three candidates, which is the case where the conditions $\mathbb{P}_k(x) \geq 0, \forall x \in C, k \in \{1, 2, 3\}$, are necessary and sufficient for the data to be consistent with the size-independent model. As noted earlier, in all seven cases this set of conditions is satisfied.

Before we turn to the election by election analysis of these seven data sets, we provide a general overview of the results.

- For five of the seven data sets, our analysis via the size-independent model rules out majority cycles, while the remaining two data sets are ambiguous in that respect. However, none of the analyses provides convincing evidence for the presence of a majority cycle.
- Only one data set satisfies our probabilistic generalization of Sen's value restriction condition, and that case could easily have been produced by statistical chance from a distribution that is not value restricted. Thus, we cannot hope to rely on that condition to predict transitive majority preference relations in any of the other six cases. More generally, based

---

[9] Regenwetter and Tsetlin (2004) investigate the size-independent model statistically, using a Bayesian approach.

[10] Falmagne and Regenwetter (1996) provide an empirical illustration on a different IEEE election in which the size-independent model does not hold. We have also applied the size-independent model to a number of other data sets, including data sets that we have referred to elsewhere as A16, A25, A29, A30, and A72 (Regenwetter and Grofman, 1998a). These were not actual subset choice data. Rather they are from voting methods where voters provided partial rankings of the candidates and where we used only information about the set of alternatives included in the partial rankings. A16 through A72 are part of a large collection of data kindly provided by N. Tideman from elections of professional organizations in the U.K. that used the single transferable vote or the alternative vote. For three of these five data sets, the size-independent model could be rejected, thus illustrating that the model is indeed empirically falsifiable in some circumstances. On the other hand, in virtually each case where the size-independent model's constraints on the data were violated, the data were also extremely sparse. For violations based on sparse data, our statistical confidence is low (Regenwetter and Tsetlin, 2004).

on the preference distributions yielded by the size-independent model, we cannot rely on domain restrictions to predict or explain the absence of cycles.

- In four of the remaining six cases, either the net probabilities are (net) value restricted (as defined in Definition 1.2.13), or we have a net preference majority (as defined in Definition 1.2.14), either of which is enough to account for the absence of a cycle.

In order to use the equations in Theorem 4.1.2 in this section, we use the notation $C(X) = \frac{\mathbb{P}(V=X)}{\mathbb{P}(S=|X|)}$, as before, but we now define $C = C(\{a\})$, $D = C(\{b\})$, $E = C(\{c\})$, $CD = C(\{a, b\})$, $CE = C(\{a, c\})$, and $DE = C(\{b, c\})$.

TIMS E1: The E1 ballots were first reported by Fishburn and Little (1988). The frequencies with which zero or all candidates are chosen do not provide any information about ranking probabilities, since each of these choices is consistent with any ranking.

The estimates of the marginals $\mathbb{P}_k(x)$ of Equation (4.1) are given in Table 4.1. For TIMS E1, we compute the quantity C of Theorem 4.1.2 as $C = \frac{66}{66+350+290} = .09$, using Equation (4.1) and the raw frequencies shown in Table 4.1. As a consequence, $\mathbb{P}_1(a) = .09$, as reported in Table 4.1. Similarly, we have $D = \mathbb{P}_1(b) = \frac{350}{66+350+290} = .50$, as reported in Table 4.1. In addition, $CD = \frac{175}{175+105+442} = .24$, and $DE = \frac{442}{175+105+442} = .61$. Accordingly, $\mathbb{P}_2(b) = CD + DE - D = .36$, as can be seen in Table 4.1, as well.

The estimated marginal ranking probabilities $\mathbb{P}_k(x)$ in Table 4.1 are all nonnegative, and thus the necessary and sufficient conditions for the data to be consistent with a size-independent model with three alternatives are satisfied.

We can analytically derive the possible underlying ranking probabilities that are consistent with the given marginal ranking probabilities using Theorem 4.1.2. Accordingly, the first entry in Equation (4.2) of Theorem 4.1.2 is $C + CD + DE = .948$. After substitution of the remaining relevant quantities, Equation (4.2) in Theorem 4.1.2 becomes

$$
\begin{pmatrix} \mathbb{P}_{abc} \\ \mathbb{P}_{bca} \\ \mathbb{P}_{cab} \\ \mathbb{P}_{acb} \\ \mathbb{P}_{bac} \\ \mathbb{P}_{cba} \end{pmatrix} = \begin{pmatrix} .948 \\ 1.201 \\ 1 \\ -.855 \\ -.706 \\ -.589 \end{pmatrix} + \lambda \begin{pmatrix} -1 \\ -1 \\ -1 \\ +1 \\ +1 \\ +1 \end{pmatrix}, \quad \text{with } \lambda \in \Big[.855, .948\Big],
$$

where the range of λ has been computed by substituting the relevant quantities into Formula (4.3). When $\lambda = .948$, which is its largest possible value, then $\mathbb{P}_{abc} = 0$. We can thus reparametrize the above equation by defining $\tau = \lambda - .948$. In order to carry out our simplification, we subtract .948 from the first three entries of the column vector immediately following the equality sign, and add .948 to the bottom three entries. This leads to the following simplification.

$$
\begin{pmatrix} \mathbb{P}_{abc} \\ \mathbb{P}_{bca} \\ \mathbb{P}_{cab} \\ \mathbb{P}_{acb} \\ \mathbb{P}_{bac} \\ \mathbb{P}_{cba} \end{pmatrix} = \begin{pmatrix} 0 \\ .253 \\ .052 \\ .093 \\ .242 \\ .359 \end{pmatrix} + \tau \begin{pmatrix} 1 \\ 1 \\ 1 \\ -1 \\ -1 \\ -1 \end{pmatrix}, \quad \text{with } \tau \in [0, .093].
$$

We apply analogous reparametrizations to all other analyses without further comment.

Figure 4.1 shows all possible preference probabilities, net probabilities NP (in parentheses), and pairwise net preference probabilities that are consistent with the size-independent model and the TIMS E1 data. As we have just computed, the probability of the ranking abc is not unique. Rather, based on the subset choice frequencies, and using the size-independent model as a tool to reconstruct compatible ranking probabilities, the probability of the preference order abc is equal to τ, where $\tau \in [0, .093]$. Similarly, the probability of bac is $.242 - \tau$. Note that neighboring orders in the graph differ in their sign of τ (more precisely they differ in whether τ is being added or subtracted). As τ changes, three ranking probabilities increase, and three ranking probabilities decrease.

In this data set, there are no linear orders whose net probabilities change sign with changing values of τ. We will see in later examples that this is not a mathematical necessity of the model. Note again that the range of τ is not a (statistical) confidence interval. Rather, there exists a continuum of analytical solutions and the possible values of τ completely characterize all these possible solutions. The three linear orders that have a positive net probability regardless of the value of τ are shaded in grey in the figure, whereas the three linear orders that have a negative net probability (the reverse ones of the previous three) are displayed on white background.

Once we have estimated the possible ranking probabilities, we can compute all possible marginal pairwise preference probabilities that are consistent with those ranking probabilities. Figure 4.1 also gives the

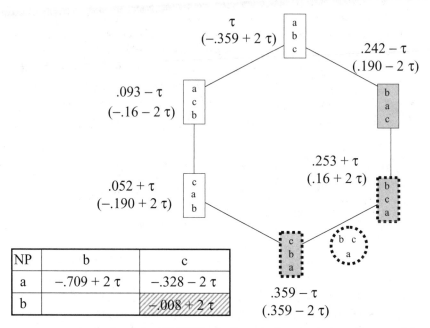

FIGURE 4.1: Analysis of the TIMS E1 election via the size-independent model. Possible probability distributions $\mathbb{P}$ and net probabilities $N\!P$ (in parentheses) on the rankings are shown, with $\tau \in [0, .093]$. Shaded rankings have positive net probability for all values of τ. The inset table provides the pairwise net preference probabilities $N\!P_{ab}$, $N\!P_{ac}$, and $N\!P_{bc}$. Pairwise net preference probabilities on white background are negative for all values of τ, whereas the one on grey and white striped background changes sign as τ varies. The three possible majority preference relations are marked with bold dotted frames.

corresponding pairwise net probabilities $N\!P_{ab}$, $N\!P_{ac}$, and $N\!P_{bc}$. For any feasible value of τ, $N\!P_{ab}$ and $N\!P_{ac}$ are negative, whereas $N\!P_{bc}$ can be positive or negative, depending on the value of τ. Accordingly, the first two net probabilities are displayed on white background, whereas the last one is shaded with grey and white stripes. We find that there is no uniquely determined Condorcet winner. The solution space for the probability distribution is not narrow enough to eliminate either b or c as a winner. This confirms Fishburn and Little's (1988) difficulty in discriminating between the two alternatives in terms of being able to clearly designate one of them as <u>the</u> underlying Condorcet winner.

In light of the size-independent model, it is easy to see from the net probabilities (in parentheses) in Figure 4.1 that for any acceptable value of τ, $N\!P$ is value restricted (as defined in Definition 1.2.13). In fact, regardless of the value of τ, the same three linear orders, namely *bac*, *bca*, and *cba*, always have positive net probabilities. (As mentioned earlier, these three linear orders are shaded in grey.) From this fact or from the pairwise net probability matrix we can derive that there exists a transitive majority preference relation. We find three possible majority preference relations: When $\tau \in [0, .004)$, we have the linear order $c \succ b \succ a$, which has a net preference majority (as defined in Definition 1.2.14) in that range of τ; when $\tau = .004$ (.004249 to be more precise), we obtain the weak order $\{(b, a), (c, a)\}$; when $\tau \in (.004, .093]$, we obtain the linear order $b \succ c \succ a$, which has a net preference majority when $\tau > .065$. These three possible majority preference outcomes are indicated in Figure 4.1 with bold dotted frames.[11] Overall, we get c or b, or both, as Condorcet winners, depending on the specific value for τ that we use to generate a solution for the size-independent model ranking probabilities. These and related results are summarized in Table 4.2.

TIMS E2: Like TIMS E1, the E2 ballot was also first reported and analyzed by Fishburn and Little (1988). The subset frequencies and the estimates of the marginals $\mathbb{P}_k(x)$ of the size-independent model are reported in Table 4.1. As the marginal ranking probabilities derived via the size-independent model are nonnegative, we conclude that this probabilistic model is able to provide an appropriate account for the E2 election. For reasons of brevity, we omit a figure analogous to Figure 4.1. We find, once again, three possible majority preference relations that are compatible with these ranking probabilities. When $\tau \in [0, .152)$, we obtain the linear order $c \succ b \succ a$, which has a net preference majority when $\tau < .116$; when $\tau = .152$ (.151894 to be more precise), we obtain the weak order $\{(b, a), (c, a)\}$; when $\tau \in (.152, .197]$, we obtain the linear order $b \succ c \succ a$, which has a net preference majority when $\tau > .152$. We find again that (a.s.) value restriction is violated. Net value restriction holds whenever $\tau \in [.063, .187]$. Overall, we obtain transitive majorities for all feasible values of τ because everywhere in the solution space either net value restriction or net preference majority, or both, hold. These and related results are summarized in Table 4.2.

MAA 1: The MAA data were first reported and analyzed in Brams (1988). The estimated marginals $\mathbb{P}_k(x)$ of Equation (4.1) for MAA 1 are reported in Table 4.1. All these estimates are positive, which is consistent with the model. According to the size-independent model, $\mathbb{P}$ is not (a.s.) value restricted (because the ranking probability solution is not

---

[11] Note that the weak order is relevant only at the aggregate majority level. The size-independent model assumes that individual preferences are strict linear orders.

TABLE 4.2: *Overview of Results and Model Comparisons for Majority Outcomes ≻, (a.s.) Value Restriction and Sen's Value Restriction (VR), Generalized Net Value Restriction (NVR), and Net Majority (NM), Computed Via the Size-Independent Model (as a function of the value of τ) and the Topset Voting Model, for Seven Real or Mock Approval Voting Elections*

Data Set	τ	Size-Independent Model				Topset Voting Model			
		≻	VR	NVR	NM	≻	VR	NVR	NM
TIMS E1	[0, .004)	c ≻ b ≻ a			Y				
	.004	{(b,a),(c,a)}	N	Y	N	b ≻ c ≻ a	N	Y	Y
	(.004, .065]	b ≻ c ≻ a							
	(.065, .093]				Y				
TIMS E2	[0, .063)	c ≻ b ≻ a			N				
	[.063, .116)				Y				
	[.116, .152)				Y				
	.152	{(b,a),(c,a)}	N	Y	N	c ≻ b ≻ a	N	Y	Y
	(.152, .187]	b ≻ c ≻ a			Y				
	(.187, .197]				N				
MAA 1	[0, .024)	a ≻ c ≻ b			Y				
	.024	{(a,b),(c,b)}	N	Y	N	c ≻ a ≻ b	N	N	N
	(.024, .094]	c ≻ a ≻ b							
	(.094, .145]				Y				
MAA 2	[0, .104]	b ≻ c ≻ a	N	Y	Y	b ≻ c ≻ a	N	N	Y
IEEE	[0, .063)	cycle			N				
	.063	intransitivity		N	N				
	(.063, .086)	a ≻ c ≻ b			Y				
	[.086, .108)				Y				
	.108	{(a,b),(a,c)}	N	Y	N	a ≻ b ≻ c	N	N	N
	(.108, .124]				N				
	(.124, .154]	a ≻ b ≻ c			Y				
	(.154, .199)				Y				
	.199	intransitivity		N	N				
	(.199, .242]	cycle			N				
SJDM	[0, .027)	cycle			N				
	.027	intransitivity		N	N				
	(.027, .064)	b ≻ a ≻ c			Y				
	[.064, .088)				Y				
	[.088, .1)				Y				
	.1	{(a,c),(b,c)}	N	Y	N	b ≻ a ≻ c	N	N	N
	(.1, .118]	a ≻ b ≻ c			Y				
	(.118, .136)				Y				
	.136	intransitivity		N	N				
	(.136, .163]	cycle			N				
SSCW	0	{(a,b),(a,c)}	Y	Y	N	a ≻ c ≻ b	N	N	N

unique). However, N^P is value restricted regardless of the particular value of τ. As for TIMS E2, we omit a figure for the probability distributions on rankings and the net probabilities. It is easy to derive that the following majority preference solutions are possible: When $\tau \in [0, .024)$, we have the linear order $a \succ c \succ b$, which has a net preference majority in that case; when $\tau = .024$ (.023946 to be more precise), we have the weak order $\{(a, b), (c, b)\}$; when $\tau \in (.024, .145]$, we have the linear order $c \succ a \succ b$, which has a net preference majority when $\tau \in (.094, .145]$. Again, we obtain transitive majorities regardless of the value of τ because everywhere in the solution space net value restriction holds, and, in addition, in parts of the solution space net preference majority holds as well. These and related results are summarized in Table 4.2.

MAA 2: The MAA 2 data were also first reported and analyzed in Brams (1988). The possible ranking probabilities here are shown in Table 4.1. We find a violation of (a.s.) value restriction, but nevertheless, net value restriction holds everywhere in the solution space. The possible probability distributions and net probabilities (given in parentheses), as well as the pairwise net preference probabilities for MAA 2, are reported in Figure 4.2. One linear order changes from positive to negative net probability as τ increases from 0 to .104 (and thus its reverse changes from negative net probability to positive net probability). These two linear orders are accordingly shaded with grey and white stripes. As the pairwise net probabilities do not change sign as τ varies, each of them is either positive (shaded in grey) or negative (not shaded). There is, therefore, a unique majority preference relation, namely $b \succ c \succ a$. The latter also has a net majority, regardless of the value of τ. The majority preference relation is marked with a boldface frame in Figure 4.2. These and related results are summarized in Table 4.2.

The next two data sets illustrate situations in which the size-independent model does not rule out the possibility of a majority cycle. However, in both cases, the part of the solution space that is consistent with a cycle is small.

IEEE: The IEEE election was first reported in Brams and Nagel (1991). As can be seen from Table 4.1, the estimated marginal probabilities for IEEE are all nonnegative, and thereby consistent with the model. There are two areas of the solution space which do not produce Condorcet candidates or transitive majority preference relations, namely when $\tau \in [0, .063]$ and when $\tau \in [.199, .242]$. Taken together, these two areas produce both possible cycles, namely $\{(a, b), (b, c), (c, a)\}$ and

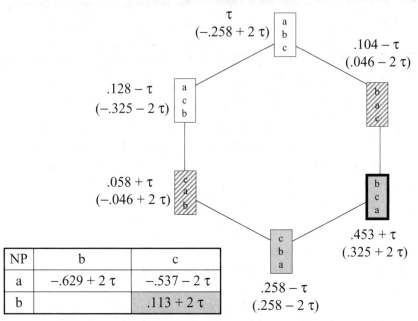

FIGURE 4.2: Analysis of the MAA 2 election via the size-independent model. Possible probability distributions $\mathbb{P}$ and net probabilities $N\!P$ (in parentheses) on the rankings are shown, with $\tau \in [0, .104]$. The shaded rankings have positive net probability for all values of τ, whereas the striped rankings have net probabilities with changing sign as τ varies. The inset table provides the pairwise net preference probabilities $N\!P_{ab}$, $N\!P_{ac}$, and $N\!P_{bc}$. Pairwise net preference probabilities on white background are negative for all values of τ, whereas the shaded one is negative for all values of τ. The (unique) majority preference order $b \succ c \succ a$ is marked with a boldface frame.

$\{(a, c), (c, b), (b, a)\}$, as well as two additional intransitive majority relations, namely $\{(b, c), (c, a)\}$ and $\{(a, b), (b, c)\}$. In all other cases, i.e., in the bigger part of the solution space where $\tau \in (.063, .199)$, we find that a is the unique Condorcet winner. This is the case even though there are still three different majority preference relations possible, namely $a \succ c \succ b$ when $\tau \in (.063, .108)$, the weak order $\{(a, b), (a, c)\}$ when $\tau = .108$ (.108330 to be more precise), and $a \succ b \succ c$ when $\tau \in (.108, .199)$. We find net value restriction when $\tau \in [.086, .154]$ and a net majority when $\tau \in (.063, .108)$ and when $\tau \in (.124, .199)$. These and related results are summarized in Table 4.2.

This case illustrates that the size-independent model does not force the existence of a transitive majority preference relation. On the other hand, we do not believe that this result provides clear empirical evidence

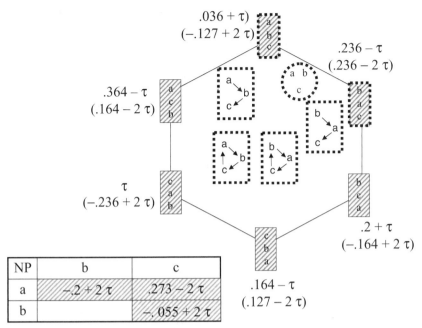

FIGURE 4.3: Analysis of the SJDM election via the size-independent model. Possible probability distributions $\mathbb{P}$ and net probabilities NP (in parentheses) on the rankings are shown, with $\tau \in [0, .164]$. The inset table provides the pairwise net preference probabilities NP_{ab}, NP_{ac}, and NP_{bc}. All net probabilities change sign as τ varies, thus all rankings and all pairwise net probabilities are shaded with grey and white stripes. The seven possible majority preference relations are marked with dotted boldface frames.

for the presence of a majority cycle either: The ranking probabilities are extremely underdetermined, with τ taking values in a huge range and yielding altogether <u>seven different</u> possible majority outcomes.

SJDM: The SJDM data were first analyzed in Regenwetter and Tsetlin (2004). As can be seen from Table 4.1, SJDM is the sparsest data set. The estimated marginal probabilities are all nonnegative, and therefore consistent with the model. The possible ranking probabilities, net preference probabilities, and pairwise net preference probabilities for SJDM are reported in Figure 4.3. We find that (a.s.) value restriction is violated because the ranking probabilities are not uniquely determined. Again, we find <u>seven different</u> possible solutions for the majority preference relation: When $\tau \in [0, .027)$, we obtain the majority cycle $\succ = \{(b, a), (a, c), (c, b)\}$. When $\tau = .027$ (.02727 to be more precise), we obtain the intransitive relation $\succ = \{(b, a), (a, c)\}$. When $\tau \in (.027, .1)$, we obtain the majority ordering $b \succ a \succ c$, which has a net majority when $\tau \in (.027, .088)$. When $\tau = .1$, we obtain the weak order $\succ= \{(a, c), (b, c)\}$. When $\tau \in (.1, .136)$, we obtain the linear order $a \succ b \succ c$, which has a net majority when $\tau \in (.100, .136)$. When $\tau = .136$ (.136364, to be more precise), we obtain the intransitive relation $\succ= \{(a, b), (b, c)\}$. When $\tau \in (.136, .163]$, we obtain the majority cycle $\succ= \{(a, b), (b, c), (c, a)\}$. We obtain net value restriction for $\tau \in [.064, .118]$. In Figure 4.3, the binary relations with bold dotted frames are the seven possible majority preference outcomes over the possible values of τ. They include two linear orders, one weak order, two cycles, and two other nontransitive binary relations. All linear orders and all entries in the pairwise net preference table are shaded with grey and white stripes because each net probability is positive for some values of τ and negative for some values of τ. These and related results are summarized in Table 4.2. Overall, this analysis is another toss-up because the ranking probabilities and net probabilities, as well as the corresponding majority relations, are highly unidentifiable (nonunique).

SSCW: The SSCW data were first analyzed in Brams and Fishburn (2001) and Saari (2001a). Table 4.1 reveals that, like SJDM, the SSCW data set is sparse. In this case, the solution for the probability distribution on linear orders is unique, i.e., the conditions of Theorem 4.1.3 are satisfied, and as a consequence, (a.s.) value restriction holds. The resulting unique transitive majority preference relation is the strict weak order $a \succ b, a \succ c$, framed in bold, where b and c are tied. Since (a.s.) value restriction holds, net value restriction holds as well. We do not have a net majority here. These and related results are summarized in Table 4.2.

All in all, even though the descriptive model that we employ here is quite simple, it works in all seven three-candidate elections we study. We now summarize our findings. The probabilistic version of Sen's value restriction holds in one data set; however, we suspect that the sparseness of data is the real reason for having some empty cells, which in turn are responsible for the necessary and sufficient condition of value restriction holding.[12] None of the other six data sets yields (a.s.) value restriction, so we cannot use Sen's result to predict a transitive majority preference relation in any of those six cases. In four of the remaining six data sets, we have transitive majority preference relations throughout the solution space. Here, net value restriction virtually always holds and those parts

---

[12] An alternative explanation would be that preferences are so extremely homogeneous that some empirical cells are automatically empty. We do not believe that this is a viable explanation.

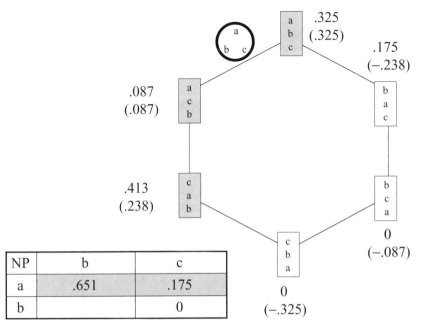

FIGURE 4.4: Analysis of the SSCW election via the size-independent model. Unique solutions are shown for the probability distribution ℙ and net probabilities *NP* (in parentheses) on the rankings. The shaded rankings have positive net probability. The inset table provides the pairwise net preference probabilities NP_{ab}, NP_{ac}, and NP_{bc}. The shaded pairwise net preference probabilities are positive. The (unique) majority preference relation is marked with a bold dotted frame.

of the solution space that do not yield net value restriction do have a net preference majority for some ordering. Two data sets fail to rule out majority cycles. Both of those data analyses suffer from much ambiguity regarding the possible/plausible majority preference relations in that each of them allows for seven different possible majority preference relations. No data set unambiguously suggests the presence of a majority cycle. These results (summarized in Table 4.2) further support the major claim of this book that majority cycles are much less important (theoretically and empirically) than the literature has suggested them to be.

4.3.2 Analyses Using the Topset Voting Model

The bottom part of Table 4.1 provides the approval voting scores. As mentioned earlier, the orderings by approval voting scores automatically match the majority preference relations according to the topset voting model. Since the topset voting model is statistically vacuous, we report only the most important results about the majority outcomes, such as our findings about net value restriction and net majority preference relations. Our probabilistic version of Sen's value restriction in terms of probability distributions over linear orders, introduced in Definition 1.2.8 of Chapter 1, does not apply here because the topset voting model assumes that individual preferences are weak orders. Instead, we check Sen's original value restriction on the weak order (relative) frequencies, and we find that none of the seven data sets satisfies Sen's value restriction. The majority outcomes are as follows.

TIMS E1: Through the lens of the topset voting model, this data set satisfies $NetNB(a)$, and the weak order $\{(b, a), (b, c)\}$ has a net preference majority. Either of these is sufficient to guarantee the absence of majority cycles. The majority preference relation is $b \succ c \succ a$.

TIMS E2: The topset voting model yields that this data set also satisfies $NetNB(a)$, this time with the weak order $\{(c, a), (c, b)\}$ having a net preference majority. The majority preference relation is $c \succ b \succ a$.

MAA 1: The topset voting model yields neither net value restriction nor net preference majority. Nevertheless, majority preferences form a strict linear order, namely $c \succ a \succ b$. This illustrates Theorem 2.3.8 which states that majority preferences can be transitive without either net value restriction or net majority holding.

MAA 2: According to the topset voting model, net value restriction is violated, but the weak order $\{(b, a), (b, c)\}$ has a net preference majority. The majority preference relation is $b \succ c \succ a$.

IEEE, SJDM, AND SSCW: The topset voting model, in all three cases, suggests that neither net value restriction nor net majority is satisfied. Nonetheless, the majority preference relation is a complete linear order, namely $a \succ b \succ c$ for IEEE, $b \succ a \succ c$ for SJDM, and $a \succ c \succ b$ for SSCW. Thus, these three elections give three more illustrations of the result in Theorem 2.3.8 that transitive majority preferences require neither net value restriction nor net majority as prerequisites.

These and related results are summarized in Table 4.2.

4.3.3 Model Dependence of Majority Outcomes, Net Value Restriction, and Net Majority

The overview of results, given in Table 4.2 for the size-independent model and the topset voting model, helps us to illustrate the problem of model dependence.

In six of the seven data sets, both models find Sen's value restriction (and its generalization to a.s. value restriction, in the size-independent model) violated. Even though the size-independent model usually does not uniquely pin down the majority ordering, the majority ordering found under the topset voting model always happens to match the majority ordering of the size-independent model associated with the largest range of values for τ. For MAA 2, we can pin down the entire majority ordering in a robust fashion, because it is unique across all values of τ and matches across models. For TIMS E1, TIMS E2, and MAA 1, we can pin down the majority loser in a very robust fashion, because it is unique across all values of τ and it matches across models. Even for SJDM, in the subspace where majority preferences are transitive, the majority loser is robust. In IEEE, we are able to pin down the majority winner in a robust fashion within the ranges of τ that guarantee transitivity. In SSCW we also pin down the majority winner in a robust fashion across the two models. Depending on whether we use linear orders (size-independent model) or weak orders (topset voting model), we find model dependent patterns of results for the (generalized) net value restriction and the net majority conditions.

Now consider the presence or absence of cycles. The topset voting model forces the absence of a cycle. However, more importantly, the analysis of the size-independent model suggests that our evidence against the presence of majority cycles in any of these elections is reasonably robust over possible values of τ (i.e., across many or all of the submodels of the size-independent model that are associated with particular values of τ).

4.4 DISCUSSION

This chapter provides further tools for the development of behavioral social choice theories. Here, we discuss methods for embedding the social choice analysis of subset choice data (where no paired comparisons or full rankings are directly observed) into a psychological representation of preferences and choice behavior. By formulating social choice concepts in terms of plausible (and, ideally, empirically testable) cognitive models of individual choice behavior, we take a model-based approach to the question of whether or not weak stochastic transitivity holds and whether or not a Condorcet winner exists in empirical subset choice data. We envisage future similar developments for a broad range of other empirical rating, ranking, or choice paradigms that also do not provide full rankings or all paired comparisons.

We have applied the two models presented here to seven three-candidate real or mock approval voting elections. In all seven instances the topset voting model necessarily fits the data, and in all seven cases the size-independent model satisfactorily fits, even though it need not fit all conceivable data. Thus, we are able to apply these techniques to test for the existence of a Condorcet winner and a transitive majority preference relation. Under the topset voting model we (automatically) find a transitive majority preference relation in every instance, even though it turns out that Sen's value restriction is never satisfied. Even net value restriction and the net majority conditions are both violated for four of our seven data sets under the topset voting model. Under the size-independent model we find five instances of unambiguously transitive majority preference relations and two cases which are ambiguous. Of the five unambiguous cases, in only one do we find (a.s.) value restriction holding. In the other four unambiguous cases, sometimes net majority, sometimes net value restriction, and sometimes both, account for the transitivity. The two ambiguous cases where we cannot rule out intransitive majority preferences under the size-independent model are ones with seven different possible majority outcomes. The most robust findings we report here are the absence of Sen's value restriction in six of the seven data sets, as well as the identity of the majority loser in most of the elections. The identity of the majority winner and the answers to questions about net value restriction and net majority turn out to be, by and large, model dependent.

We discuss both model dependence and robustness. The complexity of these issues is compounded by the fact that models are able to represent reality only to varying degrees. An inadequate model may erroneously fit a given set of data, and an adequate model may erroneously fail to fit a given set of data.[13] In particular, statistical models are always approximations to a complex reality. As a consequence, just because a testable model fails to be satisfied for some sets of data, this does not mean that we should discard that model in situations where it is able to account for the observed data. Similarly, even if a model is technically rejected by a given set

---

[13] For instance, sparse data sets may accidentally fail to generate data points that are inconsistent with the model, whereas extremely large data sets tend to generate excessive statistical power, i.e., a tendency to overemphasize slight discrepancies between predicted and observed data. Since virtually every model is necessarily an imperfect reflection of a more complex reality, we can virtually always get a model statistically rejected by collecting a sufficiently large sample of data. Conversely, even if a model fits empirical data adequately, we know always that the model may still be only an idealization of a more complex reality.

of data, the majority preferences (or other quantities of interest) derived through the lens of that model may nevertheless be a good approximation of reality. In that latter case, we would say that the majority preferences (or other quantities) are robust under model violations. For instance, we know that the independence assumptions entering the size-independent model are probably unrealistic. Nevertheless, in our opinion, the majority preferences inferred through the size-independent model may still be robust under model violations, in the sense that a slightly more realistic model (but still formulated in terms of linear order preferences) is unlikely to dramatically change our results.[14] For an excellent overview of model estimation and testing for discrete data, as well as methodological issues arising in that context, see, for instance, Bishop et al. (1975).

In the next chapter we consider a statistical sampling and inference framework for majority relations. This framework allows us to place upper and lower bounds on the probability of majority cycles and any other possible majority outcomes, based on "pairwise margins" among candidates. Throughout all previous chapters we make theoretical and empirical points showing that majority cycles do not pose the overwhelming threat that they are commonly suggested to pose. The statistical sampling and inference framework in Chapter 5 allows us to move to what we see as a much more important issue, namely the question of whether or not majority outcomes generated under conditions of uncertainty, such as sampling, are 'correct' or 'incorrect' majority outcomes. We develop a methodology to determine the sample size required for the majority preference relation in a sample of that size to accurately reflect the majority preference of the population (that the sample was drawn from) at any level of confidence. Vice versa, for any given sample size we quantify the confidence we can have that the majority preference in that sample matches the majority preference in the population that the sample is meant to reflect.

---

[14] Parallel issues arise in investigations of majority/plurality preferences of different racial and ethnic groups in real-world elections, where data on individual preference rankings are not available and must be inferred from demographic and election outcome information about aggregation units, such as voting precincts (Grofman, 1991, 1995, 2000; Grofman and Merrill, 2004, 2005). These authors have also looked at model dependence in other contexts, e.g., see Grofman (2004).

III

A GENERAL STATISTICAL SAMPLING AND BAYESIAN INFERENCE FRAMEWORK

5

Majority Rule in a Statistical Sampling and Bayesian Inference Framework

Chapter Summary

This chapter presents theoretical and empirical results concerning majority rule both in a statistical sampling and a Bayesian inference framework. For instance, suppose we have a population of preference relations, and a random sample (taken with replacement) of preference relations from that population. Using the term majority preference relation as in Chapter 2, we call a sample majority preference relation the *correct majority relation* whenever it matches the population majority preference relation, and otherwise we call it an *incorrect majority relation*. Based on any given paired comparison or ranking probabilities in the population (i.e., culture) of reference, we derive upper and lower bounds on the probability of a correct (respectively, incorrect) majority preference relation in a random sample (with replacement) from that population. Using Bayesian updating, we also present upper and lower bounds on the probabilities of majority preference relations in the population given a sample. These bounds enable a quite precise understanding of the possible majority preference relations (cycles or not) as well as their probabilities.

This work is closely related to the concept of Condorcet efficiency: The *Condorcet efficiency* of a social choice procedure is often operationalized as the probability that the procedure yields the majority winner (or majority ordering) in random samples, given that a majority winner exists (or given that the majority ordering is transitive) in such random samples. Consequently, the Condorcet efficiency is in effect a conditional probability that two sample statistics coincide, given certain side conditions. We raise a different issue of Condorcet efficiencies:

What is the probability that the outcome of a social choice procedure, applied to a sample, matches the majority winner of the population from which the sample was drawn? We apply the same logic to majority preferences.

We think of sampling in a broad sense: Data generated or gathered under conditions of uncertainty need to be thought of as a sample (possibly biased) from some underlying distribution. We show that, for real-world social choice data, preference misestimation, i.e., situations where a sampling process generates observed choices that are different from the (majority) preferences of the population, is a far more important phenomenon than cycles. We demonstrate this fact by looking at the likelihood of both cycles and incorrect majority preference outcomes in samples drawn from a number of real-world data sets, including U.S. and French presidential elections and German legislative elections involving three or more candidates or parties. We find no evidence of cycles in any of the populations we examine. Using these data, we show that the potential for incorrect assessments and inferences about majority preferences or candidate/party rankings derived from sampling dramatically overwhelms the potential for obtaining sample majority cycles. The latter has previously been the sole concern of social choice theorists interested in sampling models.

Moreover, consistent with points made in Chapter 1, we develop theoretical results that show that we need not worry much about majority cycles when dealing with realistic distributions, especially if our sample is very large. However, we do need to worry about misestimation, especially when dealing with heterogeneous groups and small sets of data. We also show that variations in preference homogeneity among 'stratified' population subsamples (e.g., Communist-leaning voters in France) have important consequences for the relative importance of preference misestimation and cycles.

The chapter is organized as follows: Section 5.1 introduces the general notion of majority rule in a sampling framework, by moving from the impartial culture and related distributional assumptions to arbitrary distributions on binary relations. Section 5.2 discusses how our approach relates to the issue of Condorcet efficiency. Section 5.3 moves from sampling to Bayesian inference, in which we take a set of data as a given and attempt to make inferences about the majority preferences in the population from which the data originated. Section 5.4 provides various empirical illustrations, using real world survey data, by estimating the probabilities of various majority outcomes in a sample, given a known population, or in a population, given known data. The chapter concludes with a discussion in Section 5.5.

5.1 MAJORITY RULE IN A GENERAL SAMPLING FRAMEWORK

Arrow's *Impossibility Theorem* (1951, 1963) shows that it is impossible to find a deterministic universal preference aggregation method for a finite set of voters that satisfies a certain set of simple axioms of rationality.[1] Thus, every (deterministic) preference aggregation rule requires paying a price in terms of violating one or more of Arrow's axioms. One possible price to pay for using majority rule is to violate the axiom of transitivity: majority rule preferences need not be transitive.[2] In order to be able to weigh this cost by its probability, researchers have investigated the theoretical probability and the empirical frequency of majority cycles.

As we discuss in Chapter 1, one of the most influential strands of research along those lines has been the impartial culture work that investigates the effect of sample size and number of candidates on the probability of majority rule cycles in samples drawn from a uniform distribution (DeMeyer and Plott, 1970; Gehrlein, 1988; Jones et al., 1995). In Chapter 1, we already make a case against the use of the impartial culture assumption. We now investigate what happens in random samples drawn from (almost) arbitrary distributions, not just the impartial culture. Besides moving away from the impartial culture, however, we also shift our focus from cycles to other issues that we believe are more important.

Suppose that a society uses majority rule as defined in Chapter 2. We already make the case in other chapters that majority cycles are very unlikely. Suppose that, nevertheless, a cycle is observed and that this cycle prevents the existence of a Condorcet winner.[3] Then this means that a social choice by majority rule is, in effect, prevented or postponed and that

---

[1] These axioms are commonly referred to as *collective rationality, unrestricted domain, the Pareto property, independence of irrelevant alternatives,* and *nondictatorship.* Later work shows that one can avoid the impossibility result either by generalizing the approach to *nondeterministic* methods, leading to a *probabilistic dictator* (Pattanaik and Peleg, 1986; Tangiane, 1991), or by considering an infinite set of voters (Fishburn, 1970a).

[2] However, another possible price to pay is to drop Arrow's "unrestricted domain" requirement. As we argue in this book, the latter is a very attractive option, since many distributions of preferences, while being well-defined distributions, are descriptively implausible and unattractive candidates for a behavioral theory of preference distributions in mass electorates.

[3] Of course, if there are more than three candidates, cycles are conceivable that do not involve the candidates 'at the top' of the majority preference relation.

majority rule may need to be replaced by some other procedure.[4] To us there exist potentially more dramatic costs to society than a social choice by majority rule being prevented and decision making being delayed by the need to use some other procedure. The potential for a much more severe cost to society arises when there is a possibility that decisions are based on incorrect assessments of the majority preference relation. This cost is compounded when the incorrect assessment remains unnoticed and/or uncorrected. For example, during the 2000 U.S. presidential election, the world was transfixed for several weeks with the question of whether the 'correct' presidential candidate would receive a majority of the electoral college vote.

We do not know of any empirical work on the frequency of 'incorrect' election outcomes. Indeed, the 2000 election controversy has largely been regarded as a unique event rather than as a reason to view election ballots and tallies as inherently probabilistic in nature. In this chapter we view ballot casting and tallying as probabilistic processes and we investigate the simplest nontrivial case where the recorded ballot counts can be thought of as resulting from a random sample from an underlying population. We emphasize that any process with an uncertain real-valued outcome is, by definition, a real random variable. Whenever several independent observations (with replacement, or without replacement in the case of a very large population) of such a random variable are drawn, this set of observations is a random sample. In particular, to the extent that mistakes in the ballot casting and vote tally processes occur independently and with fixed probabilities, they can be conceptualized as the results of a random sampling process.

We develop methods for evaluating the likelihoods of correct and incorrect assessments of majority rule preferences (as well as the likelihood of cycles) for any given number of ballots. Similarly, we also provide methods for evaluating the number of ballots needed to assess the correct majority preference with any given level of (statistical) confidence.

Whenever we draw a random sample from a population, we refer to the population majority preference relation as the *correct majority preference relation*. (This relation may or may not be known.) Whenever the majority preference relation in a sample does not match the majority preference relation in the population that the sample was drawn from, we call the sample majority preference relation an *incorrect majority preference*

---

[4] For example, Black (1958) proposed using the Borda score whenever a majority cycle makes it impossible to elect a majority winner.

relation. We provide the conceptual framework and the mathematical tools to evaluate the probability of a correct or incorrect majority preference relation in a random sample from a given population. We also discuss correct and incorrect inferences about population majority preferences extrapolated from sample data. This methodology may provide some helpful tools for election officials, observers, and, ultimately, society to assess the probability that a decision correctly reflects the population's majority preferences.[5]

We rely on the general concept of majority rule introduced in Chapter 2, which is applicable to virtually any kind of preference, choice, ranking, or rating data. As we show in that chapter, we lose no generality by assuming that the preferences of a population are accurately captured by a probability distribution over asymmetric binary relations. As we also discuss in earlier chapters, obvious special cases are when individual preferences are linear orders or strict weak orders. Using a basic property of probabilities of joint events, we derive upper and lower bounds on the probability of any possible majority ordering in a sample, given a population distribution. It turns out that this seemingly innocuous approach yields surprisingly strong results: Whenever the population majorities are not tied, the upper and lower bounds on the sample majority preference probabilities are very tight, even for relatively small sample sizes. The analogue holds for population majority preferences, given sample data.

Our approach contrasts with the commonly studied case of drawing random samples from the impartial culture. The latter can be thought of as an example of the sampling problem where the population has a uniform distribution over preference relations, and thus the population majority is completely tied.[6] Our tools put virtually no constraint on the type of binary relations (or utility functions) that represent individual preferences, and we place no constraint on the possible distributions of individual preferences. In contrast, the distributional assumptions in the recent literature, e.g., the maximal culture condition over linear orders (Gehrlein and Lepelley, 1999), the impartial weak order condition (Gehrlein and

---

[5] This statement applies regardless of whether the society's majority preference relation is transitive or not. Of course, it is not desirable to have a transitive majority preference in a sample when the population majority is cyclic. Even if a cycle (in the sample) effectively prevents a social choice by majority rule, and may force the consideration of other decision processes, such as the Borda count, that cycle is valuable as a portrait of society's distribution of preferences (if the cycle is indeed the correct majority preference).

[6] As before, we use the term *population* in the statistical sense. We think of a *culture* as a special case of a population.

Valognes, 2001), the existence of cardinal utilities (Tangian, 2000), or the impartial culture over weak orders (Van Deemen, 1999) are extremely restrictive. However, we do assume that data are obtained by random sampling.

Following Van Deemen's (1999) recommendation, our illustrations are based on realistic distributions. We construct probability distributions from observed relative frequencies in real-world survey data. Our method of bounds yields general and important theoretical results because it does not depend on constraining theoretical assumptions about voter preferences. On the contrary, recall that we consider an extremely broad domain of permissible preference states. As we show in our empirical illustrations, this method of bounds often allows us to infer properties of the population with surprising accuracy, for moderate to large sample sizes. Moreover, when we have groups with very homogeneous preferences (i.e., large pairwise margins), the method yields extremely precise results, even for remarkably small samples.

5.1.1 Pairwise Majority in a Sample Drawn from a Given (Population) Probability Distribution over Binary Relations

As previously, we assume a fixed finite set C of choice alternatives, candidates, parties, or consumption bundles. A binary relation on C is a set $B \subseteq C \times C$ of ordered pairs of elements in C. If B is a binary relation describing a person's state of preference, and $(a, b) \in B$, then this person prefers a to b. In other words, this person finds that a is *better than b*, and we also frequently write this as $a B b$. See Chapter 2 and Appendix B for details about the notation, axioms, definitions, and interpretation of binary relations. To ease the notation, we denote alternatives, candidates, and political parties in this chapter with small letters.

We assume throughout this chapter that the possible states of preference form a collection $\mathcal{B}$ of asymmetric binary relations over C. We are interested in situations where the distribution of individual preferences over a population can be conceptualized as a probability distribution over $\mathcal{B}$. We discuss the use of probabilistic representations in more detail in Chapter 2. Here we emphasize three key circumstances in which such a probabilistic framework may be called for:

1. Relative frequencies are a special case of a probability measure, and thus the proportion of people out of a given group that have a

particular state of preference can be quantified with a probability measure on the set of possible states of preference.

2. It is often the case that people experience uncertainty as to their own preferences, and thus any preference statements they provide may be generated through an internal sampling process (Burden, 1997; Mackelprang et al., 1975). Important examples of probabilistic models relevant to such issues are Luce's choice model (Luce, 1959, 1977), Tversky's elimination by aspects model (Tversky, 1972), Thurstonian (normal) models (Thurstone, 1927a,b), generalized extreme value models (Ben-Akiva and Lerman, 1985; McFadden, 1998), and various other types of random utility models (Barberá and Pattanaik, 1986; Falmagne, 1978; Fishburn, 1992). Marley (1989a,b) presents an integrative framework that includes various of these models as special cases.

3. The same models are often alternatively interpreted as capturing the researcher's uncertainty about the (possibly deterministic) preferences of a group of respondents rather than the uncertainty of the respondents themselves.

Each of these scenarios allows us to describe the overall distribution of preferences in a population by a single probability distribution over preference relations.

In this and the next subsection, we study properties of random samples drawn from a given population preference distribution. As in Chapter 1, p_B denotes the probability of the relation $B \in \mathcal{B}$ in the population. For example, suppose for a moment that $B = abc$, a complete linear ranking where a is single best, and c is single worst. Then $p_B = p_{abc}$ and, in a sampling framework, this denotes the probability that a person drawn at random from the population has the linear preference order abc. For any $\mathcal{R} \subseteq \mathcal{B}$, we write $p_\mathcal{R}$ for the sum of all p_B, $B \in \mathcal{R}$. To make the notation more readable, we write p_{aBb} for $p_\mathcal{R}$ when $\mathcal{R} = \{B \in \mathcal{B} \text{ such that } aBb\}$. So, for example, in the case of complete linear orders of 3 candidates (without indifference), $p_{aBb} = p_{abc} + p_{acb} + p_{cab}$. We use the analogous notation for the observed frequency of each binary relation in a sample, e.g., $N_{aBb} = N_{abc} + N_{acb} + N_{cab}$ (for complete rankings over 3 candidates without indifference). As before, we use boldface letters to denote random variables and regular font to denote numbers.

We assume throughout the chapter that sampling is done independently (and, in particular, with replacement). Therefore, the sampling distribution of preference relations has a multinomial distribution.[7] We first derive the sampling probability $P(N_{aBb} > N_{bBa})$ that a is preferred to b by a (strict) majority (consistent with the definitions of $\succ$ in Definition 1.2.5, and Definition 2.1.3), in a sample of size N, given the probabilities of all binary relations (i.e., p_B, $B \in \mathcal{B}$) in the population.[8] If there are no indifferences in the population, i.e., $B \cup B^{-1} = \mathcal{C} \times \mathcal{C}$, for all $B \in \mathcal{B}$, then $N_{aBb} + N_{bBa} = N$, and N_{aBb} has a binomial distribution with number of trials N and probability of success p_{aBb}.

Before we study that distribution, we introduce some further notation. Let $f_{Bin}(X, N, p)$ denote the probability that the binomial random variable X equals X, with number of trials N and probability of success p, and let $F_{Bin}(X, N, p)$ denote its cumulative distribution, i.e.,

$$F_{Bin}(X, N, p) = \sum_{i=0}^{X} \frac{N!}{i!(N-i)!} p^i (1-p)^{N-i} = \sum_{i=0}^{X} f_{Bin}(i, N, p).$$

Also, to deal with even and odd N, we use the *floor* of $\frac{N}{2}$, defined standardly as

$$\left\lfloor \frac{N}{2} \right\rfloor = \begin{cases} \frac{N}{2} & \text{if } N \text{ is even,} \\ \frac{N-1}{2} & \text{if } N \text{ is odd.} \end{cases} \tag{5.1}$$

As in Chapter 1, we write aEb if and only if $(a, b) \notin B$, $(b, a) \notin B$, and so aEb denotes the situation where a and b are *equivalent* (hence the notation). A person in this state of preference has no preference either way, i.e., s/he is indifferent between the two options.[9]

Returning to the probability that a is preferred to b by a majority in a sample, with replacement, of size N, we obtain that, if indifference (i.e., aEb) is allowed, then $p_{aBb} + p_{aEb} + p_{bBa} = 1$, and $N_{aBb} \mid N_{aEb}$ (i.e., N_{aBb} given N_{aEb}) has a binomial distribution with number of trials $N - N_{aEb}$ and probability of success $\frac{p_{aBb}}{p_{aBb}+p_{bBa}}$.[10] The following proposition is immediate.

---

[7] Other sampling schemes that have been studied before, such as "anonymous preference profiles," can lead to distributions other than the multinomial (Berg, 1985; Berg and Bjurulf, 1983; Gehrlein and Fishburn, 1976a).

[8] Recall that in Chapter 2 we project all binary relations down to their asymmetric parts. Notice also that a is strictly majority preferred to b in the sample if and only if $N_{aBb} > N_{bBa}$, regardless of the value of N_{aEb}.

[9] Of course, since we only consider asymmetric relations, we always have aEa for any choice of a, and thus automatically $p_{aEa} = 1$.

[10] Conditioning on N_{aEb} is equivalent to conditioning on $N - N_{aEb}$.

Proposition 5.1.1 *The probability that a is preferred to b by a strict majority in a sample of size N is given by*

$$P(N_{aBb} > N_{bBa})$$

$$= \sum_{N_{aEb}=0}^{N} \left(\begin{array}{l} f_{Bin}(N_{aEb}, N, p_{aEb}) \\ \qquad \times \ \left(1 - F_{Bin}\left(\left\lfloor \frac{N-N_{aEb}}{2} \right\rfloor, N - N_{aEb}, \frac{p_{aBb}}{p_{aBb}+p_{bBa}} \right) \right) \end{array} \right).$$

$$(5.2)$$

Furthermore, for preferences without indifference, i.e., $p_{aEb} = 0, a \neq b$, the probability that a is preferred to b by a strict majority in a sample of size N is given by

$$P(N_{aBb} > N_{bBa}) = 1 - F_{Bin}\left(\left\lfloor \frac{N}{2} \right\rfloor, N, p_{aBb} \right).$$

$$(5.3)$$

It is important to note that Proposition 5.1.1 is valid for any number of candidates and regardless of the exact nature of the asymmetric preference relations in $\mathcal{B}$. More specifically, Equation (5.2) applies to the full unconstrained domain of feasible (without loss of generality, asymmetric) binary preference relations (and other representations considered in Chapter 2), whereas Equation (5.3) utilizes what is tantamount to a domain restriction, namely that individual preferences among the pair a, b are complete (with probability one).[11]

5.1.2 Upper and Lower Bounds on the Probabilities of Majority Preference Relations Based on Probabilities of Pairwise Majorities

We now show how to evaluate the probability that any given complete, asymmetric binary relation $\succ \subseteq \mathcal{C} \times \mathcal{C}$ is the majority preference relation, when we know for each pair (a, b) the probability that a is strictly majority preferred to b. Here, we discuss the approach in a sampling framework, and in Section 5.3 we discuss the same method in a Bayesian inference framework.

Suppose we know p_{aBb} and p_{aEb} (and hence p_{bBa}) of the population distribution, for each pair (a, b). Then Equation (5.2) provides the probability $P(N_{aBb} > N_{bBa})$ that a is strictly majority preferred to b in a sample (of size N) drawn from the population.

---

[11] See Appendix B for the relevant definitions.

We first point out (without proof) a basic property of the probability of a joint event.

Proposition 5.1.2 *For any collection of events $A_1, A_2, \ldots, A_K$, the probability of the joint event $A = A_1 \cap A_2 \cap \ldots \cap A_K$ has the following upper and lower bounds:*

$$\max \left(0, 1 - \sum_{i=1}^{K} \left(1 - P(A_i) \right) \right) \leq P(A) \leq \min_i P(A_i). \tag{5.4}$$

Later, we exploit the simple fact that if the probabilities of some events A_i are close to 0 or 1, then these bounds may become very close to each other, and therefore they may become very good approximations for the probability of the joint event.

We write $\succ_p$ for the majority preference relation in a population and $\succ_s$ for the majority preference relation in a sample when these preferences are known or given, and we write $\succ_p$ and $\succ_s$ for the corresponding majority preference relations when they are the result of a random process. Throughout this subsection we focus on the case where $\succ_p$ is a complete asymmetric relation.

We assume for now that $a \succ_p b$, i.e., a is strictly majority preferred to b in the population. Writing $\delta_{aBb} = p_{aBb} - p_{bBa}$, we see that the assumption $a \succ_p b$ is equivalent to the assumption that $\delta_{aBb} > 0$. We refer to δ_{aBb} as the *pairwise margin* (for pairwise comparisons) of a over b in the population. Notice that in Chapters 1 and 2 we call this the "pairwise net probability" and denote it by NP_{ab}. Since this probability enters as a parameter here, we avoid the earlier notation.

Let $Err(N, \delta_{aBb}, p_{aEb}) = P(N_{bBa} \geq N_{aBb}) = 1 - P(N_{aBb} > N_{bBa})$ denote the probability that b is erroneously majority preferred to or tied with a in a sample of size N, contrary to the majority preference relation $a \succ_p b$ between alternatives a and b in the population. We can now state an obvious result.

Proposition 5.1.3 *Equation (5.2) implies that*

$$Err(N, \delta_{aBb}, p_{aEb})$$
$$= \sum_{i=0}^{N} f_{Bin}(i, N, p_{aEb}) \, F_{Bin} \left(\left\lfloor \frac{N-i}{2} \right\rfloor, N-i, \frac{\delta_{aBb} + 1 - p_{aEb}}{2(1 - p_{aEb})} \right).$$
$$\tag{5.5}$$

TABLE 5.1: *Sample Size, as a Function of the Pairwise Margin δ_{aBb} and Probability of Indifference p_{aEb}, Sufficient for $Err(N, \delta_{aBb}, p_{aEb})$ to be Less Than 0.1%*

$\delta_{aBb} \setminus p_{aEb}$	0.0	0.1	0.2	0.3	0.4	0.5	0.6	0.7	0.8	0.9
0.9	7	3								
0.8	9	8	5							
0.7	15	13	10	6						
0.6	21	20	17	13	8					
0.5	33	31	27	22	17	10				
0.4	55	51	45	38	31	24	14			
0.3	101	94	83	72	60	49	36	20		
0.2	235	215	191	166	142	117	92	65	31	
0.1	951	865	769	673	577	480	384	286	186	66

If no preferences with indifference are allowed in the population (i.e., if $p_{aEb} = 0$), then (5.3) implies that

$$Err(N, \delta_{aBb}, 0) = F_{Bin}\left(\left\lfloor \frac{N}{2} \right\rfloor, N, \frac{1 + \delta_{aBb}}{2}\right). \tag{5.6}$$

Again, Equation (5.5) applies to the full unconstrained domain of feasible (without loss of generality, asymmetric) binary preference relations, whereas Equation (5.6) utilizes what is tantamount to a domain restriction, namely that individual preferences among the pair a, b are complete (with probability one).

We also write $Err(N, \delta_{aBb})$ for $Err(N, \delta_{aBb}, 0)$. Obviously, $Err(N, \delta)$ is strictly decreasing in $\delta > 0$ and N (separately for odd and even N) and approaches 0 for $N \to \infty$. The risk $Err(N, \delta_{aBb}, p_{aEb})$ of an error regarding a, b is strictly decreasing as p_{aEb} increases. This means, in particular, that $Err(N, \delta_{aBb}, p_{aEb}) < Err(N, \delta_{aBb}, 0) = Err(N, \delta_{aBb})$.

Table 5.1 shows the sufficient sample size for $Err(N, \delta_{aBb}, p_{aBb})$ to be less than 0.1% for various values of δ_{aBb} and p_{aBb}. For instance, assume that indifference is ruled out, and that $p_{aBb} = .55 = 1 - .45 = 1 - p_{bBa}$. Then, $\delta_{aBb} = .10$, that is, a has a margin of ten percentage points over b in the population, and we need to sample at least 951 observations (with replacement) in order to be at least 99.9% sure that the sample will not accidentally contain a (reversed) majority preference of b over a.

On the other hand, if 30% of the population is indifferent between a and b, and the remaining 70% is split into 40% of the population preferring a over b and 30% preferring b over a (i.e., a still has a margin of 10 percentage points over b), then a sample size of 673 observations is sufficient to be 99.9% certain that a random sample yields the correct majority preference for the pair a, b, namely that a is strictly majority preferred to b.

For large enough N the multinomial distribution is approximated by a multivariate normal distribution, and we can use a normal approximation of (5.5). Define *adjusted pairwise margins* δ^*_{aBb} as

$$\delta^*_{aBb} = \frac{\delta_{aBb}}{\sqrt{1 - p_{aEb} - \delta^2_{aBb}}}, \tag{5.7}$$

and let $F_N(x)$ be the standard normal cumulative distribution function. Then, for large enough N, the normal approximation of $Err(N, \delta_{aBb}, p_{aEb})$ is given by the quantity $Err_N(N, \delta^*_{aBb})$, defined as

$$Err_N(N, \delta^*_{aBb}) = F_N\left(-\sqrt{N}\delta^*_{aBb}\right) = F_N\left(-\sqrt{N}\frac{\delta_{aBb}}{\sqrt{1 - p_{aEb} - \delta^2_{aBb}}}\right). \tag{5.8}$$

Note that Err_N approaches zero as N approaches infinity. (For an illustration, see Table 5.4.)

We now apply the method of bounds of Proposition 5.1.2 to the probabilities of possible majority relations in a sample. For m alternatives, let $M = \frac{m(m-1)}{2}$ denote the total number of pairwise margins. From the properties of the multinomial distribution or, alternatively, from (5.8), it follows that, as N goes to infinity, the probability of obtaining the correct majority relation in the sample goes to 1, provided the pairwise margins are nonzero. Notice that, from this perspective, the impartial culture assumption has a rather odd feature in that it is *impossible* for a random sample of any odd size to match the majority preference relation of the population.

Now index all adjusted pairwise margins (given by (5.7)) in such a way that $\delta^*_1 \leq \delta^*_2 \cdots \leq \delta^*_M$. Consider the case when there is a unique minimal adjusted pairwise margin i.e., $\delta^*_1 < \delta^*_2$, and let (a, b) be the pair such that $\delta^*_1 = \delta^*_{aBb}$, with $a \succ_p b$. Let $\succ^* = \left(\succ_p \cup\{(b, a)\}\right)\backslash\{(a, b)\}$, i.e., $\succ^*$ agrees with $\succ_p$, except that, while $a \succ_p b$, we have $b \succ^* a$. Then, using (5.8), we obtain the following theorem.

Theorem 5.1.4 *If a unique minimal adjusted pairwise margin exists, then the following holds, with $\succ^*$ defined as above.*

$$\lim_{N\to\infty} P(\succ_S = \succ^* \mid \succ_S \neq \succ_p) = 1.$$

In words, for large enough sample size the only 'possible' incorrect (sample) majority relation is the majority relation $\succ^* = \Big(\succ_p \cup\{(b,a)\}\Big)\backslash\{(a,b)\}$ in which for all pairs, except the pair (a,b) with the smallest pairwise margin, the majority preference relation is the same as in the population.

The proof is in Appendix C. Intuitively, the theorem follows from the fact that the reversal of the majority relation over the candidate pair with the smallest pairwise margin is more likely than the reversal of the majority relation over one or more other pairs of candidates. The relevance of this theorem can be seen in Figure 5.2 and Table 5.3 and is discussed below.

A case of particular interest involves the following property.

Definition 5.1.5 *Moderate stochastic transitivity with strict inequalities* holds in the population if

$$\left.\begin{array}{r}\delta^*_{aBb} > 0 \\ \delta^*_{bBc} > 0\end{array}\right\} \Rightarrow \delta^*_{aBc} > \min(\delta^*_{aBb}, \delta^*_{bBc}) \qquad (\forall a, b, c \in \mathcal{C}).$$

This property is similar to *moderate stochastic transitivity* (Luce and Suppes, 1965), which has each strict inequality sign replaced by weak inequality sign ($\geq$), and which is applied to the pairwise margins, with indifference (usually) ruled out.

Theorem 5.1.6 *If moderate stochastic transitivity with strict inequalities holds in the population, then for any sufficiently large (finite) sample drawn from this population the next most probable majority preference relation after the population majority preference relation is a transitive one.*

The proof is in Appendix C.

Notice that, of course, the next most probable majority preference relation, after the population majority relation, has probability zero when the population is unanimous.

Before we move from sampling to inference, we comment on the relationship of this work to the concept of Condorcet efficiency.

5.2 THE CONDORCET EFFICIENCY OF MAJORITY RULE

The Condorcet efficiency of social choice functions remains a topic of great interest in the contemporary social choice literature (Gehrlein, 1999; Gehrlein and Lepelley, 1999, 2001; Gehrlein and Valognes, 2001; Lepelley et al., 2000). The basic idea behind this concept is to use majority rule as a benchmark to evaluate the outcomes of other social choice functions.

One of the best known social choice functions, besides majority rule, is a method attributed to Borda. The *Borda score* of a candidate in an individual ranking is $n - i$ when there are n candidates and the candidate is at rank i in that individual ranking. The Borda score of a candidate over a set of ranking ballots is the sum of Borda scores over all ballots. The *Borda winner* is the candidate with the highest Borda score. A *Borda loser* is the candidate with the lowest Borda score. Similarly, a *Condorcet loser* is a candidate a, if s/he exists, who loses against all other candidates in the majority preference relation $\succ$, i.e., $x \succ a, \forall x \neq a$.

The Condorcet efficiency of the Borda score is typically operationalized as the probability that the Borda winner coincides with the Condorcet (majority) winner, given that a unique Condorcet winner exists. Related concepts of Condorcet efficiency for the example of the Borda score are, among others: (i) the probability that the Borda loser is the Condorcet loser, given that a unique Condorcet loser exists; (ii) the probability that the ordering according to Borda scores is the same as the ordering according to majority rule, given that this majority ordering is transitive.

We make three important observations:

1. The Condorcet efficiency (of any social choice function) is operationalized as a conditional probability.
2. The Condorcet efficiency is usually derived from a hypothetical probability distribution over the actual preferences. This hypothetical distribution has often been taken to be a uniform distribution over a (possibly constrained) set of preference relations, e.g., the impartial culture on linear or weak orders discussed in Chapter 1.
3. The event in question, namely that the Borda (or other social choice function) outcome coincides with the Condorcet outcome, is the outcome of a random sampling process from the given hypothetical distribution.

More abstractly, the Condorcet efficiency of any social choice function (SCF) is usually operationalized as the (conditional) probability that the

SCF and majority rule coincide in samples from some specified probability distribution over preference relations, given that the sample majority preference is not degenerate (i.e., given that it is transitive or given that it has a unique top element). The prototypical case is the conditional probability that an SCF (such as that given by plurality, Borda, approval voting, the single transferable vote, or anti-plurality) elects the Condorcet winner, given that a unique Condorcet winner exists. To calculate such a (conditional) probability requires assuming a probability distribution that underlies the calculation. The most common assumption is that the underlying preferences are distributed according to a uniform distribution over some set of preference relations (impartial culture). In statistical terms, the standard definition of Condorcet efficiency is therefore the conditional probability that two sample statistics, namely the sample SCF outcome and the sample majority outcome, coincide, conditioned upon the event that the sample majority outcome satisfies certain conditions (unique Condorcet winner, or transitivity, etc.), in samples drawn from a specified distribution over preference relations.

Our approach here differs from previous work in two key respects: (1) We draw the reader's attention to a different type of Condorcet efficiency, namely the probability that various sample statistics based on an SCF coincide with the population majority preferences of the population that the sample of a given size was drawn from. (2) In line with Van Deemen (1999), we move from stylized theoretical a priori distributions to a very broad class of theoretical distributions (which are not cultures of indifference) and to 'realistic' distributions of preferences, i.e., distributions that are inspired by real world survey data.

We investigate the canonical case of the sample majority winner and the sample majority preference ordering being the two statistics under consideration. At first sight, it might appear that large samples would automatically have the same majority preferences as the distribution from which they are drawn. However, the standard literature on random samples from the impartial culture (on linear orders) proves the contrary. In the impartial culture, the majority preference relation is a complete tie, which even large samples of odd size can never recover. In other words, the most frequently studied case of odd size samples from the impartial culture is an example of a sampling process which entirely fails to correctly represent the underlying population, even as sample size goes to infinity, because it rules out a majority tie in the sample.

Thus, even in the limit, it is not entirely obvious how sampling affects the likelihood of accurate representation of majority preferences. For finite samples of the size we typically encounter in reality, the effect of sampling is far from trivial. As we show in Table 5.1, the accuracy of samples of different sizes is closely related to the values of the pairwise margins and, for any fixed sample size, varies dramatically across distributions.[12]

5.3 MAJORITY RULE IN A BAYESIAN INFERENCE FRAMEWORK

In the previous two sections we discuss majority rule outcomes in random samples from known populations. We now turn to the inverse problem of drawing inferences about a population from data. Suppose that we have a random sample of size N of asymmetric binary preference relations, and we want to draw an inference about the probability of majority winners and majority preference relations in the population from which the sample was drawn.

The natural approach is a Bayesian updating framework. Here, any possible population probability distribution over a collection of finite binary relations $\mathcal{B}$ is conceptualized as a set of values $p = (p_B)_{B \in \mathcal{B}}$ with the restriction that $\sum_{B \in \mathcal{B}} p_B = 1$. The numbers p_B are the parameters of a multinomial distribution. In order to take into account the uncertainty in the values of these parameters, we consider a family of jointly distributed random variables $\boldsymbol{p} = (\boldsymbol{p}_B)_{B \in \mathcal{B}}$ satisfying the constraint that $\sum_{B \in \mathcal{B}} \boldsymbol{p}_B = 1$ (everywhere). The distribution of $\boldsymbol{p}$ captures the probability that $\boldsymbol{p}$ takes any particular parameter values. In particular, we are interested in the probability that the population exhibits any particular majority preference relation $\succ$ for a given set of data. This translates into finding the probability

$$P(\succ_{\boldsymbol{p}} = \succ) = P\left(\left[\bigcap_{a \succ b} \boldsymbol{p}_{aBb} > \boldsymbol{p}_{bBa}\right] \cap \left[\bigcap_{c \not\succ d} \boldsymbol{p}_{cBd} \leq \boldsymbol{p}_{dBc}\right]\right). \quad (5.9)$$

Clearly, $\succ$ has to be asymmetric, since otherwise $P(\succ_{\boldsymbol{p}} = \succ) = 0$. If, furthermore, $\succ$ is complete, then (5.9) reduces to

$$P(\succ_{\boldsymbol{p}} = \succ) = P\left(\bigcap_{a \succ b} \boldsymbol{p}_{aBb} > \boldsymbol{p}_{bBa}\right). \quad (5.10)$$

The first step towards finding the probability in Equation (5.10) is to estimate the distribution of $\boldsymbol{p}$ given the sample $D = (N_B)_{B \in \mathcal{B}}$, i.e., $P(\boldsymbol{p} \mid D)$. Following a general Bayesian approach (e.g., Heckerman, 1998), Bayes'

---

[12] We hinted already at the importance of pairwise margins in Section 1.4.

formula yields

$$P(D \cap p) = P(D \mid p)P(p) = P(p \mid D)P(D).$$

Here $P(p)$ is the prior probability density of the jointly distributed random variables p (before observing the data), i.e., an assumption about this distribution or prior information, and $P(p \mid D)$ is the posterior probability density of p (after observing the sample of data), i.e., it is the distribution that we wish to estimate.

Clearly, $P(D \mid p)$ is a multinomial distribution given by

$$P(D \mid p) = \frac{N!}{\prod\limits_{B \in \mathcal{B}} N_B!} \prod_{B \in \mathcal{B}} p_B^{N_B}, \qquad \sum_{B \in \mathcal{B}} N_B = N.$$

This leads us to the following proposition (stated without the routine proof).

Proposition 5.3.1 *The posterior distribution* $P(p \mid D)$ *is given by*

$$P(p \mid D) = \frac{P(D \mid p)P(p)}{P(D)} = \frac{P(p)}{P(D)} \frac{N!}{\prod\limits_{B \in \mathcal{B}} N_B!} \prod_{B \in \mathcal{B}} p_B^{N_B}$$

$$= constant * P(p) \prod_{B \in \mathcal{B}} p_B^{N_B},$$

where "constant" is given by the normalization condition: $\int P(p \mid D)dp = 1$.

Now it is time to make an assumption about $P(p)$. A convenient and common assumption is that $P(p)$ has a Dirichlet distribution with density

$$P(p) = \frac{\Gamma(\alpha)}{\prod\limits_{B \in \mathcal{B}} \Gamma(\alpha_B)} \prod_{B \in \mathcal{B}} p_B^{\alpha_B - 1}, \qquad \sum_{B \in \mathcal{B}} \alpha_B = \alpha,$$

where $\Gamma(\alpha)$ is a gamma function (for integers, $\Gamma(N+1) = N!$), α_B are the parameters of the prior probability distribution, and $\sum_B p_B = 1$. The reason we use the Dirichlet distribution is that it provides a very flexible and general class of distributions which can approximate almost any 'reasonable' prior distribution, and also because it belongs to the natural conjugate family for multinomial distributions. That is, when $P(p)$ is Dirichlet, and $P(D \mid p)$ is multinomial, then $P(p \mid D)$ is Dirichlet.

We have the following proposition (stated without the routine proof).

Proposition 5.3.2 *If the prior distribution $P(p)$ is Dirichlet and the sample size is N, then the posterior distribution $P(p \mid D)$ is also Dirichlet with density*

$$P(p \mid D) = \frac{\Gamma(\alpha + N)}{\prod_{B \in \mathcal{B}} \Gamma(\alpha_B + N_B)} \prod_{B \in \mathcal{B}} p_B^{N_B + \alpha_B - 1}. \tag{5.11}$$

Equation (5.11) provides a general framework for the estimation of majority preferences in the population given a sample. The direct calculation of the probability of any possible majority preference relation from the Dirichlet distribution requires multidimensional integration. The latter is analytically intractable and computationally intensive. On the other hand, we can use upper and lower bounds if we know the probabilities with which any given candidate is preferred to any other given candidate by a majority.

When there are only two clases, i.e., $p_1 + p_2 = 1$, then p_1 has a Beta distribution. Therefore, a specific case of the Dirichlet distribution is the Beta distribution with cumulative distribution function

$$F_\beta(x, \alpha_1, \alpha_2) = \frac{\Gamma(\alpha_1 + \alpha_2)}{\Gamma(\alpha_1)\Gamma(\alpha_2)} \int_0^x t^{\alpha_1 - 1}(1 - t)^{\alpha_2 - 1} dt, \quad 0 \le x \le 1.$$

Theorem 5.3.3 *Given N_{aBb} and N_{bBa} in the sample, and given the parameters α_{aBb} and α_{bBa} of the prior distribution, the posterior probability that a is preferred to b by a majority in the population is given by*

$$P\big((a \succ_p b) \mid D\big) = F_\beta\left(\frac{1}{2}, N_{bBa} + \alpha_{bBa}, N_{aBb} + \alpha_{aBb}\right). \tag{5.12}$$

A proof of Theorem 5.3.3 is in Appendix C.

Notice that $P\big((a \succ_p b) \mid D\big)$ does not depend on the number of indifference relations (N_{aEb}) in the sample or on α_{aEb} in the prior distribution.

The appropriate choice of priors to adequately incorporate prior information plays an important role in Bayesian statistics. We do not concentrate on this choice, but illustrate our results by choosing priors that give the highest weight to the sample information. This is equivalent to the assumption that before observing a sample we have no information about p, so $P(p)$ has a 'flat' distribution (diffuse relative to the sample information), i.e., that each set of parameters is equally probable. In particular, a 'flat' distribution can be described as a Dirichlet distribution with $\alpha_B \le 1, \forall B \in \mathcal{B}$. Given this fact, and for convenience below, we assume that $\alpha_{aBb} = \alpha_{bBa} = 1$ in Equation (5.12).

TABLE 5.2: $Err_p(N, \delta)$ *in the Inference Framework as a Function of Sample Size N and Pairwise Margin* δ

δ \ N	10	50	100	500	1,000	10,000	50,000	100,000
0.9	0.002	2.5E-12	3.3E-23	1.8E-109	4.9E-217	0.000	0.000	0.000
0.8	0.006	1.2E-09	8.5E-18	4.4E-82	3.7E-162	0.000	0.000	0.000
0.7	0.015	1.5E-07	1.4E-13	6.7E-61	8.9E-120	0.000	0.000	0.000
0.6	0.033	7.4E-06	3.5E-10	5.2E-44	5.1E-86	0.000	0.000	0.000
0.5	0.064	1.8E-04	1.9E-07	1.6E-30	4.5E-59	0.000	0.000	0.000
0.4	0.113	0.002	2.8E-05	6.5E-20	6.3E-38	0.000	0.000	0.000
0.3	0.183	0.017	0.001	7.3E-12	6.2E-22	4.7E-201	0.000	0.000
0.2	0.274	0.080	0.023	3.7E-06	1.1E-10	7.2E-90	0.000	0.000
0.1	0.382	0.242	0.160	0.013	0.001	7.0E-24	3.1E-111	3.9E-220
0.05	0.441	0.363	0.310	0.132	0.057	2.9E-07	2.5E-29	1.2E-56
0.02	0.476	0.444	0.421	0.328	0.264	0.023	3.9E-06	1.3E-10
0.01	0.488	0.472	0.460	0.412	0.376	0.159	0.013	0.001
0	0.500	0.500	0.500	0.500	0.500	0.500	0.500	0.500

Note that under the assumption of diffuse priors, the choice of a Dirichlet distribution is made only for analytical convenience. For large sample sizes, any other diffuse prior distribution would lead to virtually the same numerical results.

Paralleling Subsection 5.1.2, we denote by $Err_p(N, \delta)$ the probability that the results of a pairwise comparison in the population and in the sample differ, with the additional assumption here of a diffuse prior distribution. However, the interpretation of Err is different here, since we take the sample information as a given and consider inferences from the sample about the population. We obtain the following proposition.

Proposition 5.3.4 *Let* $N = N_{aBb} + N_{bBa}$, $\delta = \frac{N_{aBb} - N_{bBa}}{N}$. *Then* $Err_p(N, \delta)$ *is given by*

$$Err_p(N, \delta) = F_\beta \left(\frac{1}{2}, N\frac{1+\delta}{2} + 1, N\frac{1-\delta}{2} + 1 \right). \tag{5.13}$$

Equation (5.13) follows directly from Equation (5.12), after the substitution $\alpha_{aBb} = \alpha_{bBa} = 1$ and the use of the following equality:

$$1 - F_\beta \left(\frac{1}{2}, N_{bBa} + 1, N_{aBb} + 1 \right) = F_\beta \left(\frac{1}{2}, N_{aBb} + 1, N_{bBa} + 1 \right).$$

Table 5.2 provides an overview of the values of $Err_p(N, \delta)$ as a function of N and δ.

Having Equation (5.12) for the pairwise majority probability or (5.13) for the probability of erroneous pairwise majority preferences, we can use the method of upper and lower bounds, exactly as we do in Subsection 5.1.2, to obtain bounds on the probability of majority preference relations in a population based on a random sample from that population.

5.4 EMPIRICAL ILLUSTRATIONS

5.4.1 Majority Misestimation: An Alternative View of Majority Cycles and Social Homogeneity

According to traditional arguments, as long as majority cycles cannot be ruled out, the concept of majority rule may be ill defined and therefore democratic decision making may be at risk. Although this chapter bears on the likelihood of cycles, that topic is not its main focus.

1. Our first central point is that, for small numbers of alternatives and realistic distributions of preferences, the problem of cycles is much less important than the problem of misestimation, i.e., that the majority preferences in a sample diverge from those of the underlying population. Appropriate political representation is feasible not when majority preferences in a sample are revealed to be transitive, but when the (transitive or intransitive) majority preferences so revealed are those of the underlying population. Our later analysis reveals that, regardless of whether the probability of cycles is low or (relatively) high, the probability of a cycle is, in all cases, lower than the probability of obtaining a transitive majority preference order that misrepresents the majority preferences of the population.
2. We also argue that the degree of homogeneity, i.e., the degree to which members of a population share common beliefs, knowledge, goals, and preferences, is the key determinant for how representative the majority preferences in a random sample of a given size will be of the majority preferences in the population of reference. While this statement may seem obvious, we draw the reader's attention to the real and striking differences that have to be expected for different populations or different subgroups of a given population. The degree of homogeneity is closely related to the size of the smallest pairwise margin: Small margins indicate a large degree of disagreement and thus low homogeneity. Highly homogeneous populations or samples will have large pairwise margins, and thus

will tend to suffer less from incorrect representation (even for small samples). By analogy, we conjecture that some types of domain restrictions go hand in hand with large pairwise margins and, consequently, with accurate representation.

In the empirical illustrations that follow, we focus on the collective preferences of national electorates over presidential candidates or political parties and, for illustrative purposes, on the preferences of six important subgroups within one of these electorates. Knowledge of the majority preferences of national electorates – as well as the preferences of important subgroups within those electorates – is valuable to various groups and individuals, especially to the elected representatives of the electorate. On one view, such representatives, in their own voting on issues, should reflect the (majority) preferences of their constituents on the available options.

Ideally, representatives would determine constituency majority preferences by eliciting individual preferences from every member of their constituency. Although technological advances may eventually make this ideal technically feasible, requiring every voter to provide information about their preference ordering imposes a considerable burden on the electorate. Instead, it is more natural to employ more selective information gathering techniques, such as sample polls. These techniques all share the common feature that the representative infers his or her constituency's majority preferences from a sample of constituents' opinions. This raises the central question we pose here: "How likely is it that the majority preference order of such a sample accurately reflects the preferences of the entire constituency from which the sample is drawn?" Similarly, the representative might wish to know: "How likely is it that such a sample contains a majority cycle?" Given that polling is expensive, a closely related important issue is to determine a sufficient sample size for accurate representation of a population majority preference by a sample.

EMPIRICAL METHODOLOGY. To empirically tackle the questions above, we can take three different routes:

1. Using simulation methods we can take random samples (with replacement) from distributions like the ones we discuss in previous chapters.[13] We can repeat each sampling procedure, say, 10,000 times and record the proportion of times a sample yields a majority cycle, the proportion of times a sample yields the "correct" majority

---

[13] In some of what follows, we treat the observed relative frequency distribution in a survey as a finite population from which we draw random samples with replacement.

winner, and the proportion of times a sample yields the "correct" majority preference order (where "correct" is being used to refer to the majority preferences in the full survey).

2. We can use the analytical tools of Section 5.1, including the method of bounds, to derive analytical constraints on the sampling outcomes.

3. We can use the Bayesian inference tools of Section 5.3 to make inferences from survey data about the likely majority preferences in the population from which the survey data were obtained.

We start with the general sampling framework. To minimize confusion, since we are talking about sampling from data sets that are themselves random samples, we use the terms "survey" and "survey data" to refer to the relative frequency distribution in the national survey data.

To illustrate the overwhelmingly greater danger of misestimation compared to cycles in realistic distributions, on the one hand, and the role of social homogeneity, on the other, we now illustrate both points with empirical analyses. These examples illuminate the relationship between social homogeneity and the sample size required for accurate representation.

We discuss three examples in detail. The first example illustrates a case where accurate representation is easy to obtain (i.e., requires moderate sample size). The second, less typical, example shows that even large samples may not rule out the possibility of completely misevaluating majority preference orders. This example is based on a highly heterogeneous population and demonstrates that finding a "correct" representation can be a real and challenging problem in such a case. The third example illustrates the other extreme case, one where accurate representation is amazingly good even for a sample of only three voters, because virtually all members of that population think alike.

Based on important real world distributions, all three examples demonstrate that, contrary to the standard findings suggested by samples from the impartial culture, cycles are not a serious problem in realistic random samples. The issue, rather, is accurate representation in random samples. These examples further emphasize our point made in Chapter 1 that the impartial culture is a misleading worst case scenario for inferences about the likelihood of cycles.

The three primary data sets that we draw on for our illustrations are national election surveys in three different countries, namely the 1996 American National Election Study (ANES), the 1969 German National Election Study (GNES), and the 1988 French National Election Study

(FNES), restricted to Communist respondents. We study these survey preference distributions in previous chapters and report them already in Figure 2.14 (1996 ANES), Figure 1.1 (1969 GNES), and Figure 2.15 (1988 FNES Communists). Besides these three data sets that form our main emphasis, we later report some results on several additional survey data sets.

5.4.2 Majority Outcomes in Random Samples from the 1996 ANES

Recall that the weak order preference distribution of the 1996 ANES is given in Figure 2.14. We may treat this distribution as a 'realistic population distribution' (without claiming that it is the 'real population distribution') in order to illustrate our points. We report in Chapter 2 that the survey majority ordering, now treated as our population majority ordering, is $c \succ_p d \succ_p p$.[14] We are particularly interested in answering the following three questions: "what are the probabilities that a sample drawn from the 1996 ANES survey data set of a given size (a) has transitive majority preferences, (b) has the same majority winner (i.e., Clinton) as the survey respondents as a whole, (c) has the same majority preference order (i.e., Clinton is majority winner and Perot is majority loser) as the survey respondents as a whole?"

When we draw 5-person samples with replacement repeatedly (10,000 times) from the distribution on weak orders of the 1996 ANES survey set, roughly 97% of the majority orders are transitive, and so only about 3% of these samples exhibit intransitive majority preferences. About 63% of the 5-person samples yield the correct majority winner. These findings might suggest that even a very small sample of respondents from the 1996 ANES survey would reproduce the full survey's majority winner more than half the time. However, only 29% of the 5-person samples generate the correct majority order, i.e., a majority preference order that matches $c \succ_p d \succ_p p$, suggesting that obtaining the majority preference order with higher probability requires a larger sample.

---

[14] Note that Figure 2.14 reports probabilities and net probabilities only to two significant digits. In this section, we use three significant digits. In particular, as a consequence of the extra precision, our pairwise margins, which are each the sum of five weak order net probabilities, differ somewhat from the pairwise net probabilities reported in Figure 2.14. All simulations use survey relative frequencies to five significant digits as input. Also, recall that we use small letters in the text to denote candidate/party choices in this chapter.

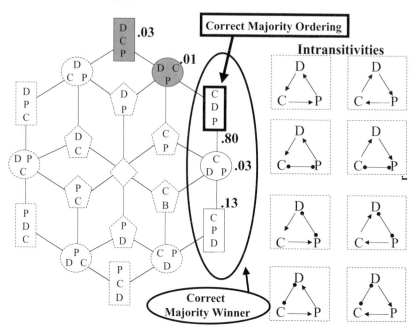

FIGURE 5.1: Simulation results for samples of size 50 from the 1996 ANES for Clinton, Dole, and Perot. The graph of partial orders is given on the left-hand side, together with the proportions of times that each partial order is the majority preference relation in a simulated sample of size 50. The correct majority ordering is displayed with the boldfaced frame. Majority outcomes with the correct winner are shown inside of the oval. Intransitive majority outcomes are shown on the right-hand side and failed to occur in any simulated sample of size 50.

It is apparent that the threat of misestimation of the transitive sample outcomes $(100\% - 3\% - 29\% = 68\%$ out of all samples) dwarfs the threat of error due to cycles (3%). Similarly, we are far more likely to generate a 5-person sample with a transitive majority preference order whose majority first choice fails to match that of the survey than we are to generate a sample with an intransitive majority preference (34% vs. 3%).

Figure 5.1 shows the result from a similar Monte Carlo simulation in which we repeatedly (as before, 10,000 times) draw samples (with replacement) of size $N = 50$ from the 1996 ANES. The figure reports the proportion of times that we observe each of the possible majority preference relations in the sample for size 50. For individuals, only the thirteen strict weak orders of Figure 2.14 are possible preference states. However, once we consider (sample) majority preference relations, then fourteen additional possibilities occur. These are the majority preference relations represented by the additional six semiorders in the partial order graph and the additional eight intransitive majority preference relations that are shown in the boxes to the right of the figure (including the forward and backward cycles). In the boxes on the right-hand side, lines with arrows represent strict majority preferences; lines with dots at their ends indicate majority ties.

The two shaded majority preference relations in Figure 5.1 are majority outcomes with incorrect majority winners. None of the majority relations with a dashed frame occurred in a single sample of size 50 among 10,000 repeated samples in the simulation. These include all eight possible intransitive majority outcomes. This means, in particular, that we have not obtained a single cycle in 10,000 samples of size 50 from the 1996 ANES. The rankings that are inside the large oval are those majority preference relations that yield the correct majority winner, i.e., all rankings in which Clinton is strictly in first place. The survey's majority preference ranking, $c \succ_p d \succ_p p$, is bordered in bold and identified with an arrow. About 80% of our random samples of size 50 yield that majority preference relation, but about 96% yield the correct majority winner. Comparing $n = 50$ with $n = 5$, we find that the larger sample size reduces variability in the majority preference distribution. As mentioned above, there are no longer any intransitivities, so the threat of a cycle is nonexistent. The proportion of samples that obtain the "correct" majority winner rises from 63% for $N = 5$ to 96% for $N = 50$, while the proportion of samples that recover the complete "correct" majority preference order rises from 29% for $N = 5$ to 80% for $N = 50$. Thus, for a sample size of 50, we still have a problem of misestimation, but we no longer have a problem of intransitivity.

Finally, if we turn to a sample size of 100, we again find no intransitivities. We also find that about 92% of all 100-person samples give the correct majority preference order, and more than 99% of all 100-person samples yield the correct majority winner. Completely contrary to expectations about sample size effects derived from the impartial culture (e.g., Shepsle and Bonchek, 1997) but in line with common sense, larger group (sample) sizes are better for majority rule decisions. For this distribution, even samples in the hundreds are sufficient to virtually guarantee correct majority outcomes, and samples in the dozens virtually guarantee the absence of majority cycles.

We do not include further figures like Figure 5.1 for other sample sizes. We refer the reader to Regenwetter et al. (2002a) for a large number of additional such figures. Table 5.3 provides a comparison of the Monte Carlo

TABLE 5.3: *Probabilities That One Candidate is Preferred to Another by a Majority in the Sample as a Function of Sample Size for the ANES 1996 Survey (Provided to Two Significant Digits in Figure 2.14) for Clinton, Dole, and Perot.*

	Social Welfare Order	$d \succ c \succ p$	$d \sim c \succ p$	$c \succ d \succ p$	$c \succ d \sim p$	$c \succ p \succ d$
Sample Size						
50	Upper Bound	0.024	0.010	0.841	0.034	0.125
	Monte Carlo	0.03	0.01	0.80	0.03	0.13
	Lower Bound	0	0	0.807	0.000	0.091
101	Upper Bound	0.003	0.001	0.930	0.013	0.057
	Monte Carlo	0	0	0.93	0.01	0.06
	Lower Bound	0	0	0.926	0.009	0.053
500	Upper Bound	<1E-9	<1E-9	1.000	6.08E-05	3.15E-04
	Monte Carlo	0	0	1	0	0
	Lower Bound	0	0	1.000	6.08E-05	3.15E-04

simulation results with our analytical results using the upper and lower bounds of Propositions 5.1.2 and 5.1.3 in samples of size $n = 50, 101$, and 500, respectively. Using our analytical tools, the table indicates that even a random sample of 50 voters is virtually certain to correctly identify the majority preference of Clinton over Perot, and to have an 84% chance of correctly ranking Dole over Perot (by a majority in the sample). This is consistent with what we find in Monte Carlo simulations. From Table 5.3 we can see that a sample of size 50 has a 96% chance of correctly ranking Clinton ahead of Dole by majority rule, and an 84% chance of correctly ranking Dole ahead of Perot. A group of 50 is virtually guaranteed to correctly rank Clinton ahead of Perot by majority rule.

For samples of size 50, the upper bound on the probability of correctly recovering the correct majority order is .841, the lower bound is .807. In our Monte Carlo simulation, we determined the proportion of times we are able to correctly recover the population majority preference in a sample of size 50 to be 80% (based on simulating 10,000 repeated samples). For $N \geq 100$ the upper and lower bounds become extremely close and match the Monte Carlo simulations.

These illustrations show that our upper and lower bounds provide a surprisingly accurate assessment of the sampling probabilities for several of the most probable majority relations in the sample (as long as the pairwise margins in the population are nonzero). In summary, for *N* of several hundred the correct majority order is virtually guaranteed, whereas for even rather small N, the sample majority order $c \succ_s p \succ_s d$ has much higher probability than any other incorrect majority order, or any cycle, in particular. This illustrates Theorem 5.1.4, with $\succ^* = \{(c, p), (p, d), (c, d)\}$.

5.4.3 Majority Outcomes in Random Samples from the 1969 GNES

The 1969 GNES linear order distribution is given in Figure 1.1 of Chapter 1. The three choice alternatives are c (CDU/CSU), f (FDP), and s (SDP), the major German parties.[15] The correct majority ranking in the survey is $c \succ_p s \succ_p f$, and the pairwise margins are $\delta_{cBs} = 0.02$, $\delta_{cBf} = 0.6$, $\delta_{sBf} = 0.58$. Figure 5.2 shows the results for all odd samples (i.e., samples with an odd number of respondents) from the 1969 GNES and compares them to outcomes of such samples from the impartial culture. According to Theorems 5.1.4 and 5.1.6, if we now draw random samples (with replacement) from the survey, the probability of the correct majority winner in such a sample approaches 1 much more slowly (with increasing sample size) than does the probability of transitive majority preferences in the sample. Figure 5.2 shows that the probability of a majority cycle for odd size samples drawn from the impartial culture are systematically higher than the corresponding probabilities derived from our realistic distribution, the 1969 GNES.

Figure 5.2 treats the 1969 GNES survey data as a population from which we can draw random samples (with replacement). We plot (1) upper and (2) lower bounds on the probability of the correct majority winner, (3) an upper bound on the probability of no majority winner (for odd N this translates into an upper bound on the probability of cycles),[16] and (4) for comparison, the probability of cycles when drawing an (odd) sample of corresponding size from an impartial culture (instead of the 1969 GNES).

5.4.4 Majority Outcomes in Random Samples from the 1988 FNES for Communist Party Identifiers

To illustrate the issues involved in sampling from important subnational voting constituencies, we now move to the 1988 French National Election

---

[15] Notice that in Figure 1.1 we use capital letters whereas we use small letters in the text for ease of exposition.

[16] In samples from the 1969 GNES our best lower bound on the probability of cycles is zero, and therefore not displayed in the figure.

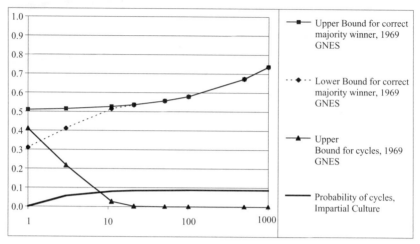

FIGURE 5.2: Results about sampling from the 1969 GNES. Bounds on probabilities of the correct majority winner and of no majority winner are shown, along with the probability of no majority winner in samples from the impartial culture (for odd sample size). The horizontal axis displays the sample size, the vertical axis displays the probability.

Study (FNES) survey data set, more specifically to the subgroup of respondents who identified themselves as Communists. The survey distribution for the three most important candidates is displayed in Figure 2.15. Recall that in that distribution 53% of the French Communists have the preference order *mbc* (*m*: Mitterrand; *b*: Barre; *c*: Chirac), and that 92% strictly prefer Mitterrand to each of his two opponents.[17] Figure 2.15 also displays the pairwise preference margins and the implied survey majority preference order, which we treat here as the population majority preference order $m \succ_p b \succ_p c$.

The large amount of agreement among Communists is a clear indication that Communist respondents in the 1988 FNES are highly homogeneous in their preferences. We find that all our simulated samples of size three yield the correct majority winner, and all our simulated samples of size more than 20 match the entire majority order of the population. Meanwhile we note that we have not encountered a single majority cycle (or other intransitivity) in our extensive Monte Carlo simulation.[18]

---

[17] Recall that Figure 2.15 uses capital letters although here we use small letters.

[18] We simulated samples sizes of 2, 3, 4, 5, 8, 9, 20, 21, 50, 51, 100, 101, 500, 501, 1000, 1001, 2000, 2001, 5000, 5001, 10000, and 10001, each 10,000 times.

Given the homogeneity of the Communists' candidate rankings, these results make perfect sense. Since the overwhelming majority of all Communist partisans strictly prefer Mitterrand, and an absolute majority display the individual preference relation *mbc*, even modest-sized samples of Communist partisans are likely to reflect the majority preferences of the Communist survey data as a whole.

Hence for the French Communists we conclude that neither majority cycles in voter samples nor unrepresentative majority preferences among samples are a serious problem for political representation, provided the sample size reaches double digits. And for extremely small samples (e.g., $N = 3$) the problem is again unrepresentative sample majority preference orders, not cyclical majority preferences.

5.4.5 Summary of Results for Samples from ANES, GNES, and FNES Surveys

We have also investigated random samples from the weak (respectively linear) order preference distributions of the 1968 ANES, 1980 ANES, 1992 ANES, 1996 ANES, 1969 GNES, 1972 GNES, 1976 GNES, various subgroups other than the Communist respondents of the 1988 FNES, as well as the full 1988 FNES survey. For the sake of brevity we omit the large number of figures that would be required in order to display the survey probabilities and the sample majority preference probabilities for various sample sizes. We note here only that the dispersion of majority outcomes in the sampling distributions from the three surveys discussed so far gives a representative idea of the diversity in probability distributions over sample majority preference orders that we find overall. In all cases, cycles play a rather minor or even negligible role. In virtually all cases, the threat of misestimation is substantial for small sample sizes, and in some cases (such as the 1969 GNES, and to lesser extents the 1972 GNES, and the 1992 ANES) misestimation remains a severe problem even for larger samples of several hundreds, and even thousands, of respondents.

Table 5.4 provides an overview of these analyses. We report the minimum adjusted pairwise margin δ^* for various data sets, as well as an upper bound on the accidental reversal of a pairwise majority preference in a sample of size N, for $N = 200$ and $N = 1000$. We use the normal approximation, $Err_N(N, \delta^*)$, given by (5.8). It is obvious from the table that, for each sample size, as the minimum adjusted pairwise margin in the survey data increases, so does, in general, the lower bound on the confidence that a sample from that data set correctly recovers the majority

TABLE 5.4: *Overview of Misestimation in ANES, GNES, FNES. We Report the Minimum Adjusted Pairwise Margin δ* for Various Data Sets, As Well As an Upper Bound on the Accidental Reversal of a Pairwise Majority Preference in a Sample of Size N, for N = 200 and N = 1000. We Use the Normal Approximation, $Err_N(N, \delta^*)$, Given by (5.8). We Report Results for the Full ANES of 1968, 1980, 1992, and 1996; the Full GNES of 1969, 1972, and 1976; the Full FNES of 1988; As Well As Six National Subgroups of the 1988 FNES, Namely Those Who Identified Themselves as Middle Class, Communists, Socialists, UDF, Unionists, or Working Class, Respectively*

Data Set	δ^*	$Err_N(200, \delta^*)$	$Err_N(1000, \delta^*)$
ANES 1968	0.054	.22	.04
ANES 1980	0.064	.18	.02
ANES 1992	0.086	.11	.003
ANES 1996	0.140	.024	.000005
GNES 1969	0.020	.39	.26
GNES 1972	0.111	.06	.0002
GNES 1976	0.022	.38	.243
FNES 1988	0.221	.0009	$< 10^{-11}$
FNES 1988 (Middle Class)	0.035	.31	.13
FNES 1988 (Communists)	0.709	$< 10^{-12}$	$< 10^{-12}$
FNES 1988 (Socialists)	1.741	$< 10^{-12}$	$< 10^{-12}$
FNES 1988 (UDF)	0.951	$< 10^{-12}$	$< 10^{-12}$
FNES 1988 (Unionists)	0.392	$< 10^{-7}$	$< 10^{-12}$
FNES 1988 (Working Class)	0.479	$< 10^{-11}$	$< 10^{-12}$

preference order of the full survey. In other words, the confidence in correct majority outcomes (for any given sample size) increases with the size of the minimal pairwise margin.

We reach three important conclusions about sampling voter preferences from these election surveys and predict by extension that very similar conclusions will be obtained by random sampling from other real-world distributions:

1. Misestimation of the majority winner and of the majority preference order occurs frequently in small samples. By contrast, majority cycles are extremely rare for all sample sizes. This suggests strongly that misestimation, not cycles, poses the most serious threat to political representation when we are seeking to judge the preferences of an electorate from incomplete or noisy data. The fact that moderate stochastic transitivity with strict inequalities appears to be

descriptive of many data underscores this point because, in such cases, the second most probable majority outcome, after the correct one, is another transitive outcome.

2. Increasing the sample size generally increases the probability of finding the correct majority preference order, and hence also of finding the correct majority winner. With respect to national electorates and, as shown below, (especially) with respect to important subnational voting constituencies, we find that the problem of misestimation becomes markedly less severe as the sample size increases. As the sample size gets very large we are virtually guaranteed to find the correct majority preference order in the sample. However, "very large" may mean tens of thousands of voters. In particular, the correct policy implications that must be drawn from this finding are that *large* committees and *high* turnout are desirable for accurate representation under majority rule.

3. Even for small or moderate sample sizes, representation will be accurate when there is a high degree of social homogeneity among members of the population from which we sample. In particular, to achieve any given level of reliability in their majority rule decisions, highly homogeneous organizations can rely on smaller committees than highly heterogeneous organizations. We conjecture that a similar conclusion will apply to many domain restricted groups because they will tend to exhibit large pairwise margins.

Note that the second finding is diametrically opposite to the conclusions that are routinely reached by sampling from the impartial culture. There, for odd sample size, increasing the sample size increases the likelihood of a cycle. Furthermore, for odd sample size and linear order preferences, correct representation is impossible when drawing from the impartial culture, even as sample size goes to infinity. Thus the problem of misestimation is most acute when the underlying population is heterogeneous, in the sense that voters display high levels of disagreement about the merits of the competing alternatives.

Recall that each survey in Chapters 1 and 2 diverges widely from the impartial culture. We find the same pattern in all additional survey data sets. This observation supports the common-sense intuition that, in actual elections, political representation is best studied by exploring the preference structure of the electorate under review, not by extrapolating from the impartial culture or other (a priori) artificial distributions (Van Deemen, 1999).

5.4.6 Bayesian Inference about Majority Outcomes for the Full 1988 FNES

Now we illustrate the method of upper and lower bounds in the inference framework by analyzing survey data of the 1988 French National Election study (FNES) (Pierce, 1996). Contrary to our earlier analyses, we treat these survey data as a random sample from some underlying population or culture, and we ask inference questions about the majority preferences in that population, given the sample. Our illustrations above rely only on data about the three most important candidates in the 1988 French election. In fact, the original data consist of thermometer scores for five candidates m (Mitterrand), b (Barre), c (Chirac), l (Lajoinie), and p (Le Pen). We now include all five candidates.

After recoding the thermometer scores as strict weak orders, there are several hundred possible states of individual preference. The number of possible majority preference relations is 3^{10}. (There are 3 possible majority relations for each pair of candidates and, for 5 candidates, the number of pairs is 10.) However, according to our approach, we need to compute only the population pairwise comparison probabilities in (5.12) and the pairwise error probabilities in (5.13). The probability that the pairwise majority preferences in the population and in the sample do not coincide is extremely small for each pair. An upper bound on the probability of an incorrect majority preference relation (i.e., different from the correct majority ordering $m \succ b \succ c \succ l \succ p$) is given by the sum of the probabilities of erroneous pairwise majority preferences (across all pairs). This upper bound equals 4.2×10^{-13}, and is given by (5.4). In other words, we are virtually certain to make the correct inference for all pairwise majority comparisons. Using (5.4) we obtain that the most likely population majority ordering based on Bayesian inference from the survey is $m \succ_p b \succ_p c \succ_p l \succ_p p$ (the lower bound on its posterior probability is $1.0 - 4.2 \times 10^{-13}$ and the upper bound is $1.0 - 3.8 \times 10^{-13}$). Again, based on our bounds for the posterior distribution, the second most probable population majority ranking (given the data) is $b \succ m \succ c \succ l \succ_p p$, the probability of which is bounded from below by 3.5×10^{-13} and from above by 3.8×10^{-13}. Analogously to Theorem 5.1.4, this probability again dramatically exceeds the probability of any other majority relation different from the majority relation in the sample.

Notice in passing that all triples in this survey satisfy a property reminiscent of moderate stochastic transitivity with strict inequalities: for each triple $a \succ b \succ c$ we find $Err(aBc) < max(Err(aBb), Err(bBc))$. This implies that for each triple the most probable erroneous majority preference relation is a transitive one, not a cycle. Because all pairwise margins in 1988 FNES are high enough, the probability of an incorrect inference is minuscule. If some pairwise margins are low and the number of respondents in the survey is not very high, as is the case for the GNES 1969 (Figure 1.1), then the probability of incorrect inference can be quite high. The 818 respondents of the GNES 1969 lead one to infer an incorrect population majority preference relation with probability 0.28.

5.5 DISCUSSION

Van Deemen (1999, p. 181, last paragraph) made the following comment about the prevalent use of the impartial culture in the study of majority outcomes in random samples:

> As is well-known, the assumption of impartial culture as employed in this paper and in most other works in the field is highly implausible. It is empirically more relevant to develop probability models that use vote frequencies, for example obtained by elections, as input.

Following Van Deemen's recommendation, we focus on the analysis of real-world distributions of preferences.[19] Our approach to behavioral social choice theory reaches beyond Van Deemen's framework by allowing individual preferences to be arbitrary asymmetric binary relations and thereby greatly expanding the domain of permissible preference states. We also go beyond just analyzing the probability of the Condorcet paradox in random samples from realistic distributions.

As soon as we analyze real-world data, we face the uncertainty of how reflective these data are of the true distribution of preferences in the electorate. Therefore, Van Deemen's recommendation naturally leads to statistical considerations.

We look at the following criteria of representativity in a majority rule framework:

1. How often does the majority rule preference order in a random sample match the majority rule preference order of the distribution that the sample was drawn from?

---

[19] Rather than rely on ballot data, however, we start with survey data.

2. How often does the majority winner in a random sample match the majority winner in the distribution that the sample was drawn from?

3. How often does a random sample from a given distribution display a nontransitive majority preference relation? How much evidence do we have that a given random sample resulted from a population with a majority cycle?

On the first two questions we develop two different frameworks to conceptualize, quantify, and assess the risk of incorrect majority preference relations: (1) a statistical sampling framework, where we quantify the probability that a random sample exhibits the correct or an incorrect majority preference relation, relative to the population from which it was drawn, and (2) a Bayesian inference framework, where a random sample is used to infer or update a probability distribution over possible majority preference relations in the (unknown) population from which the data were drawn.

Our approach is similar to three other important theoretical strands of literature, namely the work on the Condorcet efficiency of various social choice methods (Gehrlein, 1999; Gehrlein and Lepelley, 1999, 2001; Gehrlein and Valognes, 2001; Lepelley et al., 2000); the work on the Condorcet jury theorem and related issues in information pooling (Austen-Smith and Banks, 1996; Ben-Ashar and Paroush, 2000; Berg, 1993; Black, 1958; Condorcet, 1785; Estlund, 1994; Falmagne, 1994; Grofman, 1975, 1981; Grofman and Feld, 1988; Grofman and Owen, 1986a,b; Grofman et al., 1983; Ladha, 1992, 1993, 1995; Miller, 1986, 1996; Nitzan and Paroush, 1985, 1986; Owen et al., 1989; Young, 1988); and the work on the impact of voter turnout on the outcome of majority rule (Gehrlein and Fishburn, 1978, 1979). We discuss the Condorcet efficiency above in Section 5.2. The Condorcet jury theorem deals with the aggregation of judgments where each individual has some fixed probability of correctly judging the 'better' of any two alternatives. This literature and related developments on the Poisson jury theorem (Gelfand and Solomon, 1973; Poisson, 1787) specifically deal with the notions of correct and incorrect judgments in a probabilistic context. Also, these theorems explicitly introduce sampling considerations in that they study the probabilities of correct judgments as a function of the decision making group. Some work on voter abstention and turnout also has similarities to our work here, in that it studies how likely the population Condorcet winner of all eligible voters coincides with the Condorcet winner of the actual voters, under certain assumptions about voter turnout.

Our approach is also similar to work that emphasizes the potential for majority rule representativeness (e.g., Adams and Adams, 2000; Feld and Grofman, 1986a, 1988, 1990; Tangiane, 1991), and it resonates as well with traditional political science concerns for substantive representation (e.g., Weissberg, 1978, and numerous other authors). Our results strongly reinforce the findings of earlier research that cycles are simply not as much of a problem in the real world as they might appear to be from the theoretical social choice literature.

The distributions from which we have drawn our samples are realistic in the sense that they reflect the distribution of preferences in large real-world surveys. As noted previously, these real-world distributions are also quite unlike symmetric distributions with pairwise majority ties such as the impartial culture. In practice, many real-world choices are from menus of choices that have been drastically limited via institutional or cultural mechanisms. We strongly endorse the view that in such realistic distributions, at least for a small number of feasible choice alternatives, cycles will be rare or nonexistent. This reinforces our conclusions of Chapter 1. Even more importantly, for a small number of alternatives, we need not worry much about majority cycles when dealing with realistic distributions, especially if our sample is "very large"; we do, however, need to worry about misestimation, especially when dealing with heterogeneous groups and "small" sample sizes.

In our analytical work, we provide explicit formulae for the probabilities of pairwise majorities in both the sampling and the inference frameworks. We also show that the concepts of upper and lower bounds using pairwise majority probabilities is extremely useful in analyzing all possible majority preference outcomes. We prove that, for any number of candidates, if there is an asymmetric complete majority preference relation in the population (sampling problem), or in the sample (inference problem), then, for a large sample, that same relation will be represented in the sample (sampling problem) or inferred from the sample (inference problem) with probability arbitrarily close to one. In particular, this shows that the probability of cycles approaches zero in large samples if the majority preferences in the population (or underlying culture) form a linear order.

A particular strength and elegance of our approach is that we derive our results with virtually no constraints on the nature of individual preferences. For instance, we avoid any strong assumptions like the ones made in a related recent paper by Tangian (2000), namely that preferences are generated by cardinal random utilities which are independent among voters. On the contrary, as we discuss in great detail in Chapter 2, rather than considering domain restrictions on voter preferences, we dramatically expand the domain of feasible individual preference states to all finite (and, without loss of generality, asymmetric) binary relations, probability distributions on such binary relations, as well as corresponding utility or random utility representations. Our general statistical approach to majority rule preferences in the present chapter is fully compatible with the general concept of majority rule discussed in Chapter 2.

6

Conclusions and Directions for Future Behavioral Social Choice Research

6.1 CONCLUSIONS

This book is a contribution to a nascent subfield of the social and behavioral sciences that we call "behavioral social choice." By *behavioral social choice (research)* we mean a scientific investigation of social choice processes in which normative theories of 'idealized' social choice are complemented by descriptive models of actual social choice behavior (i.e., *behavioral social choice theory*) and in which such theory is systematically empirically confronted with real-world data in a statistically rigorous fashion.

We view behavioral social choice research as the social choice analogue to *behavioral decision research*, as most prominently exemplified by the work of Kahneman and Tversky (Tversky, 1969; Tversky and Kahneman, 1974, 1981; Kahneman and Tversky, 1979, 2000; Kahneman et al., 1982). Behavioral decision research places a great emphasis on descriptive theories of actual decision making and choice behavior, as well as on testing descriptive theories against empirical data. We believe that social choice research has much to gain by expanding its scope and adopting a similar methodology, both in terms of theoretical insights and in terms of its applicability to real-world problems. In this book, we therefore consistently confront theory with real-world empirical evidence drawn from data sets from three different countries (and some international professional associations).[1]

---

[1] In this book we primarily use national election survey data on important real-world political choices. In addition to the simple fact that survey data sets are publicly available,

Our methodological focus is on realism in studying social choice:

- The need to expand the domain of permissible preference states beyond weak orders to more complex and more behaviorally adequate preference relations that capture important aspects of cognition.
- The need to go beyond deterministic preferences to incorporate probabilistic representations of preference and utility.
- The need to move from highly stylized (and often symmetrical) preference distributions to more realistic distributions of the sort found in the real world.
- The need to compare expected or reconstructed social choice outcomes from the perspective of alternative models, and to pay attention to model dependence issues.

We make three major theoretical contributions:

1. We show that majority cycles are likely to be far less common in mass electorates than existing theory predicts, and that misestimation of collective preferences (e.g., the discrepancy between social choice outcomes in samples and those in the population) is apt to be a greater and more probable threat to democratic theory and practice than cycles.
2. We offer models to reconstruct majority preferences from the limited and incomplete preferences recorded in real-world election ballots and survey data.
3. We provide a highly effective statistical sampling and Bayesian inference framework to evaluate the relationship between the majority preferences (cycles or not) in samples and those of the population (and vice versa).

We make four key empirical contributions:

1. We find that none of our data sets even remotely resembles a sample from the impartial culture (or from a cyclical culture).
2. We find that, in almost all of our data sets, all permissible preference relations are reported by a large number of respondents, and thus every imaginable domain restriction condition is (significantly) violated.

we prioritize survey data over experimental data in this book because studying the former allows us to examine larger bodies of voters in several countries.

3. Despite the astounding diversity of observed preference relations at the individual level, we find no compelling evidence for the presence of a majority cycle in any of our data.
4. We find, for several data sets, that generating incorrect majority outcomes, as we go from population to samples (or vice versa), is a more significant issue for democratic choice than is the potential for cycling.

Social choice theory has offered some of the most elegant and powerful results in the mathematical social sciences. These results have been of great interest to economists, political scientists, psychologists, and even philosophers interested in the normative aspects of democratic theory. Moreover, many of these results, in particular those on majority rule, have been viewed as having critical consequences for how group decision-making can be expected to take place in the real world. The general picture offered by political scientists who have interpreted social choice results is a very negative one (see esp. Riker, 1982; but see Saari, 1999, 2001a, for a more positive view). For example, such theoretical results (including simulation results based on the impartial culture) are still routinely quoted in order to support the claim that majority rule cycles are essentially inevitable when groups decide using majority rule (Shepsle and Bonchek, 1997), and that cycling makes the concept of majority rule essentially meaningless. At the same time, Arrow's impossibility result (1951, 1963) is often taken to imply that no (other) nonarbitrary, nondictatorial deterministic procedure for democratic decision making exists. Yet, there are a number of flaws with the notion that one can simply apply theoretical results to make sense of the world because many available theoretical results are based on very strong assumptions about the nature of voter distributions or the nature of preferences themselves. Theoretical (as well as empirical) results may crucially depend upon the specific assumptions on which they are based.[2]

Our results, both analytic and empirical, give rise to a new perspective on the implications of social choice theory for the possibility of democratic decision. While behavioral decision research has shown that individuals fall short of normative benchmarks (e.g., Bayesian updating, expected utility maximization), we offer the conjecture, based on our empirical and theoretical findings, that collectivities are more able to reach

---

[2] Compare Saari (1994, 1995).

normatively desirable social choices than would be expected by classical social choice theory. From a behavioral perspective, we believe that Arrow's impossibility result, while profound in its implications for understanding the analytics of social aggregation processes, directs our attention solely to what is *possible*, when we also need to pay attention to what is *probable* – given the kinds of distributions of preferences we actually observe in the real world. If we are willing to give up Arrow's "universal domain" requirement by restricting majority rule to be well defined only on those distributions that are actually observed in real-world data, then majority rule remains a strong contender to satisfy Arrow's ideal. In addition, once we recognize that domain restriction conditions such as Black's "single-peakedness" condition, a.k.a. Sen's "never-worst" (*NW*) condition – or its relatives, Sen's "never-best" (*NB*) and "never-middle" (*NM*) conditions – are not actually required to avoid majority cycles, we can continue to be optimistic that majority rule provides a solution to Arrow's challenge despite the fact that domain restrictions do not appear to be descriptive of mass electrates. Finally, when we expand the domain of permissible preferences and shift our focus to appropriate restrictions on distributions of preferences over that large domain, we find that the distributions of preferences we observe in real-world mass electorates give rise to *possibility* results rather than *impossibility* results. To put it another way, majority rule may be expected to be, by and large, transitive. Of course, that is not to say that cycles never occur in the real world; there are a handful of such reported observed cycles in the social science literature. But it is to say that cycles are not nearly as ubiquitous as theoretical concerns might have lead one to believe, and thus majority rule may remain an acceptable decision process, especially in mass electorates.

6.2 DIRECTIONS FOR FUTURE BEHAVIORAL SOCIAL CHOICE RESEARCH

While the theoretical ideas in this book are stated primarily in terms of majority rule and all our empirical results are focused on majority rule, the framework we offer is much more general. In this section we identify six important areas for future work:

1. GENERAL REPRESENTATIONS OF SCORING RULES: We envision future work that involves theoretical and empirical analyses parallel to our work on majority rule for scoring rules (a.k.a. positional voting methods) such as the plurality and Borda scores. In particular,

we are in the process of defining a general concept of scoring rules for arbitrary binary relations, probability representations over such relations, real-valued utility functions, and real-valued random utility representations and of applying that general concept to a range of empirical data sets.

2. THE THEORETICAL AND EMPIRICAL CONCORDANCE BETWEEN BORDA WINNERS AND CONDORCET WINNERS: We hope to study the concordance between Borda and Condorcet winners. We have already collected some preliminary evidence (Regenwetter and Grofman, 1998a) that majority and Borda outcomes tend to agree. However, we need to analyze more data sets and to check for robustness of results against alternative model specifications (in a fashion similar to our work on majority rule in Chapter 3). We have also begun to investigate sufficient conditions under which Borda and Condorcet will coincide in the context of probabilistic models.[3] In this context, we hope to shed new light on a centuries-old controversy about the relative merits of the Borda rule and majority rule procedures (Young, 1974, 1986, 1988).

3. MINORITARIAN PROCEDURES FOR SELECTING MULTIPLE WIN-NERS: While majoritarian or plurality-based procedures for picking winners are the most commonly used electoral rules in English-speaking countries, throughout most of the rest of the world (and, increasingly, even in English-speaking countries that are part of the European Union) various forms of proportional representation (PR) are used (Balinski and Young, 1982). The most common is the list form of PR, in which each party sends a number of candidates into office from its ranked list of candidates proportional to its vote share. Another important minoritarian procedure is the Single Transferable Vote (STV) used in Northern Ireland and in professional and educational organizations in the United Kingdom (and, to a lesser extent, in the United States) (Bowler and Grofman, 2000a,b; Brams and Fishburn, 1984; Doron and Kronick, 1977; Tideman, 1995; Tideman and Richardson, 2000a,b). STV is a particularly natural area for behavioral social choice research, because it requires the voter to fully rank order the set of candidates. On the one hand, such full rankings provide exceptionally rich data; on the

---

[3] Buhlmann and Huber (1963) and Huber (1963) contain excellent results on the 'optimality' of ranking options by Borda-type scores when the relevant selection probabilities belong to an 'exponential' family (that includes independent normals as a special case).

other hand, they suggest the need for probabilistic models of the voting process, since the requirement to rank order a large number of candidates, many of whom the voter may have little or no information about, may place a high cognitive strain on the voter. Furthermore, STV is rather controversial among social choice theorists because of its debatable normative properties. We have begun an investigation of STV, with a focus on real-world data (expanding on the tradition of Chamberlin et al., 1984, and Felsenthal et al., 1993).

4. REASONS FOR THE ABSENCE OF CYCLES: Having argued for the rarity of cycles, it is natural to try to understand in more detail why they are rare. In this book we show that particular distributional conditions are sufficient to avoid cycles. But this is still essentially a 'black box' approach in that we do not specify mechanisms that generate just those types of distributions that avoid cycles. To resolve that puzzle we have begun work on parametric models of individual choice or rankings – e.g., processes with error components, such as Mallows' phi model and other probabilistic ranking models (Critchlow et al., 1991, 1993; Doignon et al., 2004; Mallows, 1957) – which can then be expanded into models of collective behavior.

5. EXTENSIONS TO EXPERIMENTAL WORK: There is a strong experimental tradition in behavioral social choice (see e.g., Plott and Levine, 1978; Smith, 1976, 1994). Although the data used in this book originate from surveys and election ballots, it is natural to consider how experimental work, such as the large ongoing research traditions in group-decision making, coalition processes, etc., can draw on the perspectives we propose here. For example, it is conceivable that group deliberations affect the likelihood of transitive majority preferences, and there is some evidence to that effect (Dryzek and List, 2003).[4]

6. SOPHISTICATED VOTING AND STRATEGIC BEHAVIOR: One of the most influential schools of thought in economics, political science and, in particular, in social choice theory, is the game theoretic model of strategic interactions among competing players. In this book, we have not investigated strategic aspects of social choice

---

[4] For example, some processes might lead to group polarization whereas other processes might lead to greater concordance and/or acceptancce of a shared perspective on how to 'place' alternatives in some 'ideological' space.

behavior. Clearly, future work needs to expand our scope by incorporating game theoretic notions or strategic decision heuristics.[5] The main challenge we see to such extensions is that under strategic considerations, observed ratings, rankings, or choices are no longer straightforward reflections of preferences. This means that a strategic analysis will face much more severe statistical challenges to make the relevant parameters of a model statistically identifiable. We have started work on approval voting models in which each voter votes for those candidates whose utilities are above her/his expected utility of the set of available candidates. Even this relatively simple example generates major statistical challenges and requires significant simplifications in order to make the model parameters identifiable and the statistical analysis computationally tractable.

The ideas enumerated above are only a small sample of possible directions for future work. We hope that the behavioral perspective we articulate in this book will stimulate work in many different domains of behavioral social choice, and that the contributions of this volume will help reshape the field, making it more empirically relevant and better grounded in a realistic optimism about the prospects for democratic choice.

---

[5] For an example of recent work, Brams and Sanver (in press) argue that, even though approval voting need not always pick Condorcet winners, nonetheless a Condorcet winner's election under approval voting is always a strong Nash-equilibrium outcome. Barberá and Coelho (2004) recently investigated strategic issues in a k names nomination process where a chooser picks one of a set of k that were nominated by some other entity.

Appendix A

Definitions of Cultures of Preference Distributions

This Appendix serves as an Addendum to Chapter 1 and uses the notation introduced there.

The Impartial Culture

The impartial culture is a uniform distribution over all possible orders. For example, for three candidates a, b, c the *impartial culture over linear orders* is the following distribution:

$$p_{abc} = p_{acb} = p_{bac} = p_{bca} = p_{cab} = p_{cba} = \frac{1}{6}.$$

The *impartial culture over strict weak orders with exactly one tie* for three candidates is the following distribution:

$$p_{aEbBc} = p_{cBaEb} = p_{aEcBb} = p_{bBaEc} = p_{bEcBa} = p_{aBbEc} = \frac{1}{6}.$$

The probability of cycles for an infinite sample drawn from a mixture of the impartial culture over linear orders with weight k_1 and the impartial culture over weak orders with exactly one tie, with weight k_2, is given by Gehrlein and Valognes (2001):

$$P_c^\infty(p) = \frac{1}{4} - \frac{3}{2\pi} \arcsin\left(\frac{k_1 + k_2}{3k_1 + 2k_2}\right).$$

This probability equals zero if $k_1 = 0$.

The Culture of Indifference

A distribution over all (say, strict linear) orders is a *culture of indifference* (on strict linear orders) if and only if any two alternatives a, b are majority tied, i.e.,

$$p_{aBb} = p_{bBa} \quad \forall a, b \in C.$$

The Dual Culture

The *dual culture* has been defined only for linear orders over three alternatives. It is given by the following distribution:

$$p_{abc} = p_{cba} = p_1,$$
$$p_{bac} = p_{cab} = p_2,$$
$$p_{acb} = p_{bca} = \frac{1}{2} - p_1 - p_2.$$

In the special case when there are only three candidates and individual preferences are only linear orders, the culture of indifference is identical to the dual culture. The probability of cycles for an infinite sample drawn from the dual culture is given by

$$P_c^\infty(p) = \frac{1}{4} - \frac{1}{2\pi}\Big(\arcsin(1 - 4p_1) + \arcsin(1 - 4p_2)$$
$$+ \arcsin(4p_1 + 4p_2 - 1)\Big).$$

This formula is given in Gehrlein (1999). $P_c^\infty(p)$ is maximized by $p_1 = p_2 = \frac{1}{6}$, i.e., by the impartial culture over linear orders.

The Impartial Anonymous Culture

In the *impartial anonymous culture* the sample size n is fixed and each profile of length n is equally probable. If individual preferences are linear orders, then for three candidates and odd sample size the probability of cycles is given by

$$1 - \frac{15(n+3)^2}{16(n+2)(n+4)} = \frac{1}{16}\frac{n^2 + 6n - 7}{(n+2)(n+4)} = \frac{1}{16}\left(1 - \frac{15}{n^2 + 6n + 8}\right).$$

This formula is given in Gehrlein and Fishburn (1976a). As we can see, for an infinite sample size the probability of cycles is $\frac{1}{16}$. The impartial anonymous culture as such does not fall under our sampling framework because a profile in an impartial anonymous culture cannot be rewritten as a random sample from a fixed probability distribution.

The Maximal Culture

Under the *maximal culture* assumption the frequency of each possible order is selected at random from a uniform distribution over $0, 1, \ldots, L$ where $L > 0$ is some positive fixed integer. The total number of voters is thus not fixed under the maximal culture assumption.

If individual preferences are linear orders, then for three candidates the probability of cycles is given by

$$\frac{11}{120} + \frac{99L^4 + 341L^3 + 474L^2 + 305L + 109}{120(L+1)^5}.$$

This formula appears in Gehrlein and Lepelley (1997). As this formula shows, the probability of cycles under the maximal culture assumption is no less than $\frac{11}{120}$. Samples drawn from the maximal culture do not have a fixed number of voters and therefore are quite different from the random samples drawn from some particular distribution, as assumed in our framework.

Appendix B

Definitions and Notation for Binary Relations

For a standard reference with the definitions used here, see, e.g., Roberts (1979).

A *binary relation* on a fixed finite set C takes the form $B \subseteq C \times C$. For any binary relation B, its *reverse* is $B^{-1} = \{(b, a) | (a, b) \in B\}$ and let $\overline{B} = [C \times C] - B$. Given binary relations B, B', let $BB' = \{(a, c) \in C \times C \mid \exists b \text{ such that } (a, b) \in B \text{ and } (b, c) \in B'\}$. This is also commonly referred to as the *relative product* of B and B'. Let $Id = \{(c, c) | c \in C\}$ be the identity relation on C.

A binary relation is

reflexive if $Id \subseteq B$;
transitive if $BB \subseteq B$;
asymmetric if $B \cap B^{-1} = \emptyset$;
antisymmetric if $B \cap B^{-1} \subseteq Id$;
negatively transitive if $\overline{B}\overline{B} \subseteq \overline{B}$;
strongly complete if $B \cup B^{-1} = C \times C$;
complete if $B \cup B^{-1} \cup Id = C \times C$.

A binary relation B is a *partial order* if it is reflexive, transitive, and antisymmetric.

A *strict partial order* is a partial order B which is irreflexive (i.e., $B \cap Id = \emptyset$).

An *interval order* is a strict partial order B with the additional property $B\overline{B}^{-1}B \subseteq B$. The key idea behind interval orders (Fishburn, 1970b, 1985) is that we cannot always distinguish between choice alternatives that are very similar. Therefore, interval orders capture the idea that an object is preferred to another if and only if it is sufficiently superior to the other, as formally stated in Theorem 2.1.8. The threshold of distinction may depend on the objects that are being compared, i.e., it may be variable.

A *semiorder* is an interval order B with the additional property that $B B \overline{B^{-1}} \subseteq B$. A semiorder is an interval order with a fixed threshold (Luce, 1956, 1959), as formally stated in Theorem 2.1.8.

A *weak order* is a transitive and strongly complete binary relation.

A *strict weak order* is an asymmetric and negatively transitive binary relation.

A *linear order* is a transitive, antisymmetric, and strongly complete binary relation.

A *strict linear order* is a transitive, asymmetric, and complete binary relation.

In the early chapters of the book, we use "weak order" and "strict weak order" (and, similarly, "linear order" and "strict linear order") interchangeably, because each strict weak (linear) order is the asymmetric part of a weak (linear) order. Thus, majority preference relations computed from either are the same.

Throughout the book, the set of candidates is denoted by $\mathcal{C}$. We write $\mathcal{WO}$ for the collection of all weak orders over $\mathcal{C}$, $\mathcal{SWO}$ for the collection of all strict weak orders over $\mathcal{C}$, $\mathcal{SO}$ for the collection of all semiorders over $\mathcal{C}$, $\mathcal{IO}$ for the collection of all interval orders over $\mathcal{C}$, $\mathcal{PO}$ for the collection of all partial orders over $\mathcal{C}$, $\mathcal{SPO}$ for the collection of all strict partial orders over $\mathcal{C}$, $\mathcal{PO}(k)$ for the collection of all partial orders of dimension at most k over $\mathcal{C}$, and $\mathcal{SPO}(k)$ for the collection of all strict partial orders of dimension at most k over $\mathcal{C}$.

Appendix C

Proofs of Theorems and Observations

Proof of Theorem 1.1.1. To simplify the exposition and following the notation used elsewhere, we write $x \succ y$ for "x is majority preferred to y." Suppose that among three alternatives a, b, c one pair is not majority tied in the population, e.g., $a \succ b$ (i.e., $p_{aBb} > p_{bBa}$). Then, because the weak majority preference is transitive, either $a \succ c$ or $c \succ b$ (or both) in the population. We consider each case in turn.

   i. $a \succ c$. Then the probability of the cycle $a \succ b, b \succ c, c \succ a$ in a sample is bounded from above by $P(N_{cBa} > N_{aBc})$. The probability $P(N_{cBa} > N_{aBc})$ goes to zero as sample size goes to infinity, because $p_{aBc} > p_{cBa}$ by assumption. (This type of analysis using bounds on the probability of a particular majority relation is described in detail in Chapter 5.) Similarly, the probability of the cycle $b \succ a, a \succ c, c \succ b$ in a sample is no more than $P(N_{bBa} > N_{aBb})$ which also goes to zero as sample size goes to infinity, because $p_{aBb} > p_{bBa}$ by assumption.

   ii. $c \succ b$. By assumption, we also have that $a \succ b$. So if $a \sim c$, we have $a \sim c \succ b$; if $a \succ c$, we have $a \succ c \succ b$; and if $c \succ a$, we have $c \succ a \succ b$. Each is transitive, and so we have no cycles.

   Therefore, combining i. and ii., if the probability of cycles is greater than zero as sample size approaches infinity, then the distribution of individual preferences in the population that governs the sampling process has to satisfy a culture of indifference. ∎

   The following Lemma, which is a straightforward extension of Fishburn and Gehrlein (1980) and Gehrlein (1999), is used in the proofs below. We write $p_{aBb \cap aBc}$ for $\sum_{B \in \mathcal{D}} p_B$ when $\mathcal{D} = \{B \in \mathcal{B} | aBb\} \cap \{B' \in \mathcal{B} | aB'c\}$.

Lemma C.0.1 *For a culture of indifference, the following formula holds for 3 candidates:*

$$P_c^\infty(p) = \frac{1}{4} - \frac{1}{2\pi}\left(\arcsin\left(\frac{\omega_{ab,ac}}{\sigma_{ab}\sigma_{ac}}\right) + \arcsin\left(\frac{\omega_{ab,bc}}{\sigma_{ab}\sigma_{bc}}\right)\right.$$
$$\left. + \arcsin\left(\frac{\omega_{ac,bc}}{\sigma_{ab}\sigma_{bc}}\right)\right),$$

where $\omega_{ab,ac}$ and σ_{ab} for any alternatives a, b, c are given by

$$\omega_{ab,ac} = p_{aBb\cap aBc} - p_{aBb\cap cBa} - p_{bBa\cap aBc} + p_{bBa\cap cBa}$$

$$= p_{aBbBc} + p_{aBbEc} + p_{aBcBb} - p_{cBaBb} - p_{bBaBc}$$

$$\quad + p_{bBcBa} + p_{bBEcBa} + p_{cBbBa}, \tag{C.1}$$

$$\sigma_{ab}^2 = 1 - p_{aEb} = 1 - p_{aEbBc} - p_{cBaEb} - p_{aEbEc}. \tag{C.2}$$

Proof of Lemma C.0.1. We make use of the following notation:

$$p_1 = p_{aBbBc}, \ p_2 = p_{aBbEc}, \ p_3 = p_{aBcBb}, \ p_4 = p_{aEcBb}, \ p_5 = p_{cBaBb},$$

$$p_6 = p_{aEbBc}, \ p_7 = p_{aEbEc}, \ p_8 = p_{cBaEb}, \ p_9 = p_{bBaBc}, \ p_{10} = p_{bBaEc},$$

$$p_{11} = p_{bBcBa}, \ p_{12} = p_{bBEcBa}, \ p_{13} = p_{cBbBa}. \tag{C.3}$$

Let $(N_i)_{i=1,\dots,13}$ denote the number of occurences of the weak orders $i = 1, \dots, 13$ in a sample of size n, and so $\sum_{i=1}^{13} N_i = n$, where i is the index used in (C.3). The distribution of weak orders in the sample is given by a multinomial distribution. For $n \to \infty$ this multinomial distribution converges to a multivariate normal distribution. The means $(\mu_i)_{i=1,\dots,13}$ are given by $\mu_i = np_i$, the variances $(\sigma_i^2)_{i=1,\dots,13}$ are given by $\sigma_i^2 = np_i(1 - p_i)$, and the covariances $(\omega_{ij})_{i,j=1,\dots,13}^{i \neq j}$ of variables N_i and N_j are given by $\omega_{ij} = -np_i p_j$. Writing ω_{ii} for σ_i^2, we note that the variance-covariance matrix $\Omega = (\omega_{ij})_{i,j=1,\dots,13}$ is given by

$$\omega_{ij} = \begin{cases} np_i(1 - p_i) & \text{if} \quad i = j, \\ -np_i p_j & \text{if} \quad i \neq j. \end{cases}$$

Equivalently, we can write $\omega_{ij} = -np_i p_j + np_i\delta_{ij}$, where δ_{ij} is given by

$$\delta_{ij} = \begin{cases} 1 & \text{if} \quad i = j, \\ 0 & \text{if} \quad i \neq j. \end{cases}$$

If we use a (column-) vector $\vec{p} = (p_i)_{i=1,\ldots,13}$ to denote the probabilities of the preferences in the population, then the variance–covariance matrix can be expressed as $\Omega = -n\vec{p}^T\vec{p} + n\Lambda$, where $\vec{p}^T$ is $\vec{p}$ transposed and Λ is the diagonal matrix $\lambda_{ij} = p_i\delta_{ij}$. We now restate our given constraints on p:

$$p_{aBb} = p_{bBa}, \; p_{aBc} = p_{cBa}, \; p_{bBc} = p_{cBb}, \tag{C.4}$$

$$\sum_{B\in\mathcal{B}} p_B = 1, \; p_B \geq 0 \quad \forall B \in \mathcal{B}. \tag{C.5}$$

For any $x, y \in \{a, b, c\}$, $x \neq y$, D_{xy} (as in the word difference) denotes the number of weak orders in the sample in which xBy minus the number of weak orders in the sample in which yBx. Accordingly, x is preferred to y by a strict majority in the sample if and only if $D_{xy} > 0$. By definition $D_{xy} = -D_{yx}$. Alternative $x \in \{x, y, z\} = \{a, b, c\}$ is the majority winner in the sample if and only if $D_{xy} > 0$ and $D_{xz} > 0$. In vector form D_{xy} may be expressed as $D_{xy} = \vec{I}_{xy}^T\vec{N}$, where $\vec{I}_{xy}$ is a vector of indicators in $\{1, -1, 0\}$ and $\vec{N} = (N_i)_{i=1,\ldots,13}$. The mean of D_{xy} is then given by $n\vec{I}_{xy}^T\vec{p}$. For example

$$\vec{I}_{ab}^T = (1 \;\; 1 \;\; 1 \;\; 1 \;\; 1 \;\; 0 \;\; 0 \;\; 0 \;\; -1 \;\; -1 \;\; -1 \;\; -1 \;\; -1),$$
$$D_{ab} = \vec{I}_{ab}^T\vec{N} = N_{aBbBc} + N_{aBbEc} + N_{aBcBb} + N_{aEcBb} + N_{cBaBb}$$
$$- N_{bBaBc} - N_{bBaEc} - N_{bBcBa} - N_{bEcBa} - N_{cBbBa}.$$

The random variables D_{ab}, D_{ac}, and D_{bc} are linear combinations of jointly normally distributed random variables, so they are jointly normally distributed themselves. Because of the constraints given in (C.4) their means equal zero, i.e., $\vec{I}_{ab}^T\vec{p} = 0$. It is known that if the joint distribution of two variables is normal with correlation ρ then the probability that they both exceed their means is $\frac{1}{4} + \frac{1}{2\pi}\arcsin(\rho)$ (see, for instance, Rose and Smith, 2002, p. 231 or Rose and Smith, 1996; Stuart and Ord, 1998). Accordingly, if $\rho_{ab,ac}$ is the correlation between D_{ab} and D_{ac}, then the probability that a is the majority winner equals $\frac{1}{4} + \frac{1}{2\pi}\arcsin(\rho_{ab,ac})$.

Given the variance–covariance matrix for the variables $(N_i)_{i=1,\ldots,13}$ we now develop the correlations between the normalized terms $\frac{D_{ab}}{n}$, $\frac{D_{ac}}{n}$, and $\frac{D_{bc}}{n}$.

The variance σ_{ab}^2 of $\frac{D_{ab}}{n}$ is given by

$$\sigma_{ab}^2 = \frac{1}{n}\vec{I}_{ab}^T\Omega\vec{I}_{ab} = \vec{I}_{ab}^T(-\vec{p}^T\vec{p} + \Lambda)\vec{I}_{ab} = \vec{I}_{ab}^T\Lambda\vec{I}_{ab}$$
$$= p_{aBb\cup bBa} = (1 - p_{aEbBc} - p_{cBaEb} - p_{aEbEc}).$$

Notice that if $\sigma_{ab} = 0$ then the probability of cycles is zero because in the sample a is then always tied with b. From now on we assume that all σ are nonzero.

The covariance of $\frac{D_{ab}}{n}$ and $\frac{D_{ac}}{n}$ is given by

$$\omega_{ab,ac} = \frac{1}{n}\vec{I}^T_{ab}\Omega\vec{I}_{ac} = \vec{I}^T_{ab}\Lambda\vec{I}_{ac} = p_{aBb\cap aBc} - p_{aBb\cap cBa} - p_{bBa\cap aBc} + p_{bBa\cap cBa}$$

$$= p_{aBbBc} + p_{aBbEc} + p_{aBcBb} - p_{cBaBb} - p_{bBaBc} + p_{bBcBa}$$

$$+ p_{bEcBa} + p_{cBbBa}.$$

So the probability that a is the majority winner is given by

$$\frac{1}{4} + \frac{1}{2\pi}\arcsin(\rho_{ab,ac}) = \frac{1}{4} + \frac{1}{2\pi}\arcsin\left(\frac{\omega_{ab,ac}}{\sigma_{ab}\sigma_{ac}}\right).$$

The same logic applies for computing the probability that b or c is the majority winner. As a consequence, the probability of cycles in samples of size n as $n \to \infty$ is then given by

$$P^{\infty}_c(p) = \frac{1}{4} - \frac{1}{2\pi}\left(\arcsin\left(\frac{\omega_{ab,ac}}{\sigma_{ab}\sigma_{ac}}\right) + \arcsin\left(\frac{\omega_{ab,bc}}{\sigma_{ab}\sigma_{bc}}\right)\right.$$

$$\left. + \arcsin\left(\frac{\omega_{ac,bc}}{\sigma_{ab}\sigma_{bc}}\right)\right),$$

i.e., the Lemma holds. ∎

Proof of Theorem 1.1.2. By Lemma C.0.1,

$$P^{\infty}_c(p) = \frac{1}{4} - \frac{1}{2\pi}\left(\arcsin\left(\frac{\omega_{ab,ac}}{\sigma_{ab}\sigma_{ac}}\right) + \arcsin\left(\frac{\omega_{ab,bc}}{\sigma_{ab}\sigma_{bc}}\right)\right.$$

$$\left. + \arcsin\left(\frac{\omega_{ac,bc}}{\sigma_{ab}\sigma_{bc}}\right)\right), \qquad \text{(C.6)}$$

where $\omega_{ab,ac}$ and σ_{ab} for any alternatives a, b, c are given by (C.1) and (C.2), respectively.[1]

---

[1] Note that (C.6) generalizes, to any culture of indifference over weak orders, the earlier formulae for (1) the probability of cycles drawn from a mixture of impartial cultures over linear orders and over weak orders with exactly one tie (Fishburn and Gehrlein, 1980); and for (2) the probability of cycles in samples drawn from a dual culture (Gehrlein, 1999).

To find the value of p at which the probability of cycles reaches its maximum, we need to find the minimum of the function

$$F = \arcsin\left(\frac{\omega_{ab,ac}}{\sigma_{ab}\sigma_{ac}}\right) + \arcsin\left(\frac{\omega_{ab,bc}}{\sigma_{ab}\sigma_{bc}}\right) + \arcsin\left(\frac{\omega_{ac,bc}}{\sigma_{ac}\sigma_{bc}}\right).$$

Substituting new variables

$$\sigma_3 = \frac{\sigma_{ab}}{\sqrt{1 - p_{aEbEc}}}, \qquad \sigma_2 = \frac{\sigma_{ac}}{\sqrt{1 - p_{aEbEc}}}, \qquad \sigma_1 = \frac{\sigma_{bc}}{\sqrt{1 - p_{aEbEc}}},$$

$$\omega_1 = \frac{\omega_{ab,ac}}{1 - p_{aEbEc}}, \qquad \omega_2 = \frac{\omega_{ab,bc}}{1 - p_{aEbEc}}, \qquad \omega_3 = \frac{\omega_{ac,bc}}{1 - p_{aEbEc}},$$

we need to find the minimum of

$$\arcsin\left(\frac{\omega_1}{\sigma_2\sigma_3}\right) + \arcsin\left(\frac{\omega_2}{\sigma_1\sigma_3}\right) + \arcsin\left(\frac{\omega_3}{\sigma_1\sigma_2}\right),$$

under the constraints that

$$\omega_1 + \omega_2 + \omega_3 = 1, \tag{C.7}$$

$$|\omega_i| \leq 1, \quad 0 < \sigma_i \leq 1. \tag{C.8}$$

These constraints follow from (C.1) and (C.2). Now we are going to show that the desired minimum occurs at

$$\omega_i = \frac{1}{3}, \qquad \sigma_i = 1, \quad i = 1, 2, 3.$$

First, if $\omega_i > 0$ for $i = 1, 2, 3$, then the minimum is clearly achieved when $\sigma_i = 1$ for $i = 1, 2, 3$. So we now consider the case where one of the ω_i is negative. In that case, it follows from the restrictions on ω_i for $i = 1, 2, 3$, that the other two are positive. Suppose that $\omega_3 < 0$. Because $\arcsin(x)$ is monotonically increasing in x, we see that $\frac{\partial F}{\partial \sigma_3} < 0$. Thus $\sigma_3 = 1$ at the minimum. Substituting $\omega_3 = z\sigma_1\sigma_2$ we can express F as

$$F = \arcsin\left(\frac{\omega_1}{\sigma_2\sigma_3}\right) + \arcsin\left(\frac{1 - \omega_1 - z\sigma_1\sigma_2}{\sigma_1\sigma_3}\right) + \arcsin(z)$$

$$= \arcsin\left(\frac{\omega_1}{\sigma_2\sigma_3}\right) + \arcsin\left(\frac{1 - \omega_1}{\sigma_1\sigma_3} - \frac{z\sigma_2}{\sigma_3}\right) + \arcsin(z).$$

From this representation it is clear that $\frac{\partial F}{\partial \sigma_1} < 0$, and so $\sigma_1 = 1$ at the minimum. Writing

$$F = \arcsin\left(\frac{1 - \omega_2 - z\sigma_1\sigma_2}{\sigma_2\sigma_3}\right) + \arcsin\left(\frac{\omega_2}{\sigma_1\sigma_3}\right) + \arcsin(z)$$

we get $\frac{\partial F}{\partial \sigma_2} < 0$ and so $\sigma_2 = 1$ at the minimum. Thus we have the following necessary condition for F to reach its minimum:

$$\sigma_1 = \sigma_2 = \sigma_3 = 1.$$

Now the problem is reduced to finding the minimum of

$$\arcsin(\omega_1) + \arcsin(\omega_2) + \arcsin(\omega_3)$$

under the constraints

$$\omega_1 + \omega_2 + \omega_3 = 1, \quad |\omega_i| \leq 1.$$

Substituting $\omega_1 = 1 - \omega_2 - \omega_3$, we thus need to find the minimum of

$$\arcsin(1 - \omega_2 - \omega_3) + \arcsin(\omega_2) + \arcsin(\omega_3).$$

Now

$$\frac{\partial F}{\partial \omega_3} < 0 \Leftrightarrow 1 - \omega_2 - \omega_3 > \omega_3,$$

$$\frac{\partial F}{\partial \omega_3} > 0 \Leftrightarrow \omega_3 > 1 - \omega_2 - \omega_3.$$

Since the minimum has to be at the point where the derivative changes its sign from negative to positive, we conclude that at the minimum

$$\omega_3 = \frac{1 - \omega_2}{2}.$$

However, from the fact that $|\omega_i| \leq 1$, and that we are dealing with the case $\omega_2 > 0$, we obtain that $\omega_2 < 1$, and so we have $\omega_i > 0, i = 1, 2, 3$. Since the function $\arcsin(x)$ is increasing and convex in x for $x \geq 0$, F reaches its minimum for $\omega_1 = \omega_2 = \omega_3 = \frac{1}{3}$. Thus, at the minimum, $\sigma_i = 1$, $\omega_i = \frac{1}{3}$, $i = 1, 2, 3$. The desired result then follows by substituting these values in (C.1) and (C.2), and by using the definition of p_B. Thus, we obtain that the probability of cycles reaches its maximum for

$$p_{abc} = p_{acb} = p_{cab} = p_{bac} = p_{bca} = p_{cba} = \frac{1 - p_{aEbEc}}{6},$$

$$0 \leq p_{aEbEc} < 1. \quad \blacksquare$$

Proof of Observation 1.2.6

REFLEXIVITY of $\succsim$: $c \succsim c \Leftrightarrow NP_{cc} \geq 0$. The latter holds since $NP_{cc} = 0, \forall c \in C$.

STRONG COMPLETENESS of $\succsim$: $\forall c, d \in C$, either $NP_{cd} \geq 0$ or $NP_{dc} = -NP_{cd} \geq 0$.

IRREFLEXIVITY of $\succ$: This follows immediately from the fact that $NP_{cc} = 0, \forall c \in C$.

ASYMMETRY of $\succ$: $\forall c, d \in C$, if $NP_{cd} > 0$ then $NP_{dc} = -NP_{cd} < 0$.

It is clear that $\succ$ is the asymmetric part of $\succsim$. The rest of the Observation follows immediately. ∎

Proof of Theorem 1.2.15. Transitivity holds on C if and only if transitivity holds on each triple $\{c, d, e\}$ in C. Thus, there is no loss of generality in setting $C = \{c, d, e\}$ and $\Pi = \{cde, ced, dce, dec, ecd, edc\}$. Recall that at most three rankings have (strictly) positive net preference probabilities.

FIRST, suppose that none is positive, i.e., that all net ranking probabilities are zero. Then transitivity holds because all alternatives are tied, i.e., $\succ = \varnothing$, $\succsim = C \times C$, and net value restriction holds (but there is no ranking with a net preference majority).

SECOND, suppose that exactly one net ranking probability NP_π is positive (i.e., four net ranking probabilities are zero). Then transitivity holds since $\succsim = \succ = \pi$. Net value restriction holds, with $NP_{cde} = 0 \Rightarrow NP_{dce} \neq NP_{ced}$ (including possible relabelings), and π has a net preference majority.

THIRD, suppose that exactly two net ranking probabilities are null, without loss of generality assume that $NP_{cde} = -NP_{edc} = 0$. Then $NM(d)$ holds, and therefore net value restriction also holds.

a) If $NP_{dce} > 0$ & $NP_{dec} > 0$ (and thus $NP_{dce} \neq NP_{ced}$) then transitivity follows:

$$NP_{dce} > NP_{dec} \Rightarrow \succsim = \succ = dce \text{ with a net preference majority,}$$
$$NP_{dce} = NP_{dec} \Rightarrow \succ = \{(d, c), (d, e)\}; \succsim = \{(d, c), (d, e), (c, e), (e, c)\},$$
$$NP_{dce} < NP_{dec} \Rightarrow \succsim = \succ = dec \text{ with a net preference majority;}$$

b) If $NP_{dce} < 0$ & $NP_{dec} < 0$ (and thus $NP_{dce} \neq NP_{ced}$) then transitivity follows:

$$NP_{dce} > NP_{dec} \Rightarrow \succsim = \succ = ced \text{ with a net preference majority,}$$
$$NP_{dce} = NP_{dec} \Rightarrow \succ = \{(c, d), (e, d)\}; \succsim = \{(c, d), (e, d), (c, e), (e, c)\},$$
$$NP_{dce} < NP_{dec} \Rightarrow \succsim = \succ = ecd \text{ with a net preference majority;}$$

c) If $NP_{dce} > 0$ & $NP_{dec} < 0$ then

$$NP_{dce} > NP_{ced} \Rightarrow \succsim = \succ = dce \text{ with a net preference majority,}$$

$$NP_{dce} < NP_{ced} \Rightarrow \succsim = \succ = ced \text{ with a net preference majority,}$$

$$NP_{dce} = NP_{ced} \Rightarrow \begin{cases} \succ = \{(c, e)\}; \\ \succsim = \{(d, c), (c, d), (d, e), (e, d), (c, e)\}; \quad (\dagger) \end{cases}$$

where ($\dagger$) is a violation of transitivity for R.

d) If $NP_{dce} < 0$ & $NP_{dec} > 0$ then

$$NP_{ecd} > NP_{dec} \Rightarrow \succsim = \succ = ecd \text{ with a net preference majority,}$$

$$NP_{ecd} < NP_{dec} \Rightarrow \succsim = \succ = dec \text{ with a net preference majority,}$$

$$NP_{ecd} = NP_{dec} \Rightarrow \begin{cases} \succ = \{(e, c)\}; \\ \succsim = \{(d, c), (c, d), (d, e), (e, d), (e, c)\}; \quad (\ddagger) \end{cases}$$

where ($\ddagger$) is a violation of transitivity for R.

FOURTH, the only remaining possibility is that three net probabilities are positive (and the others are negative, i.e., $NP_{xyz} = 0$ cannot occur). There are eight such cases:

$$NP_{cde} > 0 \text{ \& } NP_{dce} > 0 \text{ \& } NP_{ced} > 0, \tag{C.9}$$

$$NP_{cde} > 0 \text{ \& } NP_{dce} > 0 \text{ \& } NP_{dec} > 0, \tag{C.10}$$

$$NP_{cde} > 0 \text{ \& } NP_{ecd} > 0 \text{ \& } NP_{ced} > 0, \tag{C.11}$$

$$NP_{cde} > 0 \text{ \& } NP_{ecd} > 0 \text{ \& } NP_{dec} > 0, \tag{C.12}$$

$$NP_{edc} > 0 \text{ \& } NP_{dce} > 0 \text{ \& } NP_{ced} > 0, \tag{C.13}$$

$$NP_{edc} > 0 \text{ \& } NP_{dce} > 0 \text{ \& } NP_{dec} > 0, \tag{C.14}$$

$$NP_{edc} > 0 \text{ \& } NP_{ecd} > 0 \text{ \& } NP_{ced} > 0, \tag{C.15}$$

$$NP_{edc} > 0 \text{ \& } NP_{ecd} > 0 \text{ \& } NP_{dec} > 0. \tag{C.16}$$

The cases (C.9)–(C.11) and (C.14)–(C.16) are all equivalent through relabeling of alternatives: Starting each time from (C.9), the relabeling $c \leftrightarrow d$ yields (C.10), $d \leftrightarrow e$ yields (C.11), $c \to d \to e \to c$ yields (C.14), $c \to e \to d \to c$ yields (C.15), and $c \leftrightarrow e$ yields (C.16). Similarly, (C.12) is equivalent to (C.13) through, for instance, the relabeling $c \leftrightarrow e$. We thus need to consider only (C.9) and (C.12).

If (C.9) holds, then net value restriction holds, $c \succ e$ and, furthermore,

$$NP_{cde} < NP_{ced} + NP_{dce} \Rightarrow \begin{cases} d \succsim c \Rightarrow d \succ e \\ e \succsim d \Rightarrow c \succ d, \end{cases}$$

$$NP_{cde} \geq NP_{ced} + NP_{dce} \Rightarrow \succsim = \succ = cde,$$

each of which implies transitivity for both $\succsim$ and $\succ$.

If (C.12) holds (and thus net value restriction is violated) we obtain transitivity if and only if one of the three rankings cde, ecd, and dec has a net preference majority: Suppose that each of the three has a net probability strictly smaller than the sum of the other two. Then $\succsim=\succ=$ $\{(c, d), (d, e), (e, c)\}$, a violation of transitivity. Also, if one of the three has a net probability equal to the sum of the other two, say $NP_{cde} = NP_{ecd} +$ NP_{dec}, then $\succ= \{(c, d), (d, e)\}$, $\succsim= \{(c, d), (d, e), (c, e), (e, c)\}$, which both violate transitivity. ∎

Proof of Observation 2.3.6. We provide a counterexample for strict weak orders, which suffices also as a counterexample for strict partial orders and more general settings. Let $NP \begin{pmatrix} b \\ c \\ a \end{pmatrix} = NP \begin{pmatrix} c \\ b \\ a \end{pmatrix} = NP \begin{pmatrix} c \\ a \\ b \end{pmatrix} =$ $NP \begin{pmatrix} b \\ a\ c \end{pmatrix} = NP \begin{pmatrix} b\ c \\ a \end{pmatrix} = NP \begin{pmatrix} c \\ a\ b \end{pmatrix} = -.2$. It is straightforward to check that $NW(a)$ holds but no other net value restriction condition is satisfied. ∎

Proof of Theorem 2.3.8. The proof is by counterexample. Take $NP \begin{pmatrix} a \\ b \\ c \end{pmatrix} = .004$, $NP \begin{pmatrix} b \\ a \\ c \end{pmatrix} = .003$, $NP \begin{pmatrix} a \\ c \\ b \end{pmatrix} = .002$, $NP \begin{pmatrix} b\ c \\ a \end{pmatrix} = .002$, with the remaining net probabilities equal to zero. Then net value restriction does not hold, nor is there a binary relation with a net majority. Nevertheless, $\succ= \begin{matrix} a \\ b \\ c \end{matrix}$ and $\succsim=\succ \cup Id$ (where Id is the identity relation) are transitive social welfare orders. A graphical display of this counterexample is given in Figure 2.10. Notice that this result holds unaltered when we allow individuals to have arbitrary binary preferences: If a large proportion of the population has cyclic preferences, i.e., we add a net probability of the forward cycle to the above list, then the social welfare order remains unchanged in this example as long as

$$-.001 < NP \begin{pmatrix} a \\ \bigcirc \\ c\ b \end{pmatrix} < .007.$$ This can happen even when more than half of the population has cyclic preferences. ∎

Proof of Theorem 2.3.9. i) This follows directly from Theorem 2.1.5 and Observation 2.3.5.

ii) The following is a counterexample: Suppose $P\begin{pmatrix} a \\ b \end{pmatrix} = 1$. Then net value restriction holds, $\succ = \begin{smallmatrix} a \\ b \end{smallmatrix}$, a semiorder, and thus transitive, but $\succsim =$ $\{(a, a), (a, b), (a, c), (b, b), (b, c), (c, a), (c, b), (c, c)\}$, which is not transitive because $b \succsim c \succsim a$ but not $b \succsim a$. ∎

Proof of Theorem 2.3.10. Suppose that $C = \{a, b, c\}$. To prove i) first notice that, up to a relabeling of the alternatives, there are only three possible strict weak orders with a net preference majority, namely $\begin{smallmatrix} a \\ b \\ c \end{smallmatrix}$, $\begin{smallmatrix} a\ b \\ c \end{smallmatrix}$,

or $\begin{smallmatrix} a \\ b\ c \end{smallmatrix}$. Let $\begin{smallmatrix} a \\ b \\ c \end{smallmatrix}$ have a net majority. Then $\succ = \begin{smallmatrix} a \\ b \\ c \end{smallmatrix}$ is the social welfare order.

If $\begin{smallmatrix} a\ b \\ c \end{smallmatrix}$ has a net majority, then the social welfare order $\succ$ is transitive because it must be one of the following three strict weak orders: $\begin{smallmatrix} a \\ b \\ c \end{smallmatrix}$, $\begin{smallmatrix} b \\ a \\ c \end{smallmatrix}$,

or $\begin{smallmatrix} a\ b \\ c \end{smallmatrix}$. The proof for $\begin{smallmatrix} a \\ b\ c \end{smallmatrix}$ follows the same logic.

To obtain a counterexample for ii), suppose that $P\begin{pmatrix} a \\ b \end{pmatrix} = .7$, $P\begin{pmatrix} a \\ b \\ c \end{pmatrix} =$ $P\begin{pmatrix} b \\ c \\ a \end{pmatrix} = P\begin{pmatrix} c \\ a \\ b \end{pmatrix} = .1$, with the remaining probabilities equal to zero.

Then $\begin{smallmatrix} a \\ b \end{smallmatrix}$ has a net preference majority. It is easy to check that $NP_{ab} = .8$, $NP_{bc} = .1$, $NP_{ca} = .1$, and thus we obtain majority cycles $a \succsim b \succsim c \succsim a$ and $a \succ b \succ c \succ a$ while neither $b \succsim a$ nor $b \succ a$ is the case, i.e., neither $\succsim$ nor $\succ$ is transitive. ∎

Proof of Theorem 5.1.4. By (5.4), $P(\succ_s \Rightarrow \succ^*)$ has the following lower bound:

$$Err_N(N, \delta_1^*) - (M - 1)Err_N(N, \delta_2^*) \leq P(\succ_s \Rightarrow \succ^*).$$

Also, by (5.4), the sum of the probabilities of all incorrect majority relations $P(\succ_s \neq \succ_p)$ has the following upper bound:

$$Err_N(N, \delta_1^*) + (M - 1)Err_N(N, \delta_2^*) \geq P(\succ_s \neq \succ_p).$$

Therefore

$$P(\succ_s => ^* \mid \succ_s \neq \succ_p) = \frac{P(\succ_s => ^*)}{P(\succ_s \neq \succ_p)} \geq \frac{Err_N(N, \delta_1^*) - (M - 1)Err_N(N, \delta_2^*)}{Err_N(N, \delta_1^*) + (M - 1)Err_N(N, \delta_2^*)}.$$

$$(C.17)$$

By the properties of normal distributions,

$$\lim_{N \to \infty} \frac{Err_N(N, \delta_2^*)}{Err_N(N, \delta_1^*)} = 0,$$

and so (C.17) becomes

$$\lim_{N \to \infty} P(\succ_s => ^* \mid \succ_s \neq \succ_p) = 1. \quad \blacksquare$$

Proof of Theorem 5.1.6. The proof is based on the fact that the most probable majority preference relation (after the population majority preference relation) has a reversal of majority preference relation over only one pair, with the smallest pairwise margin. Under moderate stochastic transitivity with strict inequalities, such a reversal necessarily leads to a transitive majority preference relation. We need to consider two cases.

i. For each triple, a unique minimal adjusted pairwise margin exists. Suppose that the population majority preference relation is $a \succ_p b \succ_p c$. Then, by moderate stochastic transitivity, $a \succ_p c$ cannot have the smallest adjusted pairwise margin. But reversal of either $a \succ_p b$ or $b \succ_p c$ leads to a transitive relation. The result then follows immediately from Theorem 5.1.4.

ii. There exists a triple a, b, c, $a \succ_p b \succ_p c$, such that $\delta_{aBb}^* = \delta_{bBc}^* = \delta_1^* = \delta_2^*$. From the normal approximation of the multinomial distribution, we then have that, as $N \to \infty$, each of $P(N_{bBa} > N_{aBb})$ and $P(N_{cBb} > N_{bBc})$ converges to 0. Thus, provided that the values $N_{bBa} - N_{aBb}$ and $N_{cBb} - N_{bBc}$ are not perfectly correlated,[2] we then have

$$\lim_{N \to \infty} \frac{P((N_{bBa} > N_{aBb}) \cap (N_{cBb} > N_{bBc}))}{P(N_{bBa} > N_{aBb}) + P(N_{cBb} > N_{bBc})} = 0.$$

---

[2] The values $N_{bBa} - N_{aBb}$ and $N_{cBb} - N_{bBc}$ are perfectly correlated if and only if $p_{aBbBc} + p_{cBbBa} = 1$, in which case the probability of a cycle in the triple $\{a, b, c\}$ is clearly zero for any N.

The probability of an incorrect majority relation is not less than $P(N_{bBa} > N_{aBb}) + P(N_{cBb} > N_{bBc})$ and the probabilities of the possible cycles have the following upper bounds:

$$P(a \succ_s b, b \succ_s c, c \succ_s a) \leq P(N_{cBa} > N_{aBc}),$$

$$P(b \succ_s a, c \succ_s b, a \succ_s c) \leq P((N_{bBa} > N_{aBb}) \cap (N_{cBb} > N_{bBc})).$$

Applying bounds similar to the proof of Theorem 5.1.4 we get the result

$$\lim_{N \to \infty} \frac{P(a \succ_s b, b \succ_s c, c \succ_s a) + P(b \succ_s a, c \succ_s b, a \succ_s c)}{1 - P(a \succ_s b, b \succ_s c, a \succ_s c)}$$

$$\leq \lim_{N \to \infty} \frac{P(N_{cBa} > N_{aBc}) + P((N_{bBa} > N_{aBb}) \cap (N_{cBb} > N_{bBc}))}{P(N_{bBa} > N_{aBb}) + P(N_{cBb} > N_{bBc})}$$

$$= \lim_{N \to \infty} \frac{Err_N(N, \delta_{aBc}^*)}{2 Err_N(N, \delta_1^*)} = 0.$$

In other words, the next most probable majority relation in large samples is transitive. ■

Proof of Theorem 5.3.3. Let us consider a sample in which we know N_{aBb}, N_{bBa}, and N_{aEb}, with $N_{aBb} + N_{bBa} + N_{aEb} = N$. The parameters of the prior Dirichlet distribution are given by α_{aBb}, α_{bBa}, and α_{aEb}, $\alpha_{aBb} + \alpha_{bBa} + \alpha_{aEb} = \alpha$. We introduce the following abbreviations: $G = N_{aBb} + \alpha_{aBb} - 1$ (*a* is Greater than *b*), $L = N_{bBa} + \alpha_{bBa} - 1$ (*a* is Less than *b*), and $S = N_{aEb} + \alpha_{aEb} - 1$ (*a* is the Same as *b*). Then for the posterior distribution of $p_{bBa} = l$ and $p_{aEb} = s$ ($p_{aBb} = g$ is determined by the equality $g = 1 - s - l$), we have from (5.11)

$$P(l, s \mid G, L, S) = \frac{\Gamma(G + L + S + 3)}{\Gamma(G + 1)\Gamma(L + 1)\Gamma(S + 1)} l^L s^S (1 - s - l)^G.$$

The condition that *a* is preferred to *b* by a majority in the population means that $g > l$, which is equivalent to $l < \frac{1-s}{2}$, and so the posterior probability that *a* is preferred to *b* by a majority in the population is given by

$$P((a \succ_p b) \mid D) = P\left(l < \frac{1-s}{2} \mid D\right)$$

$$= \frac{\Gamma(G + L + S + 3)}{\Gamma(G + 1)\Gamma(L + 1)\Gamma(S + 1)} \int_{s=0}^{1} s^S \left(\int_{l=0}^{\frac{1-s}{2}} l^L (1 - s - l)^G dl\right) ds.$$

Substituting $t = \frac{l}{1-s}$ yields

$$\int\limits_{l=0}^{\frac{1-s}{2}} l^L(1-s-l)^G dl = (1-s)^{L+G+1} \int\limits_0^{1/2} t^L(1-t)^G dt.$$

Denoting the cumulative beta distribution of variable x with parameters $L+1$ and $G+1$ by $F_\beta(x, L+1, G+1)$, namely

$$F_\beta(x, L+1, G+1) = \int\limits_0^x \frac{\Gamma(G+L+2)}{\Gamma(G+1)\Gamma(L+1)} t^L(1-t)^G dt,$$

we obtain that

$$P\left(\left(l < \frac{1-s}{2}\right) \mid D\right)$$

$$= \frac{\Gamma(G+L+S+3)}{\Gamma(G+1)\Gamma(L+1)\Gamma(S+1)} \frac{\Gamma(G+1)\Gamma(L+1)}{\Gamma(G+L+2)}$$

$$\times F_\beta\left(\frac{1}{2}, L+1, G+1\right) \int\limits_{s=0}^1 s^S(1-s)^{L+G+1} ds$$

$$= \frac{\Gamma(G+L+S+3)}{\Gamma(S+1)\Gamma(G+L+2)} F_\beta\left(\frac{1}{2}, L+1, G+1\right) \frac{\Gamma(G+L+2)\Gamma(S+1)}{\Gamma(G+L+S+3)}$$

$$= F_\beta\left(\frac{1}{2}, L+1, G+1\right).$$

Returning to our original notation, we get formula (5.12) in Section 4. ■

Bibliography

Adams, J. (1997). Condorcet efficiency and the behavioral model of the vote. *Journal of Politics*, 59:1252–1263.

Adams, J., and Adams, E. (2000). The geometry of voting cycles. *Journal of Theoretical Politics*, 12:131–153.

Akerlof, G. A. (1984). *An Economic Theorist's Book of Tales: Essays That Entertain the Consequences of New Assumptions in Economic Theory*. Cambridge University Press, New York.

Allais, M. (1953). Le comportement de l'homme rationnel devant le risk: Critique des postulats et axiomes de l'école americaine. (The behavior of rational man towards risk: Criticism of the postulates and axioms of the American school.) *Econometrica*, 21:503–546.

Althaus, S. L. (1998). Information effects in collective preferences. *American Political Science Review*, 92:545–558.

Althaus, S. L. (2003). *Collective Preferences in Democratic Politics: Opinion Surveys and the Will of the People*. Cambridge University Press, New York.

Arrow, K. J. (1951). *Social Choice and Individual Values*. Wiley, New York.

Arrow, K. J. (1963). *Social Choice and Individual Values*. Wiley, New York, 2nd ed.

Austen-Smith, D., and Banks, J. S. (1996). Information aggregation, rationality, and the Condorcet jury theorem. *American Political Science Review*, 90:34–45.

Balinski, M. L., and Young, H. P. (1982). *Fair Representation: Meeting the Idea of One Man, One Vote*. Yale University Press, New Haven.

Barberá, S. (1979). Majority and positional voting in a probabilistic framework. *Review of Economic Studies*, 46:379–389.

Barberá, S., and Coelho, D. (2004). On the rule of k names. Unpublished manuscript.

Barberá, S., and Pattanaik, P. K. (1986). Falmagne and the rationalizability of stochastic choices in terms of random orderings. *Econometrica*, 54:707–715.

Ben-Akiva, M. B., and Lerman, S. R. (1985). *Discrete Choice Analysis: Theory and Applications to Travel Demand*. MIT Press, Cambridge, MA.

Ben-Ashar, R., and Paroush, J. (2000). A nonasymptotic Condorcet jury theorem. *Social Choice and Welfare*, 17:189–199.

Berg, S. (1985). Paradox of voting under an urn model: The effect of homogeneity. *Public Choice*, 47:377–387.

Berg, S. (1993). Condorcet's jury theorem, dependency among jurors. *Social Choice and Welfare*, 10:87–95.

Berg, S., and Bjurulf, B. (1983). A note on the paradox of voting: Anonymous preference profiles and May's formula. *Public Choice*, 40:307–316.

Bishop, Y. M., Fienberg, S. E., and Holland, P. W. (1975). *Discrete Multivariate Analysis: Theory and Practice*. MIT Press, Cambridge, MA.

Bjurulf, B. (1972). A probabilistic analysis of voting blocks and the occurence of the paradox of voting. In Niemi and Weisberg (Eds.), *Probability Models of Collective Decision Making*. Charles Merrill, Columbus, OH.

Black, D. (1958). *The Theory of Committees and Elections*. Cambridge University Press, Cambridge.

Blair, D. H., and Pollak, R. A. (1979). Collective rationality and dictatorship. *Journal of Economic Theory*, 21:186–194.

Blau, J. H. (1979). Semiorders and collective choice. *Journal of Economic Theory*, 21:195–206.

Block, H. D., and Marschak, J. (1960). Random orderings and stochastic theories of responses. In Olkin, I., Ghurye, S., Hoeffding, H., Madow, W., and Mann, H. (Eds.), *Contributions to Probability and Statistics*, pp. 97–132. Stanford University Press, Stanford.

Böckenholt, U. (1992). Thurstonian representation for partial ranking data. *British Journal of Mathematical & Statistical Psychology*, 45:31–49.

Böckenholt, U. (2002). A Thurstonian analysis of preference change. *Journal of Mathematical Psychology*, 46:300–314.

Bogart, K., Rabinovitch, I., and Trotter, W. T. J. (1976). A bound on the dimension of interval orders. *Journal of Combinatorial Theory*, 21:319–328.

Bolotashvili, G., Kovalev, M., and Girlich, E. (1999). New facets of the linear ordering polytope. *SIAM Journal on Discrete Mathematics*, 12:326–336.

Bowler, S., and Grofman, B. (Eds.) (2000a). *Elections in Australia, Ireland, and Malta under the Single Transferable Vote*. University of Michigan Press, Ann Arbor.

Bowler, S., and Grofman, B. (2000b). STV's place in the family of electoral systems. In Bowler, S. and Grofman, B. (Eds.), *Elections in Australia, Ireland and Malta under the Single Transferable Vote*, pp. 265–270. University of Michigan Press, Ann Arbor.

Brady, H. (1990). Dimensional analysis of ranking data. *American Journal of Political Science*, 34:1017–1048.

Brady, H., and Ansolabehere, S. (1989). The nature of utility functions in mass publics. *American Political Science Review*, 83:143–163.

Brams, S. J. (1988). More voters and more votes for MAA officers under approval voting. *Focus: Newsletter of the Mathematical Society of America*, 8:1–2.

Brams, S. J. (1993). Approval voting and the good society. *Political Economy of the Good Society, Newsletter*, 3:10–14.

Brams, S. J., and Fishburn, P. C. (1983). *Approval Voting*. Birkhäuser, Boston.

Brams, S. J., and Fishburn, P. C. (1984). Some logical defects of the single transferable vote. In Lijphart, A. and Grofman, B. (Eds.), *Choosing an Electoral System*. Praeger, New York.

Brams, S. J., and Fishburn, P. C. (1985). Comment on the problem of strategic voting under approval voting. *American Political Science Review*, 79:816–818.

Brams, S. J., and Fishburn, P. C. (1988). Does approval voting elect the lowest common denominator? *PS: Political Science & Politics*, 21:277–284.

Brams, S. J., and Fishburn, P. C. (1992). Approval voting in scientific and engineering societies. *Group Decision and Negotiation*, 1:41–55.

Brams, S. J., and Fishburn, P. C. (2001). A nail-biting election. *Social Choice and Welfare*, 18:409–414.

Brams, S. J., Fishburn, P. C., and Merrill, S. I. (1988a). Rejoinder to Saari and Van Newenhizen. *Public Choice*, 59:149.

Brams, S. J., Fishburn, P. C., and Merrill, S. I. (1988b). The responsiveness of approval voting: Comments on Saari and Van Newenhizen. *Public Choice*, 59:121–131.

Brams, S. J., and Herschbach, D. R. (2001). The science of elections. *Science*, 292:1449.

Brams, S. J., and Nagel, J. H. (1991). Approval voting in practice. *Public Choice*, 71:1–17.

Brams, S. J., and Sanver, M. R. (in press). Critical strategies under approval voting: who gets ruled in and ruled out. *Electoral Studies*.

Buhlmann, H., and Huber, P. J. (1963). Pairwise comparison in tournaments. *The Annals of Mathematical Statistics*, 34:501–510.

Burden, B. (1997). Deterministic and probabilistic voting models. *American Journal of Political Science*, 41:1150–1169.

Camerer, C. F., Lowenstein, N. G., and Rabin, M. (2004). *Advances in Behavioral Economics*. Russell Sage Foundation, New York.

Campello de Souza, F. M. (1983). Mixed models, random utilities, and the triangle inequality. *Journal of Mathematical Psychology*, 27:183–200.

Chamberlin, J. R., Cohen, J. L., and Coombs, C. H. (1984). Social choice observed: Five presidential elections of the American Psychological Association. *Journal of Politics*, 46:479–502.

Chamberlin, J. R., and Featherston, F. (1986). Selecting a voting sytem. *Journal of Politics*, 48:347–370.

Cohen, M., and Falmagne, J.-C. (1990). Random utility representation of binary choice probabilities: A new class of necessary conditions. *Journal of Mathematical Psychology*, 34:88–94.

Condorcet, M. (1785). *Essai sur l'application de l'analyse à la probabilité des décisions rendues à la pluralité des voix (Essay on the application of the probabilistic analysis of majority vote decisions)*. Imprimerie Royale, Paris.

Coughlin, P. (1992). *Probabilistic voting theory*. Cambridge University Press, New York.

Critchlow, D. E., Fligner, M. A., and Verducci, J. S. (1991). Probability models on rankings. *Journal of Mathematical Psychology*, 35:294–318.

Critchlow, D. E., Fligner, M. A., and Verducci, J. S. (Eds.) (1993). *Probability Models and Statistical Analyses for Ranking Data*. Springer, New York.

Dagsvik, J. K. (1995). How large is the class of generalized extreme value random utility models? *Journal of Mathematical Psychology*, 39:90–98.

DeMeyer, F., and Plott, C. R. (1970). The probability of a cyclical majority. *Econometrica*, 38:345–354.

Dobra, J. (1983). An approach to empirical studies of voting paradoxes: An update and extension. *Public Choice*, 41:241–250.

Dobra, J., and Tullock, G. (1981). An approach to empirical studies of voting paradoxes. *Public Choice*, 36:193–195.

Doignon, J.-P., and Fiorini, S. (2003). The approval-voting polytope: Combinatorial interpretation of the facets. *Mathématiques, Informatique et Sciences Humaines*, 161:29–39.

Doignon, J.-P., and Fiorini, S. (2004). The facets and the symmetries of the approval-voting polytope. *Journal of Combinatorial Theory, Series B*, 92: 1–12.

Doignon, J.-P., Pekeč, A., and Regenwetter, M. (2004). The repeated insertion model for rankings: Missing link between two subset choice models. *Psychometrika*, 69:33–54.

Doignon, J.-P., and Regenwetter, M. (1997). An approval-voting polytope for linear orders. *Journal of Mathematical Psychology*, 41:171–188.

Doron, G., and Kronick, R. (1977). Single transferable vote: An example of a perverse social choice function. *American Journal of Political Science*, 21: 303–311.

Dridi, T. (1980). Sur les distributions binaires associées à des distributions ordinales (On the binary distributions associated with ordinal distributions). *Mathématiques et Sciences Humaines*, 69:15–31.

Dryzek, J., and List, C. (2003). Social choice theory and deliberative democracy: A reconciliation. *British Journal of Political Science*, 33:1–28.

Duggan, J. (1999). A general extension theorem for binary relations. *Journal of Economic Theory*, 86:1–16.

Enelow, J., and Hinich, M. J. (1984). Probabilistic voting and the importance of centrist ideologies in democratic elections. *Journal of Politics*, 46:459–478.

Enelow, J., and Hinich, M. J. (1989). A general probabilistic model of spatial voting. *Public Choice*, 61:101–114.

Estlund, D. M. (1994). Opinion leaders, independence, and the Condorcet jury theorem. *Theory and Decision*, 36:131–162.

Falmagne, J.-C. (1978). A representation theorem for finite random scale systems. *Journal of Mathematical Psychology*, 18:52–72.

Falmagne, J.-C. (1994). The monks' vote: A dialogue on unidimensional probabilistic geometry. In Humphreys, P. (Ed.), *Patrick Suppes, Mathematical Philosopher*, Vol. 1, pp. 239–254. Kluwer, The Netherlands.

Falmagne, J.-C. (1997). Stochastic token theory. *Journal of Mathematical Psychology*, 41:129–143.

Falmagne, J.-C., and Regenwetter, M. (1996). Random utility models for approval voting. *Journal of Mathematical Psychology*, 40:152–159.

Feld, S. L., and Grofman, B. (1986a). On the possibility of faithfully representative committees. *American Political Science Review*, 80:863–879.

Feld, S. L., and Grofman, B. (1986b). Partial single-peakedness: An extension and clarification. *Public Choice*, 51:71–80.

Feld, S. L., and Grofman, B. (1988). Ideological consistency as a collective phenomenon. *American Political Science Review*, 83:773–788.

Feld, S. L., and Grofman, B. (1990). Collectivities as actors: Consistency of collective choices. *Rationality and Society*, 2:429–448.

Feld, S. L., and Grofman, B. (1992). Who is afraid of the big bad cycle? Evidence from 36 elections. *Journal of Theoretical Politics*, 4:231–237.

Feld, S. L., and Grofman, B. (1996). Stability induced by no quibbling. *Group Decision and Negotiation*, 5:283–294.

Feld, S. L., Grofman, B., and Miller, N. R. (1989). Limits on agenda control in spatial voting games. *Mathematical and Computer Modelling*, 12:405–416.

Felsenthal, D. S., and Machover, M. (1995). Who ought to be elected and who is actually elected – An empirical investigation of 92 elections under 3 procedures. *Electoral Studies*, 14:143–169.

Felsenthal, D. S., Maoz, Z., and Rapoport, A. (1986). Comparing voting systems in genuine elections: Approval voting vs. selection-plurality. *Social Behavior*, 1:41–53.

Felsenthal, D. S., Maoz, Z., and Rapoport, A. (1990). The Condorcet-efficiency of sophisticated voting under the plurality and approval procedures. *Behavioral Science*, 35:24–33.

Felsenthal, D. S., Maoz, Z., and Rapoport, A. (1993). An empirical evaluation of 6 voting procedures – Do they really make any difference? *British Journal of Political Science*, 23:1–27.

Fishburn, P. C. (1970a). Arrow's impossibility theorem: Concise proof and infinite voters. *Journal of Economic Theory*, 2:103–106.

Fishburn, P. C. (1970b). Intransitive indifference in preference theory. *Journal of Mathematical Psychology*, 7:207–228.

Fishburn, P. C. (1975). A probabilistic model of social choice: Comment. *Review of Economic Studies*, 42:297–301.

Fishburn, P. C. (1984). Probabilistic social choice based on simple voting comparisons. *Review of Economic Studies*, 51:683–692.

Fishburn, P. C. (1985). *Interval Orders and Interval Graphs*. Wiley, New York.

Fishburn, P. C. (1990). Binary probabilities induced by rankings. *SIAM Journal of Discrete Mathematics*, 3:478–488.

Fishburn, P. C. (1992). Induced binary probabilities and the linear ordering polytope: A status report. *Mathematical Social Sciences*, 23:67–80.

Fishburn, P. C. (1998). Stochastic utility. In Barberá, S., Hammond, P. J., and Seidl, C. (Eds.), *Handbook of Utility Theory*, pp. 273–318. Kluwer, Dordrecht.

Fishburn, P. C., and Falmagne, J.-C. (1989). Binary choice probabilities and rankings. *Economic Letters*, 31:113–117.

Fishburn, P. C., and Gehrlein, W. V. (1977). Towards a theory of elections with probabilistic preferences. *Econometrica*, 45:1907–1924.

Fishburn, P. C., and Gehrlein, W. V. (1980). The paradox of voting: Effects of individual indifference and intransitivity. *Journal of Public Economics*, 14: 83–94.

Fishburn, P. C., and Little, J. D. C. (1988). An experiment in approval voting. *Management Science*, 34:555–568.

Forsythe, R., Rietz, T., Myerson, R., and Weber, R. (1996). An experimental study of voting rules and polls in three-way elections. *International Journal of Game Theory*, 25:355–383.

Garcia-Lapresta, J. L., and Martinez-Panero, M. (2002). Borda count versus approval voting: A fuzzy approach. *Public Choice*, 112:167–184.

Garman, M., and Kamien, M. (1968). The paradox of voting: Probability calculations. *Behavioral Science*, 13:306–317.

Gärtner, W. (2001). *Domain Conditions in Social Choice Theory*. Cambridge University Press, Cambridge, UK.

Gärtner, W., and Heinecke, A. (1978). Cyclically mixed preferences – A necessary and sufficient condition for transitivity of the social preference relation. In Gottinger, H. W., and Leinfellner, W. (Eds.), *Decision Theory and Social Ethics*, pp. 169–185. Reidel, The Netherlands.

Gehrlein, W. V. (1987). The impact of social homogeneity on the Condorcet efficiency of weighted scoring rules. *Social Science Research*, 16:361–369.

Gehrlein, W. V. (1988). Probability calculations for transitivity of the simple majority rule. *Economics Letters*, 27:311–315.

Gehrlein, W. V. (1989). The probability of intransitivity of pairwise comparisons in individual preference. *Mathematical Social Sciences*, 17:67–75.

Gehrlein, W. V. (1992). Condorcet efficiency of simple voting rules for large electorates. *Economics Letters*, 40:61–66.

Gehrlein, W. V. (1998a). The probability of a Condorcet winner with a small number of voters. *Economics Letters*, 59:317–321.

Gehrlein, W. V. (1998b). The sensitivity of weight selection on the Condorcet efficiency of weighted scoring rules. *Social Choice and Welfare*, 15:351–358.

Gehrlein, W. V. (1999). Condorcet efficiency of Borda rule under the dual culture condition. *Social Science Research*, 28:36–44.

Gehrlein, W. V., and Berg, S. (1992). The effect of social homogeneity on coincidence probabilities for pairwise proportional lottery and simple majority rules. *Social Choice and Welfare*, 9:361–372.

Gehrlein, W. V., and Fishburn, P. C. (1976a). Condorcet's paradox and anonymous preference profiles. *Public Choice*, 26:1–18.

Gehrlein, W. V., and Fishburn, P. C. (1976b). The probability of the paradox of voting: A computable solution. *Journal of Economic Theory*, 13:14–25.

Gehrlein, W. V., and Fishburn, P. C. (1978). Probabilities of election outcomes for large electorates. *Journal of Economic Theory*, 19:38–49.

Gehrlein, W. V., and Fishburn, P. C. (1979). Effects of abstentions on voting procedures in three-candidate elections. *Behavioral Science*, 24:346–354.

Gehrlein, W. V., and Lepelley, D. (1997). Condorcet's paradox under the maximal culture condition. *Economics Letters*, 55:85–89.

Gehrlein, W. V., and Lepelley, D. (1998). The Condorcet efficiency of approval voting and the probability of electing the Condorcet loser. *Journal of Mathematical Economics*, 29:271–283.

Gehrlein, W. V., and Lepelley, D. (1999). Condorcet efficiencies under the maximal culture condition. *Social Choice and Welfare*, 16:471–490.

Gehrlein, W. V., and Lepelley, D. (2001). The Condorcet efficiency of Borda rule with anonymous voters. *Mathematical Social Sciences*, 41:39–50.

Gehrlein, W. V., and Valognes, F. (2001). Condorcet efficiency: A preference for indifference. *Social Choice and Welfare*, 18:193–205.

Gelfand, A., and Solomon, H. (1973). A study of Poisson's models for jury verdicts in criminal and civil trials. *Journal of the American Statistical Association*, 68:271–278.

Gilboa, I. (1990). A necessary but insufficient condition for the stochastic binary choice problem. *Journal of Mathematical Psychology*, 34:371–392.

Grandmont, J.-M. (1978). Intermediate preferences and the majority rule. *Econometrica*, 46:317–330.

Grofman, B. (1975). A comment on democratic theory: A preliminary mathematical model. *Public Choice*, 21:100–103.

Grofman, B. (1981). Mathematical models of juror and jury decision making: The state of the art. In Sales, B. D. (Ed.), *Prespectives in Law and Psychology*, Vol. II: The trial processes, pp. 305–351. Plenum, New York.

Grofman, B. (1991). Statistics without substance: A critique of Freedman et al. and Clark and Morrison. *Evaluation Review*, 15:746–769.

Grofman, B. (1995). New methods for valid ecological inference. In Eagles, M. (Ed.), *Spatial and Contextual Models in Political Research*, pp. 127–149. Taylor and Francis, London.

Grofman, B. (2000). A primer on racial bloc voting analysis. In Persily, N. (Ed.), *The Real Y2K Problem: Census 2000 Data and Redistricting Technology*. The Brennan Center for Justice, New York University School of Law, New York.

Grofman, B. (2004). Downs and two-party convergence. *Annual Review of Political Science*, 7:25–46.

Grofman, B., and Feld, S. L. (1988). Rousseau's general will: A Condorcetian perspective. *American Political Science Review*, 82:567–576.

Grofman, B., and Merrill, S. I. (2004). Ecological regression and ecological inference. In King, G., Rosen, U., and Tanner, M. (Eds.), *Ecological Inference: New Methodological Strategies*, pp. 123–143. Cambridge University Press, New York.

Grofman, B., and Merrill, S. I. (2005). Evaluating proposed solutions to the problem of ecological inference. Unpublished manuscript.

Grofman, B., and Owen, G. (1986a). Condorcet models: Avenues for future research. In Grofman, B., and Owen, G. (Eds.), *Information Pooling and Group Decision Making*, pp. 93–102. JAI Press, Greenwich, CT.

Grofman, B., and Owen, G. (Eds.) (1986b). *Information Pooling and Group Decision Making*. JAI Press, Greenwich.

Grofman, B., Owen, G., and Feld, S. L. (1983). Thirteen theorems in search of the truth. *Theory and Decision*, 15:261–278.

Grofman, B., and Uhlaner, C. (1985). Metapreferences and reasons for stability in social choice: Thoughts on broadening and clarifying the debate. *Theory and Decision*, 19:31–50.

Grötschel, M., Jünger, M., and Reinelt, G. (1985). Facets of the linear ordering polytope. *Mathematical Programming*, 33:43–60.

Guilbaud, G. (1952). Les théories de l'intérêt général et le problème logique de l'aggrégation. (The theories of public interest and the logical problem of aggregation.) *Économie Appliquée*, 5:501–584.

Harless, D. W., and Camerer, C. F. (1994). The predictive value of generalized expected utility theories. *Econometrica*, 62:1251–1289.

Heckerman, D. (1998). A tutorial on learning with Bayesian networks. In Jordan, M. (Ed.), *Learning in Graphical Models*. Cambridge, MA: MIT Press.

Heiner, R. A., and Pattanaik, P. K. (1983). The structure of general probabilistic group decision rules. In Pattanaik, P. K., and Salles, M. (Eds.), *Social Choice and Welfare*, pp. 37–54. North-Holland, Amsterdam.

Heyer, D., and Niederée, R. (1989). Elements of a model-theoretic framework for probabilistic measurement. In Roskam, E. E. (Ed.), *Mathematical Psychology in Progress*, pp. 99–112. Springer, Berlin.

Heyer, D., and Niederée, R. (1992). Generalizing the concept of binary choice systems induced by rankings: One way of probabilizing deterministic measurement structures. *Mathematical Social Sciences*, 23:31–44.

Huber, P. J. (1963). Pairwise comparison and ranking: Optimum properties of the row sum procedure. *The Annals of Mathematical Statistics*, 34:511–520.

Intriligator, M. D. (1973). A probabilistic model of social choice. *Review of Economic Studies*, 40:552–560.

Joe, H. (1997). *Multivariate Models and Dependence Concepts*. Chapman and Hall, London.

Jones, B., Radcliff, B., Taber, C., and Timpone, R. (1995). Condorcet winners and the paradox of voting: Probability calculations for weak preference orders. *American Political Science Review*, 89:137–144.

Kahneman, D., Slovic, P., and Tversky, A. (1982). *Judgment under Uncertainty: Heuristics and Biases*. Cambridge University Press, Cambridge.

Kahneman, D., and Tversky, A. (1979). Prospect theory: An analysis of decision under risk. *Econometrica*, 47:263–291.

Kahneman, D., and Tversky, A. (Eds.) (2000). *Choices, Values, and Frames*. Cambridge University Press, New York.

Kemeny, J. G., and Snell, J. L. (1962). *Mathematical Models in the Social Sciences*. MIT Press, Cambridge, MA.

Klahr, D. (1966). A computer simulation of the paradox of voting. *American Political Science Review*, 60:384–390.

Koppen, M. (1995). Random utility representation of binary choice probabilities: Critical graphs yielding critical necessary conditions. *Journal of Mathematical Psychology*, 39:21–39.

Krantz, D. H., Luce, R. D., Suppes, P., and Tversky, A. (1971). *Foundations of Measurement*, Vol. 1. Academic Press, San Diego.

Kurrild-Klitgard, P. (2001). An empirical example of the Condorcet paradox of voting for a large electorate. *Public Choice*, 107:135–145.

Ladha, K. K. (1992). The Condorcet jury theorem, free speech, and correlated votes. *American Journal of Political Science*, 36:617–634.

Ladha, K. K. (1993). Condocet's jury theorem in light of the De Finetti theorem: Majority rule voting with correlated votes. *Social Choice and Welfare*, 10:69–85.

Ladha, K. K. (1995). Information pooling through majority rule voting: Condorcet's jury theorem with correlated votes. *Journal of Economic Behavior and Organization*, 26:353–372.

Laslier, J.-F. (2002). Spatial approval voting. Unpublished manuscript.

Laslier, J.-F. (2003). Analysing a preference and approval profile. *Social Choice and Welfare*, 20:229–242.

Laver, M., and Schofield, N. (1990). *Multiparty Government: The Politics of Coalition in Europe*. Oxford University Press, New York.

Lepelley, D. (1993). Concorcet's paradox. *Theory and Decision*, 15:161–197.

Lepelley, D., and Gehrlein, W. V. (2000). Strong Condorcet efficiency of scoring rules. *Economics Letters*, 58:157–164.

Lepelley, D., Pierron, P., and Valognes, F. (2000). Scoring rules, Condorcet efficiency and social homogeneity. *Theory and Decision*, 49:175–196.

Lepelley, D., and Valognes, F. (1999). On the Kim and Roush voting procedure. *Group Decision and Negotiation*, 8:109–123.

Levin, J., and Nalebuff, B. (1995). An introduction to vote counting schemes. *Journal of Economic Perspectives*, 9:3–26.

Lijphart, A., and Grofman, B. (Eds.) (1984). *Choosing an electoral system*. Praeger, New York.

Loomes, G., and Sugden, R. (1982). Regret theory – An alternative theory of rational choice under uncertainty. *Economic Journal*, 92:805–824.

Luce, R. D. (1956). Semiorders and a theory of utility discrimination. *Econometrica*, 26:178–191.

Luce, R. D. (1959). *Individual Choice Behavior: A Theoretical Analysis*. John Wiley, New York. Reprinted in 2005 by Dover Publications.

Luce, R. D. (1977). The choice axiom after twenty years. *Journal of Mathematical Psychology*, 15:215–233.

Luce, R. D. (1992). Where does subjective-expected utility fail descriptively? *Journal of Risk and Uncertainty*, 5:5–27.

Luce, R. D. (2000). *Utility of Gains and Losses: Measurement – Theoretical and Experimental Approaches*. Erlbaum, Mahwah, NJ.

Luce, R. D., and Suppes, P. (1965). Preference, utility and subjective probability. In Luce, R. D., Bush, R. R., and Galanter, E. (Eds.), *Handbook of Mathematical Psychology*, Vol. III, pp. 249–410. Wiley, New York.

Luce, R. D., and von Winterfeldt, D. (1994). What common ground exists for descriptive, prescriptive, and normative utility theories? *Management Science*, 40:263–279.

Mackelprang, A. J., Grofman, B., and Thomas, N. K. (1975). Electoral change and stability: Some new perspectives. *American Politics Quarterly*, 3: 315–339.

Mackie, G. (2003). *Democracy Defined*. Cambridge University Press, New York.

Mallows, C. L. (1957). Non-null ranking models I. *Biometrika*, 44:114–130.

Marley, A. A. J. (1968). Some probabilistic models of simple choice and ranking. *Journal of Mathematical Psychology*, 5:311–332.

Marley, A. A. J. (1989a). A random utility family that includes many of the "classical" models and has closed form choice probabilities and choice reaction times. *British Journal of Mathematical & Statistical Psychology*, 42:13–36.

Marley, A. A. J. (1989b). A random utility family that includes many of the "classical" models and has closed form choice probabilities and choice reaction times: Addendum. *British Journal of Mathematical & Statistical Psychology*, 42:280.

Marley, A. A. J. (1990). A historical and contemporary perspective on random scale representations of choice probabilities and reaction times in the context of Cohen and Falmagne's (1990, Journal of Mathematical Psychology, 34) results. *Journal of Mathematical Psychology*, 34:81–87.

Marley, A. A. J. (1991a). Aggregation theorems and multidimensional stochastic choice models. *Theory and Decision*, 30:245–272.

Marley, A. A. J. (1991b). Context dependent probabilistic choice models based on measures of binary advantage. *Mathematical Social Sciences*, 21:201–218.

Marschak, J. (1960). Binary-choice constraints and random utility indicators. In Arrow, K. J., Karlin, S., and Suppes, P. (Eds.), *Proceedings of the First Stanford Symposium on Mathematical Methods in the Social Sciences, 1959*, pp. 312–329. Stanford University Press, Stanford, CA.

McFadden, D. (1991). Advances in computation, statistical methods, and testing of discrete choice models. *Marketing Letters*, 2:215–229.

McFadden, D. (1998). Specification of econometric models. Unpublished manuscript.

McFadden, D., and Richter, M. K. (1970). Revealed stochastic preference. Unpublished manuscript, Department of Economics, University of California at Berkeley.

McKelvey, R. D. (1976). Intransitivities in multidimensional voting models and some implications for agenda control. *Journal of Economic Theory*, 12:472–482.

McKelvey, R. D. (1979). General conditions for global intransitivities in formal voting models. *Econometrica*, 47:1085–1112.

McLean, I., and Urken, A. B. (Eds.) (1995). *Classics of Social Choice*. Ann Arbor, MI: University of Michigan Press.

Miller, N. R. (1983). Pluralism and social choice. *American Political Science Review*, 77:734–747.

Miller, N. R. (1986). Information, electorates, and democracy: Some extensions and interpretations of the Condorcet jury theorem. In Grofman, B. and Owen, G. (Eds.), *Information Pooling and Group Decision Making*, pp. 173–192. JAI Press, Greenwich.

Miller, N. R. (1996). Information, individual errors, and collective performance: Empirical evidence on the Condorcet jury theorem. *Group Decision and Negotiation*, 5:211–228.

Miller, N. R., Grofman, B., and Feld, S. L. (1989). The geometry of majority rule. *Journal of Theoretical Politics*, 1:379–406.

Murakami, Y. (1968). *Logic and Social Choice*. Routledge & K. Paul, London.

Myerson, R. B. (1993). Incentives to cultivate favored minorities under alternative electoral systems. *American Political Science Review*, 87:856–869.

Myerson, R. B. (2002). Comparison of scoring rules in Poisson voting games. *Journal of Economic Theory*, 103:219–251.

Nagel, J. H. (1984). A debut for approval voting. *PS*, 17:62–65.

Niederée, R., and Heyer, D. (1997). Generalized random utility models and the representational theory of measurement: A conceptual link. In Marley, A. A. J. (Ed.), *Choice, Decision and Measurement: Essays in Honor of R. Duncan Luce*, pp. 155–189. Lawrence Erlbaum, Mahwah, NJ.

Niemi, R. (1970). The occurrence of the paradox of voting in a university election. *Public Choice*, 8:91–100.

Niemi, R. (1983). Why so much stability? Another opinion. *Public Choice*, 42:261–270.

Niemi, R., and Weisberg, H. (1968). A mathematical solution for the probability of the paradox of voting. *Behavioral Science*, 13:317–323.

Niemi, R., and Wright, J. (1987). Voting cycles and the structure of individual preferences. *Social Choice and Welfare*, 4:173–183.

Nitzan, S., and Paroush, J. (1985). *Collective Decision Making: An Economic Approach*. Cambridge University Press, New York.

Nitzan, S., and Paroush, J. (1986). Optimal decision making under dichotomous choice: The basic result and some generalizations. In Grofman, B., and Owen, G. (Eds.), *Information Pooling and Group Decision Making*, pp. 123–125. JAI Press, Greenwich.

Norpoth, H. (1979). The parties come to order! Dimensions of preferential choice in the West German electorate, 1961–1976. *American Political Science Review*, 73:724–736.

Owen, G., Grofman, B., and Feld, S. L. (1989). Proving a distribution-free generalization of the Condorcet jury theorem. *Mathematical Social Sciences*, 17: 1–6.

Pattanaik, P. K. (1971). *Voting and collective choice: Some aspects of the theory of group decision-making*. Cambridge University Press, Cambridge.

Pattanaik, P. K., and Peleg, B. (1986). Distribution of power under stochastic social choice rules. *Econometrica*, 54:909–921.

Pierce, R. (1996). *French Presidential Elections Survey, 1988*. Inter-University Consortium for Political and Social Research, Ann Arbor, MI.

Plott, C. R., and Levine, M. E. (1978). A model of agenda influence on committee decisions. *American Economic Review*, 68:146–160.

Poisson, S.-D. (1787). *Recherches sur la Probabilité Des Jugements En Matière Criminelle et En Matière Civile: Procédés Des Règles Générales Du Calcul Des Probabilités. (Research on the Probability of Criminal and Civil Judgments: Proceedings of the General Rules of Probability Calculus.)* Bachelier, Paris.

Rabinovitch, I. (1978). The dimension of semiorders. *Journal of Combinatorial Theory*, 25:50–61.

Radcliff, B. (1997). Collective preferences in presidential elections. *Electoral Studies*, 13:50–57.

Regenwetter, M. (1996). Random utility representations of finite m-ary relations. *Journal of Mathematical Psychology*, 40:219–234.

Regenwetter, M. (1997). Probabilistic preferences and topset voting. *Mathematical Social Sciences*, 34:91–105.

Regenwetter, M., Adams, J., and Grofman, B. (2002a). On the (sample) Condorcet efficiency of majority rule: An alternative view of majority cycles and social homogeneity. *Theory and Decision*, 53:153–186.

Regenwetter, M., Falmagne, J.-C., and Grofman, B. (1999). A stochastic model of preference change and its application to 1992 presidential election panel data. *Psychological Review*, 106:362–384.

Regenwetter, M., and Grofman, B. (1998a). Approval voting, Borda winners and Condorcet winners: Evidence from seven elections. *Management Science*, 44:520–533.

Regenwetter, M., and Grofman, B. (1998b). Choosing subsets: A size-independent probabilistic model and the quest for a social welfare ordering. *Social Choice and Welfare*, 15:423–443.

Regenwetter, M., Grofman, B., and Marley, A. A. J. (2002b). On the model dependence of majority preferences reconstructed from ballot or survey data. *Mathematical Social Sciences: Special issue on random utility theory and probabilistic measurement theory*, 43:453–468.

Regenwetter, M., and Marley, A. A. J. (2001). Random relations, random utilities, and random functions. *Journal of Mathematical Psychology*, 45:864–912.

Regenwetter, M., Marley, A. A. J., and Grofman, B. (2002c). A general concept of majority rule. *Mathematical Social Sciences: Special issue on random utility theory and probabilistic measurement theory*, 43:407–430.

Regenwetter, M., Marley, A. A. J., and Grofman, B. (2003). General concepts of value restriction and preference majority. *Social Choice and Welfare*, 21:149–173.

Regenwetter, M., Marley, A. A. J., and Joe, H. (1998). Random utility threshold models of subset choice. *Australian Journal of Psychology: Special issue on mathematical psychology*, 50:175–185.

Regenwetter, M., and Tsetlin, I. (2004). Approval voting and positional voting methods: Inference, relationship, examples. *Social Choice and Welfare*, 22:539–566.

Riker, W. (1958). The paradox of voting and congressional rules for voting on amendments. *The American Political Science Review*, 52:349–366.

Riker, W. H. (1961). Voting and the summation of preferences: An interpretative bibliographical review of selected developments during the last decade. *American Political Science Review*, 55:900–911.

Riker, W. H. (1965). Arrows theorem and some examples of the paradox of voting. In Claunch, J. M. (Ed.), *Mathematical Applications in Political Science*, pp. 41–60. Southern Methodist University Press, Dallas.

Riker, W. H. (1982). *Liberalism against Populism*. W. H. Freeman and Co., San Francisco.

Roberts, F. S. (1979). *Measurement Theory*. Addison-Wesley, London.

Rose, C., and Smith, M. D. (1996). The multivariate normal distribution. *Mathematica Journal*, 6:32–37.

Rose, C., and Smith, M. D. (2002). *Mathematical Statistics with Mathematica*. Springer-Verlag, NewYork.

Saari, D. G. (1994). *Geometry of Voting*. Springer-Verlag, New York.

Saari, D. G. (1995). *Basic Geometry of Voting*. Springer-Verlag, Berlin, New York.

Saari, D. G. (1999). Explaining all three-alternative voting outcomes. *Journal of Economic Theory*, 87:313–355.

Saari, D. G. (2001a). Analyzing a nail-biting election. *Social Choice and Welfare*, 18:415–430.

Saari, D. G. (2001b). *Chaotic Elections! A Mathematician Looks at Voting.* American Mathematical Society, Providence, RI.

Saari, D. G. (2001c). *Decisions and Elections: Explaining the Unexpected.* Cambridge University Press, Cambridge, UK.

Saari, D. G., and Tataru, M. (1999). The likelihood of dubious election outcomes. *Economic Theory*, 13:345–363.

Saari, D. G., and Van Newenhizen, J. (1988a). Is approval voting an 'unmitigated evil'?: A response to Brams, Fishburn, and Merrill. *Public Choice*, 59:133–147.

Saari, D. G., and Van Newenhizen, J. (1988b). The problem of indeterminacy in approval, multiple, and truncated voting systems. *Public Choice*, 59:101–120.

Sapiro, V., Rosenstone, S., and Miller, W. (1998). *American National Election Studies, 1948–1997.* Inter-University Consortium for Political and Social Research, Ann Arbor, MI.

Schofield, N., and Tovey, C. (1992). Probability and convergence for supramajority rule with Euclidean preferences. *Mathematical and Computer Modelling*, 16:41–58.

Sen, A. K. (1966). A possibility theorem on majority decisions. *Econometrica*, 34:491–499.

Sen, A. K. (1969). Quasi-transitivity, rational choice and collective decisions. *Review of Economic Studies*, 36:381–393.

Sen, A. K. (1970). *Collective Choice and Social Welfare.* Holden-Day, San Francisco.

Shapley, L. S., and Grofman, B. (1984). Optimizing group judgmental accuracy in the presence of interdependencies. *Public Choice*, 43:329–343.

Shepsle, K., and Bonchek, M. (1997). *Analyzing Politics: Rationality, Behavior and Institutions.* Norton, New York.

Shepsle, K., and Weingast, B. (1981). Structure-induced equilibrium and legislative choice. *Public Choice*, 37:503–519.

Shleifer, A. (2000). *Inefficient Markets: An Introduction to Behavioral Finance.* Oxford University Press.

Simon, H. A. (1955). A behavioral model of rational choice. *Quarterly Journal of Economics*, 69:99–118.

Smith, V. L. (1976). Experimental economics: Induced value theory. *American Economic Review*, 66:274–279.

Smith, V. L. (1994). Economics in the laboratory. *Journal of Economic Perspectives*, 8:113–131.

Sonstegaard, M. H. (1998). A shortcut method of calculating the distribution of election outcome types under approval voting. *Theory and Decision*, 44: 211–220.

Stuart, A., and Ord, J. K. (1998). Distribution theory. In *Kendall's Advanced Theory of Statistics*, Vol. 1. Oxford University Press, New York, 6th ed.

Suck, R. (1992). Geometric and combinatorial properties of the polytope of binary choice probabilities. *Mathematical Social Sciences*, 23:81–102.

Suck, R. (1995). Random utility representations based on semiorders, interval orders, and partial orders. Unpublished manuscript.

Suppes, P. (1961). Behavioristic foundations of utility. *Econometrica*, 29:186–202.

Tangian, A. (2000). Unlikelihood of Condorcet's paradox in a large society. *Social Choice and Welfare*, 17:337–365.

Tangiane, A. S. (1991). *Aggregation and Representation of Preferences: Introduction to Mathematical Theory of Democracy*. Springer-Verlag, Berlin.

Tataru, M., and Merlin, V. (1997). On the relationship of the Concorcet winner and positional voting rules. *Mathematical Social Sciences*, 34:81–90.

Thaler, R. H. (Ed.) (1993a). *Advances in Behavioral Finance*. Russell Sage Foundation.

Thaler, R. H. (1993b). *The Winner's Curse: Paradoxes and Anomalies of Economic Life*. Princeton, NJ: Princeton University Press.

Thurstone, L. L. (1927a). A law of comparative judgement. *Psychological Review*, 34:273–286.

Thurstone, L. L. (1927b). Three psychophysical laws. *Psychophysical Review*, 34:424–432.

Tideman, N. (1995). Collective decisions and voting (title tentative). In preparation.

Tideman, N., and Richardson, D. (2000a). Better voting methods through technology: The refinement-manageability trade-off in the single transferable vote. *Public Choice*, 103:13–34.

Tideman, N., and Richardson, D. (2000b). A comparison of improved STV methods. In Bowler, S., and Grofman, B. (Eds.), *Elections in Australia, Ireland and Malta under the Single Transferable Vote*, pp. 248–264. University of Michigan Press, Ann Arbor.

Timpone, R., and Taber, C. (1998). Analytic and algorithmic analyses of Condorcet's paradox – Variations on a classical theme. *Social Science Computer Review*, 16:72–95.

Trotter, W. T. (1992). *Combinatorics and Partially Ordered Sets*. Johns Hopkins, London.

Tsetlin, I., and Regenwetter, M. (2003). On the probability of correct or incorrect majority preference relations. *Social Choice and Welfare*, 20:283–306.

Tsetlin, I., Regenwetter, M., and Grofman, B. (2003). The impartial culture maximizes the probability of majority cycles. *Social Choice and Welfare*, 21:387–398.

Tullock, G. (1981). Why so much stability? *Public Choice*, 37:189–202.

Tversky, A. (1969). Intransitivity of preferences. *Psychological Review*, 76:31–48.

Tversky, A. (1972). Choice by elimination. *Journal of Mathematical Psychology*, 9:340–367.

Tversky, A., and Kahneman, D. (1974). Judgment under uncertainty: Heuristics and biases. *Science*, 185:1124–1131.

Tversky, A., and Kahneman, D. (1981). The framing of decisions and the psychology of choices. *Science*, 211:453–458.

Tversky, A., and Kahneman, D. (1986). Rational choice and the framing of decisions. *Journal of Business*, 59:251–278.

Van Deemen, A. (1999). The probability of the paradox of voting for weak preference orderings. *Social Choice and Welfare*, 16:171–182.

Van Deemen, A., and Vergunst, N. (1998). Empirical evidence of paradoxes of voting in Dutch elections. *Public Choice*, 97:475–490.

Vila, X. (1998). On the intransitivity of preferences consistent with similarity relations. *Journal of Economic Theory*, 79:281–287.

Weber, R. J. (1995). Approval voting. *Journal of Economic Perspectives*, 9:39–49.

Weissberg, R. (1978). Collective vs. dyadic representation. *The American Political Science Review*, 72:535–547.

Williamson, O., and Sargent, T. (1967). Social choice: A probabilistic approach. *Economic Journal*, 77:797–813.

Wiseman, J. (2000). Approval voting in subset elections. *Economic Theory*, 15:477–483.

Young, H. P. (1974). An axiomatization of Borda's rule. *The Journal of Economic Theory*, 9:43–52.

Young, H. P. (1986). Optimal ranking and choice from pairwise comparisons. In Grofman, B., and Owen, G. (Eds.), *Information Pooling and Group Decision Making: Proceedings of the Second University of California, Irvine, Conference in Political Economy*, pp. 113–122. JAI Press, Greenwich.

Young, H. P. (1988). Condorcet's theory of voting. *American Political Science Review*, 82:1231–1243.

Author Index

233

Subject Index